MW01118644

Voices of Foster Youth

This important book offers unique insight into the experience of foster youth from 27 countries around the world. It provides a systematic review of literature reporting the experiences of youth in care, addressing a wide range of key topics in this multidisciplinary field, and presenting the views and perceptions of these young people.

Including a meta-analysis on contact with birth parents, it examines youth's experiences of the foster care system; contact and relationships; caregiving and relationships with caregivers; placements; and emotional well-being. These five core themes embrace a wide range of crucial topics including foster youth's involvement in decisions about themselves; interactions with social workers, birth families, foster families, peers, and friends; the benefits and challenges of foster care; the stigma attached to being in care; mental health, well-being, and belonging; and developing a sense of self.

This essential volume is for students and scholars of child and adolescent development, social work, education, sociology, and public health. Illustrated with quotes from former and current foster youth, and with research-based recommendations for best practices in foster care, it is also for professional social workers, psychologists, child advocates, children's therapists, children's attorneys, youth workers, and foster parents.

Dr. Sue D. Hobbs is an associate professor in Child and Adolescent Development at California State University, Sacramento.

Ms. Jennifer M. Krebsbach is a behavior analyst and PhD student in Sociology at the University of California, Davis.

Dr. Rakel P. Larson is an associate professor of Psychology in the Behavioral Sciences department at Riverside City College.

Dr. Christine R. Wells holds a PhD in Social Psychology and is the senior member of the UCLA Statistical Consulting Group.

Dr. Karen J. Saywitz was a distinguished developmental and clinical psychologist and professor in the UCLA School of Medicine, Departments of Psychiatry and Pediatrics for over 25 years.

"*Voices of Foster Youth* offers a powerful global perspective on the experiences of foster youth. Weaving together research findings, policy recommendations, and the poignant experiences of former foster youth, it is must-read for professionals, scholars, and anyone seeking to better understand and support young people in the foster care system."
     – **Dr. Luke Wood,** *President, Sacramento State and former foster youth*

"This book offers a unique and informative exploration into foster care, combining rigorous research and real experiences. It's a vital read for anyone interested in understanding and improving the lives of foster youth through genuine, first-hand perspectives."
     – **Dr. Gail S. Goodman,** *Distinguished Professor of Psychology, University of California, Davis*

Voices of Foster Youth

Experts on Their Own Lives

**Sue D. Hobbs, Jennifer M. Krebsbach,
Rakel P. Larson, Christine R. Wells and
Karen J. Saywitz**

NEW YORK AND LONDON

Designed cover image: GettyImages/SDI Productions

First published 2025
by Routledge
605 Third Avenue, New York, NY 10158

and by Routledge
4 Park Square, Milton Park, Abingdon, Oxon, OX14 4RN

Routledge is an imprint of the Taylor & Francis Group, an informa business

© 2025 Sue D. Hobbs, Jennifer M. Krebsbach, Rakel P. Larson,
Christine R. Wells and Karen J. Saywitz

ISBN: 978-1-032-31330-6 (hbk)
ISBN: 978-1-032-31329-0 (pbk)
ISBN: 978-1-003-30921-5 (ebk)

DOI: 10.4324/9781003309215

Typeset in Times New Roman
by MPS Limited, Dehradun

Contents

About the Authors

Dr. Sue D. Hobbs is an associate professor in Child and Adolescent Development at California State University, Sacramento. She holds a PhD in Developmental Psychology from University of California, Davis. Her research revolves around child witnesses' and victims' experiences in the legal system, including best practices in forensic interviewing, children's memory and suggestibility, and the well-being of youth in foster care. Dr. Hobbs' expertise and contributions in these areas significantly contribute to the field of Developmental Psychology, offering valuable insights for professionals working with vulnerable children and adolescents.

Ms. Jennifer M. Krebsbach is a behavior analyst and PhD student in Sociology at the University of California, Davis. She holds an MA with distinction in Education, Gender Equity Studies from California State University, Sacramento and an MS in Applied Behavior Analysis (ABA) with an emphasis in Autism Studies. Her previous research includes identifying disparities between genders in journal publications, textbook authorship, ABA company ownership, fellowship/awards from professional organizations, and tenure requirements in academia. Ms. Krebsbach is dedicated to addressing societal inequities, and promoting inclusivity in adults, children, and families in education, organizations, and foster care.

Dr. Rakel P. Larson is an associate professor of Psychology in the Behavioral Sciences department at Riverside City College. She received her PhD in Cognitive and Developmental Psychology from the University of California, Riverside. Her research examines factors that predict witness/victim participation in the criminal justice process, procedural justice, eyewitness memory and suggestibility, and forensic interview techniques for eliciting reliable and high-quality memory reports from adults and children. Dr. Larson's work addresses issues affecting historically underrepresented and marginalized groups and has implications for theory, public policy, and practice.

Dr. Christine R. Wells holds a PhD in Social Psychology and is the senior member of the UCLA Statistical Consulting Group. She is a statistical consultant with over 20 years of experience assisting clients with quantitative research. Dr. Wells has advised clients on all phases of the research process, including experimental design, item and instrument development, data collection, data cleaning and verification, statistical analysis and interpretation, graphing and visualizing data, and presenting results in written and oral formats. Her areas of specialization and expertise include utilizing public-use data sets, statistical disclosure control methods, and meta-analysis. In addition to statistical consulting, Dr. Wells has co-authored numerous articles in peer-reviewed academic journals and regularly presents at professional conferences and meetings.

Dr. Karen J. Saywitz was a distinguished developmental and clinical psychologist and professor in the UCLA School of Medicine, Departments of Psychiatry and Pediatrics for over 25 years. Dr. Saywitz made seminal contributions to the burgeoning field of child trauma and maltreatment, working to ameliorate trauma experienced by child victims and witnesses in the legal system. She trained hundreds of students across the nation in the schools of medicine, psychology, social work, and law; founded programs for professionals to support maltreated youth, children, and families; lobbied at Congress; developed children's forensic interviewing protocols; authored handbooks for legal professionals; and conducted and published groundbreaking research dedicated to improving outcomes for child victims. She was a Fellow in the American Psychological Association; served in the Presidential triumvirate of the American Psychological Association's Division of Child and Family Policy and Practice; and was president-elect of the Section on Child Maltreatment. Dr. Saywitz was universally regarded as a consummate mentor and colleague who lived her values through a lifelong commitment to vulnerable children and families.

Acknowledgements

The late Dr. Karen J. Saywitz started this work at UCLA and secured original funding from the Swedish National Board of Health and Welfare (R90039–2). The present research was funded by grants awarded to Dr. Sue D. Hobbs from the California State University, Sacramento Office of Research, Innovation, and Economic Development as well as the California State University, Sacramento Office of Graduate Studies, Diversity and Equity Programs Office. We would also like to thank Rachel Stark and Samantha McClellan, California State University, Sacramento, librarians for their assistance in creating comparable search strategies for seven library databases; Mike Krebsbach for proofreading drafts; Kimberly Biddle, Gail S. Goodman, and Lynda Stone for reading and reviewing our book proposals; and Brandy Phillips, Jennifer Mayer, Olivia Wilson, Tanya Nayak, Hannah Klinger, and Sierra Harmon for their work reading and coding studies.

Preface

Voices of foster youth are key to developing policy and practices that promote healthy youth development and outcomes. Although various perspectives are valuable (e.g., foster parents, social workers, former foster youth), it is important to hear from foster youth themselves who are reporting on their contemporaneous experiences. Indeed, there are many published studies worldwide in which foster youth have been interviewed about their experiences in care. The topics of these studies vary widely, and each provides a small glimpse of foster youth's experiences and needs. While these disparate studies cover meaningful ground individually, it is important to identify common themes that span geographic boundaries.

To meet this need, we wrote a systematic literature review on research in which foster youth were interviewed about their experiences in care. A systematic literature search and review is a transparent, unbiased method to locate and synthesize research using a predetermined set of search and selection criteria. The collection of studies we identified provides a rich overview of the advantages and challenges of foster care as described by foster youth themselves. Foster youth from more than 20 countries gave their perspectives on a wide variety of topics related to their experiences in care (e.g., sense of belonging and security, knowledge of the foster care system, relationships with caregivers and social workers, and feelings about placement changes). In addition, we conducted a meta-analysis on youth's contact with their birth parents. As you navigate this book, you will find research synthesizing the perspectives of foster youth as well as direct quotes from those in care. To our knowledge, this is the first book that systematically examines these topics with this breadth and scope, specifically from the perspective of foster youth themselves.

Our unique and focused approach is of broad interest and a "must read" in this important and multidisciplinary field. This book will be useful to a diverse audience, including those in higher education and professional settings. Students, social workers, psychologists, child advocates, children's therapists, academics, researchers, children's attorneys, foster carers, youth workers, and others who professionally or personally engage with foster youth will benefit from this book. Additionally, we hope that this book will provide representation of and validate the experiences of current and former foster youth. The recommendations provided by the youth will inform best-practice guidelines for future policy and practice. As experts on their own lives, these youth should be listened to and heard.

Chapter 1

The Importance of Listening to Foster Youth

"I was invisible unless I was acting out. Then I was a monster[1]"

Millions of youth are in foster and residential care worldwide (Petrowski et al., 2017; UNICEF, 2022). Increasingly, child advocates internationally have been calling for youth to meaningfully participate in decision-making matters that affect their own welfare (Appell, 2006; Cashmore, 2002, 2014; Head, 2011; Jones, 2002). This movement recognizes youth as active agents and stakeholders in their own care rather than passive objects for concern. The United Nations Convention on the Rights of the Child (CRC) declares that youth are "entitled to participate in all decisions that affect them" and that their views should be given "due weight" (United Nations General Assembly, 1989, Article 12, p. 4).[2] In short, this means that children should have a right to be listened to, be heard, and have their concerns taken *seriously* (UNICEF, 2022). In this chapter, we first describe the prevalence and types of foster care. Then we discuss why we should listen to foster youth voices, challenges with hearing them, and then provide an overview of the current study.

"We know what we need.[3]"

What Is Foster Care?

Foster care is a type of temporary out-of-home living arrangement that can occur when biological parents are unable or unwilling to efficiently care for their children (Annie E. Casey Foundation, 2024; Petrowski et al., 2017). Thus, the goal of foster care is to provide a stable and caring environment for children to develop. Article 12 of the CRC states that every child has the right to "a standard of living adequate for the child's physical, mental, spiritual, moral and social development" and requires that caregivers "secure, within

DOI: 10.4324/9781003309215-1

their abilities and financial capabilities, the conditions of living necessary for the child's development" (United Nations General Assembly, 1989, p. 8). Youth may come to the attention of child welfare services when their basic needs (e.g., food, clothing, shelter, health care, education) are not met, when they have experienced abuse, or when their biological parents have died (Petrowski et al., 2017).

Types of Foster Care

Youth in foster care may experience various types of out-of-home placements, including kinship care, formal foster care, and residential or institutional care (Cashmore, 2014). In kinship care or network care[4], children are placed with family members, close family friends, or acquaintances. These placements can be either informally arranged by family members or through formal government intervention. (United Nations General Assembly, 2009, para. 29).

Kinship care is the most common and accepted type of placement in developing countries (Cashmore, 2014). In many African countries, child-headed households are more common in regions that have been impacted by the HIV/AIDs epidemic, which have left some youth without biological parents or other relatives to take care of them (Assim, 2013; Phillips, 2011; Zimmerman, 2005). For example, approximately one in eight children in Rwanda are cared for by older siblings (Cantwell, 2005). When children lose parental care due to being orphaned, abandoned, or other reasons, relatives and extended family members often step in to care for them (Biemba et al., 2010). There is also a cultural view in many African cultures that the care and upbringing of children is a shared responsibility of family and the broader community (Assim, 2013; Bennett, 1999).

Another type of out-of-home arrangement is formal foster care. This is when children are formally placed with a home with one family. Foster parents/caregivers are most often vetted, approved and supervised by the government or by nonprofit organizations (United Nations General Assembly, 2009, para. 29). These programs have a shorter history compared to kinship care and are more common in Western Europe, North America, and Australasia[5] (Cashmore, 2014). The purpose and planned length of care varies. For example, it may include emergency care for abandoned children who need to be immediately removed from their homes for safety or well-being issues, short- to medium-term placements for children who may be eventually reunified with their biological parents, or more long-term care for maltreated children who are unlikely to be returned home permanently or be adopted (Cashmore, 2014).

> *"I am also grateful to the people who do foster care for the right reasons with their hearts full of love and compassion to help children.[6]"*

Youth may also be placed in residential care, which is "care provided in any non-family-based group setting, such as places of safety for emergency care, transit centers in emergency situations, and all other short- and long-term residential care facilities, including group homes" (United Nations General Assembly, 2009, para. 29). Internationally, residential care encompasses a broad range of institutionalized facilities. These include large-scale institutions, such as orphanages, common in former Soviet states (Lough & Panos, 2003), small to medium "children's homes" or group facilities run by government or nonprofits in many areas (Sinclair & Gibbs, 1998), and private mental health centers and secure units in the USA (Courtney & Iwaniec, 2009). In these institutional arrangements, typically caregivers are paid staff working in shifts, who do not live onsite at the facility (Petrowski et al., 2017). These institutions vary greatly in the ages and needs they accommodate, as well as their purpose (e.g., care, housing, education, treatment). They also differ in their practices (e.g., staffing, training, links to families, length of stay, resources, aftercare, philosophy) within the institutions (Ainsworth & Thoburn, 2014). Residential services like boarding schools, madrassas, and pagodas may constitute a form of care based on the cultural context and region. For example, in some cases youth may end up living in residential-like facilities when parents are struggling to provide them access to education or other services rather than a need for protection and safety (Delap & Melville, 2011). In these cases, some youth may board at the residential facilities for access to resources and still visit their families regularly whereas others may choose not to visit their families.

The most problematic institutions are large-scale and impersonal with continually rotating staff. Such institutions hinder the development of stable relationships. Concerns about abuse and bullying from caretakers as well as other youth residents have led Western countries away from institutional models–although they may still be used for sibling groups and children with disabilities. Therapeutic group care is also a last resort to house older youth who, for some reason, cannot be placed in kinship or foster care

(Cashmore, 2014). Residential or institutional care remains common across Eastern Europe, South America, and Asia, although the Convention on the Rights of the Child has prompted "deinstitutionalization" efforts in many countries (Cantwell, 2005; Innocenti Research Centre, 2003; Thoburn, 2007).

Some youth eventually reunite with their biological parents or previous caregivers through a process of family reunification. In the United States, slightly less than 50% of youth in foster care are reunified with their families (Annie E. Casey Foundation, 2024). Biological parents who seek to be reunited with their children may be asked to take courses that teach parenting skills that promote healthy development and how to provide a stable household. Parents may also be required to receive counseling, or other treatment, such as drug rehabilitation (U.S. Department of Health and Human Services 2023).

Prevalence of Children in Foster Care

A study by UNICEF covering 142 countries and 84% of the world's children found that approximately 2.7 million children between the ages of 0 and 17 were living in institutional care (Petrowski et al., 2017). In 2021, over 200,000 children entered foster care in the United States (Annie E. Casey Foundation, 2024). However, the prevalence of children in foster care, in general, is difficult to precisely measure. Only 88 of the 142 countries examined in the UNICEF study–representing only 25% of the world's children–had foster care data that was reliably collected and could be analyzed. Data collection on the foster care populations was particularly low in South Asia, East Asia, and the Pacific. There are several factors that contribute to the lack of reliable data on the number and details of children in foster care. Administrative record-keeping is often inadequate and systems for tracking children may not be functioning properly. Quality assurance processes and data collection oversight are inconsistent or absent and there is often a lack of sufficient resources and investments devoted to collecting reliable data (Petrowski et al., 2017). Additionally, there are unregistered or unofficial institutions that operate within the foster care system that further impede reliable and valid measurement (Delap, 2011). Taken together, the prevalence of children living in foster care is likely to be conservative and underestimated.

Disparities in the Foster Care System

It is critical to talk about racial disparities in the foster care system (Kim et al., 2017; Luken et al., 2021; Yi et al., 2020). In the United States, youth of color (specifically Native American, Black, and mixed-race youth) are disproportionately represented in foster care. Moreover, families of color are more often reported and investigated for maltreatment compared to White families (Feliz et al., 2022; Kim et al., 2017; Luken et al., 2021). For example, at the time of this writing, although Black children represented 14% of youth in the population, they represented 20% of the children in foster care (National KIDS COUNT, 2022a, 2022b). One reason for this is cultural misunderstanding and the overreaching application of White parenting beliefs and practices to families of color (Adjei & Minka, 2018; One Vision One Voice, 2016). This disparity perpetuates racism and inequities that people of color have experienced for centuries. In Chapter 10, we further describe how lack of cultural understanding affects children while they are in care.

LGBTQIA+[7] youth are also disproportionately represented in the foster care system (Dettlaff et al., 2018). For example, a study conducted by Fish et al. (2019) found that sexual minority youth in the United States were 2.5 times more likely to be placed in foster care compared with heterosexual youth. LGBTQIA+ youth can experience verbal and physical harassment when disclosing their sexual orientation to family members (D'Augelli et al., 1998; Katz-Wise et al., 2016; Hatzenbuehler & Pachankis, 2016), which is associated with increased risk of foster care placement and homelessness (Berberet, 2006; Huebner et al., 2009; Winter, 2012). In general, LGBTQIA+ and gender nonconforming youth are more likely to experience family rejection, sexual abuse, parental physical abuse, and assault at school compared to cisgender, heterosexual nonminority youth (Baams, 2018; Friedman et al., 2011). Family rejection and abuse increase the risk of out-of-home and foster care placement (Mallon et al., 2002: Wilson & Kastanis, 2018). The intersection of race/ethnicity and sexual orientation/gender identity is important to consider when examining the prevalence of foster care representation (Hightow-Weidman et al., 2011). Research published in 2014 found that Black LGBTQ youth were overrepresented in the foster care system (Wilson et al., 2014). Unfortunately, there is a substantial gap in the present literature that examines the intersection of race/ethnicity and sexual/gender identities among foster care youth representation (Grooms, 2020).

Why Listen to Children in Foster Care?

Youth can provide unique perspectives regarding their foster care experiences. Meaningful information critical to youth welfare may be overlooked if their viewpoints are not considered. Even the most attentive and caring adults cannot fully take on a child's perspective and see the world through their lens, nor can they report on children's internal states. Youth's viewpoints should be considered in these matters because, in part, they are increasingly recognized as reliable informants about their own lives (Cashmore, 2014; Fox & Berrick, 2007; Saywitz et al., 2014). For example, social workers and other adults responsible for youth's care have started to take foster youth viewpoints into account when making case planning, placement, health care, and education decisions (Boshier & Steel-Baker, 2007; Cashmore et al., 2023; Clark, 2005; McTavish et al., 2012; Moore & Kirk, 2010; Nutbrown & Clough, 2009; Unrau, 2007; Weisz et al., 2011). More broadly, as experts on their own lives, foster youth offer valuable perspectives that can help shape policies and practices to reform the foster care system for the better.

> *"Listening should never be a challenge when making decisions about a foster youth and their life.*[8]*"*

Youth in care consistently express a desire to be more involved in decisions affecting them (Chapman et al., 2004; Daly, 2009; Ellermann, 2007). They generally do not want to fully control decision-making, but they do want to be informed and involved in the process. They want "to have a say, rather than their own way" (Cashmore, 2002, p. 845). Participation also prepares children in care for future independent, autonomous decision-making (Melton et al., 2014). This is particularly important for youth who will age out of the foster care system and who may not have stable, familial support.

The participation process itself may benefit children, even if final decisions do not fully reflect their input. Youth may have an increased sense of recognition, agency, empowerment, or self-esteem after participating in the process (Head, 2011; Melton et al., 2014). This is particularly salient for maltreated children, who can shift from seeing themselves as powerless victims to active agents in a system in which decisions are often made by numerous professionals and providers (Weithorn, 1983).

> *"It is important that youth feel heard because of the stress, anxiety, loneliness, and everything that leads to them being placed in the system.*[9]*"*

Additionally, children may be more satisfied with outcomes when they have a voice (Cashmore, 2002).

Procedural justice research has shown that perceived input in the process and interpersonal relationships with authority figures directly predict outcome satisfaction, along with perceived legitimacy of and compliance with decisions (Lind & Tyler, 1988; Thibaut & Walker, 1975; Tyler, 2013). This is also true for broader systems–such as the dependency system (Tyler, 1990; Tyler & Huo, 2002; Tyler & Fagan, 2008). Per procedural justice theory, quality of relationships with social workers and other important adults (e.g., foster care staff, attorneys, judges) is associated with how youth perceive their experiences in the foster care system, Moreover, the perceived quality of prior experiences (e.g., frequency of attorney contact, quality of attorney representation) predicts how favorably youth view the dependency system itself (Goldfarb et al., 2021). Even indirect methods, such as exercising children's voices through advocates or representatives who work with them on their behalf, have a positive effect on children's participation (Kennan et al., 2018).

Procedural Justice Evaluations

We explore theories of procedural justice and their implications for youth in foster care further below. The core ingredients of procedural justice are participating in the process, perceiving authority figures as making decisions fairly and without bias, being treated with dignity and respect, viewing authority figures as trustworthy, and providing their perspectives in decision-making (Mazerolle et al., 2013). Foster youth may form perceptions based on their own or through vicarious experiences (e.g., hearing about what occurred to a peer). Youth's perceptions of procedural justice can affect how they evaluate the effectiveness of authority figures (Tankebe, 2013). Foster youth may evaluate how well social workers and foster families are meeting their needs. Procedural justice evaluations have been found to be more important than the outcome in predicting whether individuals view the system and legal authorities as legitimate (e.g., Tyler & Huo, 2002).

Evaluations of, and sensitivity towards, procedural justice begin developing in early childhood during interactions with others (e.g., Killen & Smetana, 1999). For example, children's perceptions of fairness emerge by age 3 in collaborative activities (Ulber et al., 2017). Young children interpret fairness as mutual respect (Engelmann & Tomasello, 2019). Additionally, children are more likely to accept group decisions if they have been afforded an opportunity to provide input (Grocke et al., 2018). During early childhood, youth show a strong preference for procedural justice even when the outcome may be disadvantageous for themselves (Durham et al., 2018). There is also some evidence to suggest that procedural justice evaluations (e.g., opportunity to provide an input and participate) carries more weight for youth compared with adults (Murphy, 2015).

Youth perceptions about procedural matters have a downstream effect on outcomes that extend into adulthood. Legal cynicism tends to increase during adolescence and is coupled with viewing the legal system and its authorities as less legitimate (Fagan & Tyler, 2005). Adolescents who view legal authorities as more legitimate, however, tend to engage in less delinquency. Perceiving the system as more legitimate is associated with more voluntary, self-regulatory behavior, compliance with obeying the law, less recidivism, and more deference to decisions by legal authorities in adulthood (Tyler & Huo, 2002). Additionally, individuals with higher procedural justice evaluations (and therefore legitimacy) tend to be more willing to report crimes to the police (Reisig et al., 2007; Murphy & Cherney, 2012; Tankebe, 2009; Tankebe, 2013; Tyler & Fagan, 2008). Adolescents who have had negative interactions with legal authorities, such as the police, tend to be less willing to become engaged in the legal processes (Carr et al., 2007). Thus, *subjective* perceptions can have *objective* meaningful outcomes in the real world.

Meaningful Participation is Key

For procedural justice to truly matter, it must influence actual outcomes (Clark et al., 2018). In other words, what purpose does providing children with the opportunity to provide their input and participate in the process serve if it does not have any bearing on how adults will make decisions about their lives? Youth often report feeling like they are not being heard, even though others appear to listen to them, but that they perceive they are not being heard (Mitchell et al., 2010).

"I felt that I wasn't heard or taken seriously with how I felt due to me being a child. I was always told to stay in a child's place and that others knew what was best for me.[10]"

Providing input gives youth a sense that they can shape the decision-making process and allows them to feel like they are valued and an equally important member of a group (Thibaut & Walker, 1975; Tyler & Huo, 2002). Giving children the opportunity to express their views is only the first step. Allowing them to have meaningful participation suggests that their opinions and beliefs are taken seriously and considered when adults make decisions on their behalf (Cashmore, 2014, 2023). Thus, participation should not just entail that children perceive that they *could* influence the decision-making process, but that their input *does* have real-world consequences.

Challenges to Hearing Youth

There are potential challenges to youth participation in decision-making procedures. For example, youth in foster care often rely on social workers to exercise their rights. However, there are often discrepancies between children's perceptions of their rights to participate versus adults' perceptions of children's rights to participate (Cossar et al., 2016). Youth tend to believe in this right more than adults do (Taylor et al., 2001; Yitzhak Cohen & Ben-Arieh, 2021). For example, Sharon (2016) found that 64.3% of youth compared with 45.1% of social workers believed that children have a right to participate in coordinating committees. In another study, Yitzhak Cohen and Ben-Arieh (2021) found that 91.5% of children aged 8–14 in an emergency center believed they had a right to participate in decision-making, whereas less than half of the professional staff did. Child welfare professionals may view children as too vulnerable for involvement and often don't believe children can handle the responsibility that comes with participation (Atwool, 2006; Garcia-Quiroga & Salvo Agoglia, 2020; Pinkney, 2011). Some social workers report that children may lack the understanding, capability, or emotional state to express views (Sanders & Mace, 2006). Case managers may avoid involving children in decision-making due to a fear of further burdening them and to protect them from having to discuss difficult life experiences (Vis et al., 2011). That is, they may want to protect children from what they believe is undue stress (Kosher & Ben-Arieh, 2019). At times, social workers may also worry that children's involvement could negatively impact their well-being or case outcomes. Thus, training for social workers and other professionals on the benefits of participation may be needed.

Interpreting and implementing children's right to participation is complex (Archard & Uniacke, 2021). Decisions about whether to include children in decision-making requires consideration of age, development, and under-standing, as well as context and the family dynamics (Cossar et al., 2016). For instance, Article 12 of the CRC states that, "the views of the child [should be] given due weight in accordance with the age and maturity of the child" (United Nations General Assembly, 1989, p. 4). This suggests that more weight should be given to older and mature children. Practically speaking, this is left open for interpretation and may be applied inconsistently. For instance, what is the threshold for *sufficient* maturity to place more weight on one child's views over another's? Children develop and mature at different rates. Younger children's perspectives may not be given as much weight as older children, which may be particularly problematic in cases of child maltreatment in which preschool aged children are particularly susceptible for victimization (Austin et al., 2020; U.S. Department of Health and Human Services, 2023). It also presumes that adults, by nature of being older, can make competent decisions on behalf of children–which may not always be accurate.

"I felt disenfranchised as a young person, I lacked a connection with elders and a culture that felt real.[11]*"*

Cultural considerations of the rights of children are controversial, but necessary. For example, the idea that youth should be able to exert independent decision-making and autonomous decision-making has been criticized as a Western, individualistic notion (Shweder & Sullivan, 1993). The extent to which youth's input and participation is important to the process has been questioned by more collectivist cultures that emphasize group harmony over individual preferences (Iyengar & Lepper, 1999; Lahat et al., 2009). However, theories such as self-determinism, argue that autonomy represents a more universal psychological need and that core, personal needs extend cross-culturally (Cherney et al., 2008; Qin, 2017). Consistent with self-determination theory, we argue that children's right to participation is not culturally bound. While there may be cultural variations in implementing these procedural strategies for youth participation cross-culturally, there are underlying principles regarding the importance of youth's participation in matters that affect their welfare that are universal.

The Present Study

We conducted a systematic literature review and meta-analysis[12] examining youth's perspectives in foster care (see Appendix A). A systematic literature review is a method used to thoroughly search, locate, and synthesize relevant research on a given topic. It employs transparent, replicable procedures to reduce bias and error that may exaggerate or minimize effects. Our review focused on studies that used qualitative and mixed method (qualitative and quantitative) designs. This allowed us to compile information that was directly collected from foster youth about their experiences, perceptions, and behaviors (Tenny et al., 2022). Qualitative research often uses open-ended questions that ask about "how" and "why" things occur. Phenomena like experiences, attitudes, and behaviors can be difficult to accurately capture using quantitative (e.g., numbers) methods alone. Qualitative studies allow participants to elaborate on their thoughts, feelings, and experiences. While it is possible to quantify qualitative findings, the core purpose is identifying themes and patterns within the narratives. Focusing on these types of studies for our systematic review thus allowed foster care youth to talk about their experiences, in their *own* words, in rich detail. During these interviews, youth also made recommendations for best-practice guidelines for foster parents, social workers, and other adults.

For a description of the sample used in our systematic review and meta-analysis, including ages, countries, and interview topics, see Appendix B. Foster youth aged 0 to 18 from 27 countries across Asia, Africa, Europe, Australia, and North America were represented in our sample. These countries included Australia, Austria, Botswana, Bulgaria, Cambodia, Canada, England, Finland, France, Ghana, Greece, Ireland, Israel, Italy, Japan, Kenya, the Netherlands, Portugal, Romania, Scotland, Serbia, South Africa, Spain, Sweden, the United States, and Wales. Of note, in our review of the literature we did not find any published studies that interviewed participants from Central or South America.

What Lies Ahead: Themes and Takeaways by Chapter

As experts on their own lives, foster youth should be listened to and heard. The purpose of this book is to give children across the world the opportunity to express their voice by describing their experiences in foster care in their own words. Youth were interviewed about a variety of topics. Major themes that emerged across studies included around relationships with adults and peers (e.g., biological families, foster parents, foster siblings, and social workers), placement transitions in and out of care, belonging, feeling cared for, caregiver maltreatment, differences between birth and foster parents, cultural responsiveness to needs (e.g., hair care), mental health, self-advocacy, and perceptions of feelings of trust. In the following chapters, we will discuss the themes from the youth interviews that emerged in our systematic review.

Foster youth's perspectives on being in care, their feelings about the foster care system itself, and their views on court proceedings and case reviews are described in Chapter 2. Specifically, we explore youth's emotional reactions to entering and living in care, whether they find the system helpful, their level of understanding about their cases, and their experiences participating in legal meetings. Greater transparency, preparation, and participation in decision-making contribute to more positive outcomes for foster youth.

Chapter 3 examines foster youth's desire to participate in decisions made about them across areas like placements, foster homes, schools, family visits, and legal meetings. We found that inclusion of youth perspectives leads to greater belonging, wellbeing, and more positive outcomes overall.

Relationships with others are described in several chapters. Specifically, we discuss youth's contact, feelings, and perceptions about social workers (Chapter 4), birth families (Chapter 5), and foster families (Chapter 6).

Youth may experience placement changes and difficulties while in the foster care system. Chapter 7 explores the transitions youth in foster care experience when entering, moving within, and aging out of the system. Youth may experience difficulties during these various placements, including lack of resources, caring for others, building relationships, changing schools, and making friends (Chapter 8).

In Chapter 9, we discuss factors affecting foster youth psychological and socioemotional well-being, both positively and negatively, as well as youth perspectives on developing a sense of belonging within their foster families. Foster youth may feel different from others. Chapter 10 explores the stigma and bullying foster youth face because of being in care, their cultural identities and needs, self-advocacy abilities, self-esteem and confidence levels, and aspirations for the future.

This final chapter (Chapter 11) pulls together central themes around foster youth views on transitions, decision-making, relationships, support needs, cultural identity, and well-being into a summary, as well as providing a comprehensive list of recommendations youth made for improving the foster care experience.

Notes

1 Tammy, former foster youth; personal communication, November 30, 2023.
2 To date, this document has been ratified by 196 countries. Notably, the United States is one of the nations who has not signed it.
3 Tammy, former foster youth; personal communication, November 30, 2023.
4 Network care is a subset of kinship care that occurs when children are placed with family friends or acquaintances.
5 Inclusive of Australia, New Zealand, the Malay Archipelago, the Philippines, New Guinea, New Caledonia, Fiji, Micronesia, and Polynesia (Ray, 2023).
6 Yolanda, former foster youth; personal communication, December 1, 2023.
7 The current term is LGBTQIA+, which represents "Lesbian, Gay, Bisexual, Transgender, Queer and/or Questioning, Intersex, Asexual, … and the countless affirmative ways in which people choose to self-identify" (Emerson College, n.d.).
8 Diane, former foster youth; personal communication, November 30, 2023.
9 Yolanda, former foster youth; personal communication, December 1, 2023.
10 Diane, former foster youth; personal communication, November 30, 2023.

11 Michele, former foster youth; personal communication, December 1, 2023.
12 Specifically, we conducted a meta-analysis examining the number of foster youth who had contact with their biological mothers compared with their biological fathers.

References

Adjei, P. B., & Minka, E. (2018). Black parents ask for a second look: Parenting under "White" child protection rules in Canada. *Children and Youth Services Review, 94*, 511–524. 10.1016/j.childyouth.2018.08.030

Ainsworth, F., & Thoburn, J. (2014). An exploration of the differential usage of residential childcare across national boundaries. *International Journal of Social Welfare, 23*(1), 16–24. 10.1111/ijsw.12025

Annie E. Casey Foundation. (2024). Foster care explained: What it is, how it works and how it can be improved. https://www.aecf.org/blog/what-is-foster-care

Appell, A. R. (2006). Children's voice and justice: Lawyering for children in the twenty-first century. *Nevada Law Journal, 6*(3), 692–723.

Archard, D., & Uniacke, S. (2021). The child's right to a voice. *Research Publica, 27*, 521–536. 10.1007/s11158-020-09491-z

Assim, U. M. (2013). *Understanding kinship care of children in Africa: A family environment or an alternative care option* [Doctoral dissertation, University of the Western Cape]. http://hdl.handle.net/11394/3476

Atwool, N. (2006). Participation in decision-making: The experience of New Zealand children in care. *Child Care in Practice, 12*, 259–267. 10.1080/13575270600761727

Austin, A. E., Lesak, A. M., & Shanahan, M. E. (2020). Risk and protective factors for child maltreatment: A review. *Current Epidemiological Reports, 7*(4), 334–342. 10.1007/s40471-020-00252-3

Baams, L. (2018). Disparities for LGBTQ and gender nonconforming adolescents. *Pediatrics, 141*(5), 1–13. 10.1542/peds.2017-3004

Bennett, T. W. (1999). *Human rights and African customary law under the South African constitution.* Juta.

Berberet, H. M. (2006). Putting the pieces together for Queer youth: A model of integrated assessment of need and program planning. *Child Welfare, 85*(2), 361–384. http://www.jstor.org/stable/45398769

Biemba, G., Beard, J., Brook, B., Bresnaham, M., Flynn, D., & Simon, J. (2010). *The scale, scope and impact of alternative care for OVC in developing countries: A review of literature.* Center for Global Health and Development, Boston University.

Boshier, P., & Steel-Baker, D. (2007). Invisible parties: Listening to children. *Family Court Review, 45*, 548–559. 10.1111/j.1744-1617.2007.00170.x

Cantwell, N. (2005). The challenges of out-of-home care. Children without parental care: Qualitative alternatives. *Early Childhood Matters, 105*, 4–14.

Carr, P. J., Napolitano, L., & Keating, J. (2007). We never call the cops and here is why: A qualitative examination of legal cynicism in three Philadelphia neighborhoods. *Criminology, 45*(2), 445–480. 10.1111/j.1745-9125.2007.00084.x

Cashmore, J. (2002). Promoting the participation of children and young people in care. *Child Abuse and Neglect, 26*, 837–847. 10.1016/S0145-2134(02)00353-8

Cashmore, J. (2014). Children living away from home. In G. Melton, A. BenArieh, J. Cashmore, G. S. Goodman, & N. K. Worley (Eds.), *The Sage handbook of child research* (pp. 197–207). SAGE Publications Ltd.

Cashmore, J., Kong, P., & McLaine, M. (2023). Children's participation in care and protection decision-making matters. *Laws, 12*(49), 1–26. 10.3390/laws12030049

Chapman, M. V., Wall, A., & Barth, R. P. (2004). Children's voices: The perceptions of children in foster care. *American Journal of Orthopsychiatry, 74*, 293–304. https://doi.org10.1037/0002-9432.74.3.293

Cherney, I. D., Greteman, A. J., & Travers, B. G. (2008). A cross-cultural view of adults' perceptions of children's rights. *Social Justice Research, 21*, 432–456. 10.1007/s11211-008-0079-7

Clark, A. (2005). Listening to and involving young children: A review of research and practice. *Early Child Development and Care, 175*, 489–505. 10.1080/030044305 00131288

Clark, S. E., Moreland, M., & Larson, R. P. (2018). Legitimacy, procedural justice, accuracy, and eyewitness identification. *UC Irvine Law Review, 8*(1), https://escholarship.org/uc/item/4847151q

Courtney, M., & Iwaniec, D. (2009). *Residential care of children: Comparative perspectives.* Oxford University Press.

Cossar, J., Brandon, M., & Jordan, P. (2016). "You've got to trust her and she's got to trust you": Children's views of participation in the child protection system. *Child & Family Social Work, 21*(1), 103–112. 10.1111/cfs.12115

Daly, W. (2009). "Adding their flavour to the mix:" Involving children and young people in care in research design. *Australian Social Work, 62*, 460–475. 10.1080/03124070903265732

D'Augelli, A. R., Hershberger, S. L., & Pilkington, N. W. (1998). Lesbian, gay, and bisexual youth and their families: Disclosure of sexual orientation and its consequences. *American Journal of Orthopsychiatry, 68*(3), 361–371. 10.1037/h0080345

Delap, E. (2011). *Scaling down: Reducing, reshaping and improving residential care around the world* (Positive care choices: Working paper 1). London, United Kingdom: EveryChild. Retrieved November 22, 2023 from https://resourcecentre.savethechildren.net/pdf/4270.pdf/

Delap, E., & Melville, L. (2011). *Fostering better care: Improving foster care provision around the world* (Positive care choices: Working paper 2). London, United Kingdom: EveryChild. Retrieved from November 22, 2023 from https://bettercarenetwork.org/sites/default/files/Fostering%20Better%20Care%20-%20Improving%20Foster%20Care%20Provision%20Around%20the%20World.pdf

Dettlaff, A. J., Washburn, M., Carra, L., & Vogel, A. (2018). Lesbian, gay, and bisexual (LGB) youth within in welfare: Prevalence, risk and outcomes. *Child Abuse and Neglect, 80*, 183–193. 10.1016/j.chiabu.2018.03.009

Durham, Y., Durkin, A., & Tyler, T. R. (2018). The development of a preference for procedural justice for self and others. *Scientific Reports, 8*(17740), 1–8. 10.1038/s41598-018-36072-1

Ellermann, C. R. (2007). Influences on the mental health of children placed in foster care. *Family & Community Health, 30*, S23–S32. 10.1097/01.FCH.0000264878.50569.a3

Engelmann, J. M., & Tomasello, M. (2019). Children's sense of fairness as equal respect. *Trends in Cognitive Sciences, 23*(6), 454–463. 10.1016/j.tics.2019.03.001

Fagan, J., & Tyler, T. R. (2005). Legal socialization of children and adolescents. *Social Justice Research, 18*(3), 217–241. https://scholarship.law.columbia.edu/faculty_scholarship/1386

Feliz, V. A., Hobbs, S. D., Borunda, R. (2022). Strengthen and respect each thread. *International Journal of Environmental Research and Public Health, 19*(21), 14117. 10.3390/Ijerph192114117

Fish, J. N., Baams, L., Stevenson Wojciak, A., & Russell, S. T. (2019). Are sexual minority youth overrepresented in foster care, child welfare, and out-of-home placement? Findings from nationally representative data. *Child Abuse & Neglect, 89,* 203–211. 10.1016/j.chiabu.2019.01.005

Fox, A., & Berrick, J. D. (2007). A response to no one ever asked us: A review of children's experiences in out-of-home care. *Child and Adolescent Social Work Journal, 24,* 23–51. 10.1007/s10560-006-0057-6

Friedman, M. S., Marshal, M. P., Guadamuz, T. E., Wei, C., Wong, C. F., Saewyc, E. M., & Stall, R. (2011). A meta-analysis of disparities in childhood sexual abuse, parental physical abuse, and peer victimization among sexual minority and sexual nonminority individuals. *American Journal of Public Health, 101*(8), 1481–1494. 10.2105/AJPH.2009.190009

Garcia-Quiroga, M., & Salvo Agoglia, I. (2020). Too vulnerable to participate? Challenges for meaningful participation in research with children in alternative care and adoption. *International Journal of Qualitative Methods, 19,* 1–11. 10.1177/16094 06920958965

Goldfarb, D., Tashjian, S. M., Goodman, G. S., Bederian-Gardner, D., Hobbs, S. D., Cordón, I. M., Ogle, C. M., Bakanosky, S., Karr, R. K., Chae, Y., &the NYTD/CYTD Research Group. (2021). After child maltreatment: The importance of voice for youth in foster care. *Journal of Interpersonal Violence, 36*(13-14), NP7388–NP7414. 10.1177/088626051982588

Grocke, P., Rossano, F., & Tomasello, M. (2018). Young children are more willing to accept group decisions in which they have had a voice. *Journal of Experimental Child Psychology, 166,* 67–78. 10.1016/j.jecp.2017.08.003

Grooms, J. (2020). No home and no acceptance: Exploring the intersectionality of sexual/gender identities (LGBTQ) and race in the foster care system. *The Review of Black Political Economy, 47*(2), 1–17. 10.1177/0034644620911381

Hatzenbuehler, M. L., & Pachankis, J. E. (2016). Stigma and minority stress as social determinants of health among lesbian, gay, bisexual, and transgender youth: Research evidence and clinical implications. *Pediatric Clinics, 63*(6), 985–997. 10.1016/j.pcl.2016.07.003

Head, B. W. (2011). Why not ask them? Mapping and promoting youth participation. *Children and Youth Services Review, 33,* 541–547. 10.1016/j.childyouth.2010.05.015

Hightow-Weidman, L. B., Phillips, G., Jones, K. C., Outlaw, A. Y., Fields, S. D., & Smith, J. C., for the YMSM of Color SPNS Initiative Study Group, J. C. (2011). Racial and sexual identity-related maltreatment among minority YMSM: Prevalence, perceptions, and the association with emotional distress. *AIDS Patient Care and STDs, 25*(S1), S39–S45. 10.1089/apc.2011.9877

Huebner, R. C., Diaz, R. M., & Sanchez, J. (2009). Family rejection as a predictor of negative health outcomes in white and Latino lesbian, gay, and bisexual young adults. *Pediatrics, 123*(1), 346–352. 10.1542/peds.2007-3524

Innocenti Research Centre (2003). Children in institutions: The beginning of the end? UNICEF. Retrieved November 23, 2023 from https://www.unicef-irc.org/publications/pdf/insight8e.pdf

Iyengar, S. S., & Lepper, M. R. (1999). Rethinking the value of choice: A cultural perspective on intrinsic motivation. *Journal of Personality and Social Psychology, 76*(3), 349–366. 10.1037/0022-3514.76.3.349

Jones, D. P. H. (2002). Editorial: Listening to children. *Child Abuse & Neglect, 26,* 833–835. 10.1016/S0145-2134(02)00352-6

Katz-Wise, S. L., Rosario, M., Tsappis, M. (2016). Lesbian, gay, bisexual, and transgender youth and family acceptance. *Pediatric Clinics, 63*(6), 1011–1025. 10.1016/j.pcl.2016.07.005

Kennan, D., Brady, B., & Forkan, C. C. (2018). Supporting children's participation in decision making: A systematic literature review exploring the effectiveness of participatory processes. *British Journal of Social Work, 48*(7), 1985–2002. 10. 1093/bjsw/bcx142

Kim, H., Wildeman, C., Jonson-Reid, M., & Drake, B. (2017). Lifetime prevalence of investigating child maltreatment among US children. *American Journal of Public Health, 107*(2), 274–280. 10.2105/AJPH.2016.303545

Killen, M., & Smetana, J. G. (1999). Social interactions in preschool classrooms and the development of young children's conceptions of the personal. *Child Development, 70*(2), 486–501. 10.1111/1467-8624.00035

Kosher, H., & Ben-Arieh, A. (2019). Social workers' perceptions of children's right to participation. *Child & Family Social Work, 25*(2), 294–303. 10.1111/cfs.12685

Lahat, A., Helwig, C. C., Yang, S., Tan, D., & Liu, C. (2009). Mainland Chinese adolescents' judgments and reasoning about self-determination and nurturance rights. *Social Development, 18*(3), 690–710. 10.1111/i.14679507.2008.00507.x

Lind, E. A., & Tyler, T. R. (1988). *The social psychology of procedural justice*. Plenum Press.

Lough, B., & Panos, P. (2003). Rise and demise of orphanages in Ukraine. *European Journal of Social Work, 6*(1), 49–63. 10.1080/01369145032000099648

Luken, A., Nair, R., & Fix, R. L. (2021). On racial disparities in child abuse reports: Exploratory mapping the 2018 NCANDS. *Child Maltreatment, 26*(3), 267–281. 10.1177/10775595211001926

Mallon, G. P., Aledort, N., & Ferrera, M. (2002). There's no place like home: achieving safety, permanency, and well-being for lesbian and gay adolescents in out-of-home care settings. *Child Welfare, 81*(2), 407–439. https://www.jstor.org/stable/45390066

Mazerolle, L., Antrobus, E., Bennett, S., & Tyler, T. R. (2013). Shaping citizen perceptions of police legitimacy: A randomized field trial of procedural justice. *Criminology, 51*(1), 33–63. 10.1111/j.1745-9125.2012.00289.x

McTavish, M., Streelasky, J., & Coles, L. (2012). Listening to children's voices: Children as participants in research. *International Journal of Early Childhood, 44*(3), 249–267. 10.1007/s13158-012-0068-8

Melton, G. B., Gross-Manos, D., Ben-Arieh, A., & Yazykova, E. (2014). The nature and scope of child research: Learning about children's lives. In G. Melton, A. Ben-Arieh, J. Cashmore, G. S. Goodman, & N. K. Worley, (Eds.), *The Sage handbook of child research* (pp. 3–28). SAGE Publications Ltd.

Mitchell, M. B., Kuczynski, L., Tubbs, C. Y., & Ross, C. (2010). We care about care: Advice by children in care for children in care, foster parents and child welfare workers about the transition into foster care. *Child & Family Social Work, 15*, 176–185. 10.1111/j.1365-2206.2009.00657.x

Moore, L., & Kirk, S. (2010). A literature review of children's and young people's participation in decisions relating to health care. *Journal of Clinical Nursing, 19*, 2215–2225. 10.1111/j.1365-2702.2009.03161.x

Murphy, K. (2015). Does procedural justice matter to youth? Comparing adults' and youths' willingness to collaborate with police. *Policing and Society, 25*(1), 53–76. 10.1080/10439463.2013.802786

Murphy, K., & Cherney, A. (2012). Understanding cooperation with police in a diverse society. *British Journal of Criminology, 52*, 181–201. 10.1093/bjc/azr065

National KIDS COUNT (2022a). *Child population by race in the United States* [data set]. Annie E. Casey Foundation Kids Count Data Set. https://datacenter.kidscount.org/data/tables/103-child-population-by-race#detailed/1/any/false/574,1729,37,871,870,573,869,36,868,867/68,69,67,12,70,66,71,72/423,424

National KIDS COUNT (2022b). *Children entering foster care by race and Hispanic origin in the United States* [data set]. Annie E. Casey Foundation Kids Count Data

Set. https://datacenter.kidscount.org/data/tables/6272-children-entering-foster-care-by-race-and-hispanic-origin#detailed/1/any/false/574,1729,37,871,870,573,869,36, 868,867/2638,2601,2600,2598,2603,2597,2602,1353/13041,13042

Nutbrown, C., & Clough, P. (2009). Citizenship and inclusion in the early years: Understanding and responding to children's perspectives on 'belonging.' *International Journal of Early Years Education, 17*, 191–206. 10.1080/09669760903424523

One Vision One Voice (2016). *Changing the Ontario Child Welfare System to better serve African Canadians: Practice framework part 1.* Ontario Association of Children's Aid Societies. https://www.oacas.org/wp-content/uploads/2016/09/One-Vision-One-Voice-Part-1_digital_english-May-2019.pdf

Petrowski, N., Cappa, C., & Gross, P. (2017). Estimating the number of children in formal alternative care: Challenges and results. *Child Abuse & Neglect, 70*, 388–398. 10.1016/j.chiabu.2016.11.026

Phillips, C. (2011). Child-headed households: A feasible way forward, or an infringement on children's right to alternative care? Retrieved November 30, 2023 from https://files.eric.ed.gov/fulltext/ED527864.pdf

Pinkney, S. (2011). Participation and emotions: Troubling encounters between children and social welfare professionals. *Children & Society, 25*, 37–46. 10.1111/j.1099-0860.2009.00261.x

Qin, L. (2017). We have voices, too: A literature review of Chinese children's participation rights. *Journal of Social Research & Policy, 8*(1), 17–31. https://www.proquest.com/scholarly-journals/we-have-voices-too-literature-review-chinese/docview/2330960174/se-2.

Ray, M. (2023). Australasia. In *Britannica.* Retrieved November 22, 2023, from https://www.britannica.com/place/Australasia

Reisig, M. D., Bratton, J., & Gertz, M. G. (2007). The construct validity and refinement of process-based policing measures. *Criminal Justice and Behavior, 34*, 1005–1028. 10.1177/0093854807301275

Sanders, R., & Mace, S. (2006). Agency policy and the participation of children and young people in the child protection process. *Child Abuse Review, 15*, 89–109. 10. 1002/car.927

Saywitz, K. J., Larson, R. P., Hobbs, S. D., & Wells, C. (2014). *Listening to children in foster care: Eliciting reliable reports from children: Review of influential factors.* The Swedish National Board of Health and Welfare. http://www.socialstyrelsen.se/publikationer2015/2015-1-17

Sharon, R. (2016). *Children's participation and satisfaction from treatment: The case of Parent-Child Centers* [Unpublished doctoral dissertation]. The Hebrew University of Jerusalem, Israel. 10.1007/978-3-030-82479-2_8

Sinclair, I. & Gibbs, I. (1998). *Children's homes: A study in diversity.* Wiley.

Shweder, R. A., & Sullivan, M. A. (1993). Cultural psychology: Who needs it? *Annual Review of Psychology, 44*, 497–523. 10.1146/annurev.ps.44.020193.002433

Tankebe, J. (2009). Public cooperation with the police in Ghana: Does procedural fairness matter? *Criminology, 47*(4), 1265–1293. 10.1111/j.1745-9125.2009.00175.x

Tankebe, J. (2013). Viewing things differently: The dimensions of public perceptions of police legitimacy. *Criminology, 51*(1), 103–135. 10.1111/j.1745-9125.2012.00291.x

Taylor, T. J., Turner, K. B., Esbensen, F. -A., Winfree Jr., L. T. (2001). Coppin' an attitude: Attitudinal differences among juveniles toward police. *Journal of Criminal Justice, 29*, 295–305. 10.1016/S0047-2352(01)00089-7

Tenny S., Brannan. J. M., & Brannan, G. D. (2022). Qualitative study. In StatsPearls. Retrieved November 23, 2023 from https://www.ncbi.nlm.nih.gov/books/NBK470395/

Thibaut, K. & Walker, L. (1975). *Procedural justice.* Lawrence Erlbaum.

Thoburn, J. (2007). Globalisation and child welfare: Some lessons from a cross-national study of children in out-of-home care. *British Journal of Social Work*, *38*, 1–70. https://www.researchgate.net/publication/265357214

Tyler, T. R. (1990). *Why people obey the law*. Yale University Press.

Tyler, T. R. (2013). *Why people cooperate: The role of social motivations*. Princeton University Press.

Tyler, T. R., & Fagan, J. (2008). Legitimacy and cooperation: Why do people help the police fight crime in their communities. *Ohio State Journal of Criminal Law*, *6*, 231–275. http://moritzlaw.osu.edu/osjcl/Articles/Volume6_1/Tyler-Fagan-PDF.pdf

Tyler, T. R., & Huo, Y. J. (2002). *Trust in the Law: Encouraging Public Cooperation with the Police and Courts*. Russell Sage Foundation.

Ulber, J., Hamann, K., & Tomasello, M. (2017). Young children, but not chimpanzees, are averse to disadvantageous and advantageous inequities. *Journal of Experimental Child Psychology*, *155*, 48–66. 10.1016/j.jecp.2016.10.013

United Nations General Assembly (1989). *Convention on the rights of the child.* (U.N. Doc. A/Res/44/25). *United Nations Treaty Series*, *1577*, 1–15. https://www.refworld.org/docid/3ae6b38f0.html

United Nations General Assembly. (2009). Guidelines for the Alternative Care of Children (U.N Doc. A/RES/64/142). https://digitallibrary.un.org/record/673583/files/A_RES_64_142-EN.pdf

UNICEF (2022). *Child rights and why they matter: Every right, for every child.* Retrieved November 30, 2023 from https://www.unicef.org/child-rights-convention/child-rights-why-they-matter

Unrau, Y. A. (2007). Research on placement moves: Seeking the perspective of foster children. *Children and Youth Services Review*, *29*, 122–137. 10.1016/j.childyouth.2006.08.003

U.S. Department of Health and Human Services (2023). *Child Maltreatment, 2021.* https://www.acf.hhs.gov/sites/default/files/documents/cb/cm2021.pdf

Vis, S., Strandbu, A., Holtan, A., & Thomas, N. (2011). Participation and health—A research review of child participation in planning and decision making. *Child and Family Social Work*, *16*, 325–335. 10.1111/j.1365-2206.2010.00743.x

Weisz, V., Wingrove, T., Beal, S. J., & Faith-Slaker, A. (2011). Children's participation in foster care hearings. *Child Abuse & Neglect*, *35*, 267–272. 10.1016/j.chiabu.2010.12.007

Weithorn, L. (1983). Involving children in decision-making affecting their own welfare: Guidelines for professionals. In G. Melton, G. Koocher, & M. Saks, (Eds.), *Children's competence to consent* (pp. 235–260). Plenum Press.

Wilson, B. D. M., Cooper, K., Kastanis, A., & Nezhad, S. (2014). *Sexual and gender minority youth in foster care: Assessing disportionality and disparities in Los Angeles.* The Williams Institute. Retrieved November 30, 2023 from https://escholarship.org/uc/item/6mg3n153.

Wilson, B. D. M., & Kastanis, A. A. (2018). Sexual and gender minority disproportionality and disparities in child welfare: A population-based study. *Child Youth Services Review*, *58*, 11–17. 10.1016/j.childyouth.2015.08.016

Winter, C. (2012). *Responding to LGBT health disparities.* In Missouri Foundation for Health: Health Equity Series. Retrieved November 22, 2023, from https://mffh.org/wp-content/uploads/2016/04/LGBTHealthEquityReport.pdf

Yi, Y., Edwards, F. R., & Wildeman, C. (2020). Cumulative prevalence of confirmed maltreatment and foster care placement for US children by race/ethnicity, 2011-2016. *American Journal of Public Health*, *110*(5), 704–709. 10.2105/AJPH.2019.305554

Yitzhak Cohen, O., & Ben-Arieh, A. (2021). Maltreated children in emergency centers: Do they participate? And how satisfied are they? *International Journal on Child Maltreatment: Research, Public Policy, and Practice, 4,* 279–305. 10.1007/s42448-021-00081-x

Zimmerman, B. (2005). Orphan living situations in Malawi: A comparison of orphanages and foster homes. *Review of Policy Research, 22*(6), 881–917. 10.1111/j.1541-1338.2005.00180.x

Chapter 2

Children's Attitudes and Knowledge of the Foster Care System

"I'd like to know the truth about why we went into foster care[1]"

Although the foster care system was developed to care for youth who need to be removed from their biological homes, many of these youth do not understand the foster care system or how they fit within it. The ways in which foster youth approach and understand their involvement in the foster care system varied widely across studies in our systematic review. Understanding the perspectives of foster youth in relation to their role in the foster care system can help administrators more effectively provide the necessary support and services that the foster youth need to be successful. In this chapter, we will review how youth felt about being in care, how they felt about the foster care system, and their views about court proceedings and case reviews.

Youth's Feelings about Foster Care

Across studies, youth were open about their feelings about foster care, both during transitions into care and while living in care. Many youth described feeling worried and afraid when they entered into care (Dansey et al., 2018; Mitchell & Kuczynski, 2010). When children interviewed in the United Kingdom were told they were being placed into care, many worried that their needs would not be met and they would not have toys or a place to sleep. Youth also expressed concern about being able to maintain their lives as they were prior to placement (Mitchell & Kuczynski, 2010). Many youth interviewed in Canada were afraid that their friends would not want to be friends with them anymore, and some felt like their biological parents didn't love them enough to keep them from being placed in care. One youth described feeling like she needed to settle down quickly and fit in to avoid being moved to another home (e.g., Dansey et al., 2018).

DOI: 10.4324/9781003309215-2

"I thought when I first went into foster care that I wouldn't be able to see my parents ever again ... Even though my parents didn't do right, they weren't being right with me ... it doesn't mean I don't like them. But, like, it kinda feels like prison if you didn't get to see them.[2]"

Some children preferred living in foster care rather than living with their biological families. For example, in one study in Ghana, most (16 out of 27) of the children were happy their parents had sent them to foster care (Kuyini et al., 2009). In Japan, some children said they did not want to return home because they experienced maltreatment while with their biological families or because they were left alone when they were there (Bamba & Haight, 2009). Dunn et al. (2010) found that girls and children (of all genders) who were sexually or emotionally abused were more likely than boys or children (of all genders) who experienced physical abuse to report that their lives would have been worse if they had stayed with their biological parents. These youth mentioned that some days they questioned their placements, but if they thought about their situations more carefully, they realized they were better off in care than with their biological families (Hedin et al., 2012).

Conversely, some children had more negative or conflicting feelings about living in foster care. For example, Selwyn et al. (2010) found that 14% of the youth in their study stated that they were uncertain (lonely or nervous) or otherwise unhappy regarding their placement. Morrison et al. (2011) interviewed 24 children in Canada regarding their visits with biological family members. Most children understood that their biological families could not take care of them or that they were safer with their foster families. However, even in circumstances wherein the youth experienced abuse, some still wanted to return to living with their biological mothers. It is important for adults (e.g., foster carers, caseworkers) to listen to youth and validate feelings they have about their birth parents.

The System Itself

Of the youth who were interviewed about their experiences with the foster care system, some noted that they felt better off in foster care than when they were living with their biological families (Bamba & Haight, 2009; Dunn et al., 2010; Emond, 2010; Morrison et al., 2011). Of interest, this depended upon the type of care. That is, in one study conducted in the United States, youth in residential care (compared to youth in foster or kinship[3] care) were more likely to report that they would have fared better if they stayed with their biological families and had not entered care[4] (Dunn et al., 2010). There were also youth who felt like their lives would have been better if they had entered foster care sooner (e.g., Jansen & Haavind, 2011).

"Why should I believe that this place is as brilliant as you say when none of the other places have been as you envisioned? ... You can't just move me around for the hundredth time. It does something to you as a person.[5]"

Youth described an increase in their well-being based on differences in experiences between living with biological families versus when living in foster care. For example, foster youth—in all placement types—reported feeling safe in their new environments, having enough food to eat, having clean clothes to wear, getting consistent access to education, and feeling like part of a family (Dunn et al., 2010; Emond, 2010; Gayapersad et al., 2019; Hedin et al., 2011; Schiller & de Wet, 2018). Thus, at times the system was effective in providing the intended services and support for vulnerable youth (Burgund & Zegarac, 2016; Weisz et al., 2011).

There were also youth who found the system to be unhelpful, confusing, or generally unsatisfactory (Fargas-Malet & McSherry, 2018; Jansen & Haavind, 2011; Pert et al., 2017). For example, sometimes youth were unconvinced that new placements would be any better based on several poor placements in the past (e.g., Jansen & Haavind, 2011). In addition, sometimes youth felt like they were missing important information, such as why they were in care (see e.g., Aldgate, 2009; Mateos et al., 2012; Mitchell & Kuczynski, 2010). Some children were given multiple reasons for their placement into care or did not believe social workers' explanations for their placement into care. Other children asked caregivers, social workers, and teachers why they were in care and felt like no one really knew. Unfortunately, some children even blamed themselves for being in foster care (e.g., because they wore old clothes to school). Often youth reported not knowing how long they would be in care or whether they were doing well in their current placements (e.g., Aldgate, 2009; Burgund & Zegarac, 2016; Schofield et al., 2012). Others wanted to know more about their birth parents but felt like they could not ask for fear of upsetting foster carers (Mateos et al., 2012).

Although there are often support systems in place for foster youth, some youth are not aware that they exist or how to access them. For example, youth have reported not knowing if there were case or educational support plans in place for them; and if they were aware, they did not know what these plans contained (Buys et al., 2011; Southwell & Fraser, 2010). This lack of knowledge of the system's supports could be impacting foster youth in a negative way, both emotionally and academically. However, creating multidisciplinary teams (including mental health professionals, advocates, educators, and other service providers) may help foster youth to get access to services and supports they need, and could help identify what can be made available to them (even if they aren't necessarily needed at the time) (Fargas-Malet & McSherry, 2018; Pölkki et al., 2012).

Court Proceedings and Case Reviews

Part of being in the foster care system means participating in legal matters, including attending review meetings and court proceedings. Attendance at dependency court proceedings and case review meetings is not always required, and at times, youth are given a choice to attend or not (e.g., Pert et al., 2017; Schofield et al., 2012; Weisz et al., 2011). In terms of dependency court proceedings, when compared to children who did not attend, children who did attend felt happier with the judges' decisions (Weisz et al., 2011). However, youth's knowledge of their role within these proceedings appeared to be relatively low. Children who attended meetings felt like they understood the system better and knew more about their cases, but the researchers did not state the level of overall knowledge (Weisz et al., 2011). Older youth understood the court process significantly better than younger youth, however, it was still a low understanding (Block et al., 2010; Weisz et al., 2011). Of interest, in the Weisz et al. (2011) study, encouragement from judges during court proceedings predicted youth's positive feelings about their experiences in court.

In terms of case reviews, across studies, youth wanted to attend reviews to know what was being decided about them, and to make their opinions known, especially regarding school and visitation with birth families (Pert et al., 2017; Schofield et al., 2012).

> *"I like the meetings, I like to have a chat and it's nice to talk about me.[6]"*

However, many youth who did attend reported that they did not like the reviews, felt they were boring, were not sure the purpose, or found it hard to understand the jargon being used (Pert et al., 2017; Pölkki et al., 2012; Schofield et al., 2012).

> *"The meetings themselves are a bit scary, they are daunting really, so then I'm not in the right frame of mind to talk about anything and it's just … embarrassing.[7]"*

Sometimes youth described case review meetings as a way to get things they wanted or needed (e.g., change in placement, access to information), and these youth tended to see the meetings as valuable (Pert et al., 2017; Pölkki et al., 2012). Although the goal of review meetings was to ensure the youth's needs were met, these meetings did not guarantee that the youth would get the support they wanted or needed. For example, some youth felt they had to push for services they needed, including mental health services and support (Fargas-Malet & McSherry, 2018). This had the unexpected benefit of helping youth become more mature, self-reliant, and better able to evaluate which support was needed, which helped them feel more capable of speaking up for themselves in meetings and proceedings (Buys et al., 2011; Emond, 2010; Fargas-Malet & McSherry, 2018; Hedin, 2014; Kelly et al., 2019; Pert et al., 2017).

One study went in depth to obtain a comprehensive picture of how knowledgeable foster youth were about case reviews. Pert et al. (2017) interviewed 25 foster children (ages 8–17) in England about their case reviews. Only a few of the children interviewed were asked to provide input about upcoming reviews. Two children reported being visited by their social worker ahead of time. A few others were sent generic forms in the mail. None of the children were given agency to decide when or where reviews would take place. Most of the children stated that they wanted to have their case reviews at preferred locations (restaurants, activity venues, etc.). Some youth were unhappy with the large number of people that attended the review—at times not knowing who the people were. This led to them feeling confused, uncomfortable, or even angry. Many of the youth either liked having their birth parents present or wanted their birth parents to be present. In this study, only two of the 25 children (8%) felt the reviews were helpful, and while the majority of foster carers felt the meetings were helpful in general, most felt that they were not helpful for the youth. Moreover, many youth did not fully understand the purpose of the reviews and did not feel prepared for them when they occurred. This lack of understanding was associated with more negative feelings about reviews and less participation in them (Pert et al., 2017).

There were instances in which youth felt the reviews caused them more trouble than they were helpful. For example, in the Schofield et al. (2012) study, one youth described a time when adults spoke *about* him and then confronted him, rather than including him in the conversation about his behavior. Another youth was asked about her sex life by and in front of unfamiliar adults. These are from a small sample of foster youth and cannot be considered generalizable to all youth in care. However, it is important that social workers and those managing care reviews treat youth as active and respected participants. When they do, this may lead more youth to trust the system that is meant to protect them. As described in Chapters 3, 4, and 9, trust with foster families and social workers is related to better emotional outcomes, more involvement in the decision-making process, and an increase in buy-in with necessary changes.

Schofield et al. (2012) found that certain practices, such as advocacy meetings, were effective in keeping youth informed and knowledgeable about the system. In these advocacy meetings, children were informed and/or involved in decision-making (for more about youth's involvement in the decision-making process, see Chapter 3). Meeting procedures varied depending upon youth's situations. Some procedures included receiving information about upcoming placements, being told what to expect, visiting with potential upcoming foster carers, seeing photographs of foster families and foster homes, or being provided with other information, all of which can help in the transition process. The advocacy meetings often helped youth feel less anxious about where they would be living and for how long (Schofield et al., 2012). Helping foster youth to feel more supported and knowledgeable may be the key in ensuring success in foster care placement and in supporting youth's overall emotional well-being.

Summary

Foster youth's feelings about foster care varied across studies in our systematic review. Some youth were happy to be out of their biological homes, while others felt conflicted or wanted to return home. Youth typically had little understanding about what was happening in their lives. Across studies, foster youth expressed their desire to know about their biological families, why they were in care, details of their case plans, what supports were available, what others said about them, and to have input in the decisions made for and about them. Additionally, youth wanted their care teams to be transparent and to explain decisions in a way that was easier for them to understand. When youth are a part of the foster care system, there are several legal meetings and proceedings that require their attendance. Based on what we know from the studies by Weisz et al. (2011) and Block et al. (2010), it seems reasonable that court preparation programs and child advocates would be helpful for youth attending dependency court hearings. For example, children in mock trials felt better prepared and less anxious after participating in a court preparation program (see e.g., Nathanson & Saywitz, 2015). Social workers, foster families, and legal representatives can all work together to ensure that foster youth are given the tools they need to feel supported in their transition into foster care, and to understand both the foster care system and their role within it.

Notes

1 Age not given, range 8–16; Aldgate, 2009, p. 52.
2 Age 10–11; Mitchell & Kuczynski, 2010, p. 440.
3 Children in kinship care can be placed with family members or close family friends.
4 Unfortunately, the researchers did not ask youth *why* they felt it would have been better if they had stayed with their biological families.
5 Age 16; Jansen & Haavind, 2011, p. 82.
6 Age 10; Pert et al., 2017, p. 3.
7 Age 15; Pert et al., 2017, p. 3.

References

Aldgate, J. (2009). Living in kinship care: A child-centered view. *Adoption & Fostering*, *33*(3), 51–63. 10.1177/030857590903300306

Bamba, S., & Haight, W. (2009). Maltreated children's emerging well-being in Japanese state care. *Children and Youth Services Review*, *31*(7), 797–806. 10.1016/j.childyouth.2009.02.006

Block, S. D., Oran, H., Oran, D., Baumrind, N., & Goodman, G. S. (2010). Abused and neglected children in court: knowledge and attitudes. *Child Abuse & Neglect*, *34*(9), 659–670. 10.1016/j.chiabu.2010.02.003

Burgund, A., & Zegarac, N. (2016). Perspectives of youth in care in Serbia. *Child & Adolescent Social Work Journal*, *33*(2), 151–161. 10.1007/s10560-015-0413-5

Buys, N., Tilbury, C., Creed, P., & Crawford, M. (2011). Working with youth in-care: Implications for vocational rehabilitation practice. *Disability and Rehabilitation*, *33*(13-14), 1125–1135. 10.3109/09638288.2010.521614

Dansey, D., John, M., & Shbero, D. (2018). How children in foster care engage with loyalty conflict: presenting a model of processes informing loyalty. *Adoption & Fostering*, *42*(4), 354–368. http://dx.doi.org/10.1177/0308575918798767.

Dunn, D. M., Culhane, S. E., & Taussig, H. N. (2010). Children's appraisals of their experiences in out-of-home care. *Children and Youth Services Review*, *32*(10), 1324–1330. 10.1016/j.childyouth.2010.05.001

Emond, R. (2010). Caring as a moral, practical and powerful endeavour: Peer care in a Cambodian orphanage. *The British Journal of Social Work*, *40*(1), 63–81. 10.1093/bjsw/bcn102

Fargas-Malet, M., & McSherry, D. (2018). The mental health and help-seeking behavior of children and young people in care in Northern Ireland: Making services accessible and engaging. *The British Journal of Social Work*, *48*(3), 578–595. 10.1093/bjsw/bcx062

Gayapersad, A., Ombok, C., Kamanda, A., Tarus, C., Ayuku, D., & Braitstein, P. (2019). The production and reproduction of kinship in charitable children's institutions in Uasin Gishu County, Kenya. *Child & Youth Care Forum*, *48*, 797–828. 10.1007/s10566-019-09506-8

Hedin, L. (2014). A sense of belonging in a changeable everyday life – a follow-up study of young people in kinship, network, and traditional foster families. *Child & Family Social Work*, *19*(2), 165–173. 10.1111/j.1365-2206.2012.00887.x

Hedin, L., Höjer, I., & Brunnberg, E. (2011). Settling into a new home as a teenager: About establishing social bonds in different types of foster families in Sweden. *Children and Youth Services Review*, *33*(11), 2282–2289. 10.1016/j.childyouth.2011.07.016

Hedin, L., Höjer, I., & Brunnberg, E. (2012). Jokes and routines make everyday life a good life—on 'doing family' for young people in foster care in Sweden. *European Journal of Social Work*, *15*(5), 613–628. http://dx.doi.org/10.1080/13691457.2011.579558

Jansen, A., & Haavind, H. (2011). "If only" and "despite all": Narrative configuration among young people living in residential care. *Narrative Inquiry*, *21*(1), 68–87. 10.1075/ni.21.1.04jan

Kelly, C., Anthony, E. K., & Krysik, J. (2019). "How am I doing?" Narratives of youth living in congregate care on their social-emotional well-being. *Children and Youth Services Review*, *103*, 255–263. 10.1016/j.childyouth.2019.06.001

Kuyini, A. B., Alhassan, A. R., Tollerud, I., Weld, H., & Haruna, I. (2009). Traditional kinship foster care in northern Ghana: the experiences and views of children, carers and adults in Tamale. *Child & Family Social Work*, *14*(4), 440–449. http://doi.org/10.1111/j.1365-2206.2009.00616.x

Mateos, A., Balsells, M. À., Molina, M. C., & Fuentes-Peláez, N. (2012). The perception adolescents in kinship foster care have of their own needs. *Revista de Cercetare si Interventie Sociala, 38*, 25–41. http://hdl.handle.net/2445/103325

Mitchell, M. B., & Kuczynski, L. (2010). Does anyone know what is going on? Examining children's lived experience of the transition into foster care. *Children and Youth Services Review, 32*(3), 437–444. 10.1016/j.childyouth.2009.10.023

Morrison, J., Mishna, F., Cook, C., & Aitken, G. (2011). Access visits: Perceptions of child protection workers, foster parents and children who are Crown wards. *Children and Youth Services Review, 33*(9), 1476–1482. 10.1016/j.childyouth.2011. 03.011

Nathanson, R., & Saywitz, K. J. (2015). Preparing children for court: Effects of a model court education program on children's anticipatory anxiety. *Behavioral Sciences and the Law, 33*, 459–475. 10.1002/bsl.2191

Pert, H., Diaz, C., & Thomas, N. (2017). Children's participation in LAC reviews: A study in one English local authority. *Child & Family Social Work, 22*(S2), 1–10. 10.1111/cfs.12194

Pölkki, P., Vornanen, R., Pursiainen, M., & Riikonen, M. (2012). Children's participation in child-protection processes as experienced by foster children and social workers. *Child Care in Practice, 18*(2), 107–125. 10.1080/13575279.2011. 646954

Schiller, U., & de Wet, G. (2018). Communication, indigenous culture and participatory decision making amongst foster adolescents. *Qualitative Social Work, 17*(2), 236–251. 10.1177/1473325016662329

Schofield, G., Beek, M., & Ward, E. (2012). Part of the family: Planning for permanence in long-term family foster care. *Children and Youth Services Review, 34*(1), 244–253. 10.1016/j.childyouth.2011.10.020

Selwyn, J., Saunders, H., & Farmer, E. (2010). The Views of Children and Young People on Being Cared For by an Independent Foster-Care Provider. *British Journal of Social Work, 40*(3), 696–713. http://doi.org/10.1093/bjsw/bcn117

Southwell, J., & Fraser, E. (2010). Young people's satisfaction with residential care: Identifying strengths and weaknesses in service delivery. *Child Welfare, 89*(2), 209–228. https://pubmed.ncbi.nlm.nih.gov/20857888/

Weisz, V., Wingrove, T., Beal, S. J., & Faith-Slaker, A. (2011). Children's participation in foster care hearings. *Child Abuse & Neglect, 35*(4), 267–272. 10.1016/j.chiabu. 2010.12.007

Chapter 3

Youth Involvement in Decisions about Themselves

"I haven't really had involvement in my case plan. I don't really get told much about my life[1]"

While social workers may be experts in their field overall, foster youth are the true experts on their own lives (Tindall-Biggins, 2020). Indeed, the UN Convention on the Rights of the Child states that children's views should be given "due weight" when decisions are being made that can affect their lives (Office of the High Commissioner, Human Rights, 2021). This sentiment has been echoed in policies throughout the world [see e.g., The Child Protection Act, 1999; Three-Year Programme on Austrian Development Policy 2013-2015, 2012; Botswana Bill of Child Rights, 2021; The Juvenile Justice (Care and Protection of Children) Act, 2015, 2020]. Moreover, the social work profession includes many values specific to their codes of conduct and ethics, one of which states that foster youth should be given opportunities to have a say in decisions that directly affect them (International Federation of Social Workers, 2018). Unfortunately, foster youth often feel like they have little control over what occurs in their lives. One reason for this may be that adults do not trust foster youth's abilities to make realistic decisions (McLeod, 2006). However, youth are often well aware of boundaries in place within the system and are concerned with fairness and having their input considered when decisions are made on their behalf (McLeod, 2006). Including foster youth in conversations and decisions, and trusting them to be active participants, helps protect their agency and sense of competency (Fylkesnes et al., 2021).

A key focus in our work is recognizing that youth are experts in their own lives. In this systematic review, we first sought to understand how youth felt regarding their participation in decisions made about their lives. While the amount or type of say in the decision-making process can vary, in a majority of the studies we reviewed, most foster youth expressed the desire to be involved in decisions that are made about their care in at least *some* way (Balsells et al., 2017; Barnes, 2012; Dansey et al., 2018; Kiraly & Humphreys, 2013; Pert et al., 2017; Ridley et al., 2016; Rostill-Brookes et al., 2011; Schiller & de Wet, 2018; Schofield et al., 2012; Southwell & Fraser, 2010). When foster youth are not included in the decision-making process, they may not know what is going to happen to them, which can result in feelings of insecurity (Buys et al., 2011). Based on interviews across several studies in our

DOI: 10.4324/9781003309215-3

review, foster youth's participation in their care ranged from being very involved to being actively pushed out of the decision-making process. Youth who were not involved in the decision-making process were often unhappy with the choices made on their behalf. Conversely, youth who were involved felt happier and more secure (e.g., Schofield et al., 2012).

Inclusion in the Decision-Making Process

The foster care system is meant to provide support and safety to children who need to be removed from their homes and placed into alternative care. Including youth in the decision-making process can help them feel more safe and secure. There are a number of ways adults can include youth in decisions made about themselves and their care. These include decisions about placement, decisions at the foster home, decisions at school, decisions about family visits, and decisions about legal proceedings and meetings. In the following paragraphs, we will discuss these in further detail.

Decisions about Placement

Placement came up multiple times as a specific area in which youth felt like decisions were made for and about them without their knowledge or input. Children wished to be consulted and informed about initial placement, placement duration, and placement changes.

"At least told [sic] me that I was moving, instead of me having to run into my house and cry.[2]"

However, many youth said they were not asked for their opinion and felt like they were completely cut out of the decision-making process. Youth reported being unaware that they would be removed from home, when they would be changing placements, and where they would be living (Balsells et al., 2017; Burgund & Zegarac, 2016; Daly, 2009; Rostill-Brookes et al., 2011). In addition, many children told researchers that they were placed into care, or their placements were changed, and they were not told why (Daly, 2009; Dansey et al., 2018; Gayapersad et al., 2019; Kiraly & Humphreys, 2013;

Rostill-Brookes et al., 2011; Schiller & de Wet, 2018; Selwyn et al., 2010). However, there were youth who felt their social workers were helpful in finding new placements if the current one was problematic, even if problems occurred after typical business hours (Ridley et al., 2016). This openness and willingness to include youth perspectives in placement changes helps strengthen the relationships between the youth and their social workers. For example, in research with children in Sweden, those who had the opportunity to visit potential living sites showed more positive feelings about their placement. Whereas children who did not have this opportunity were visibly upset when discussing placement during interviews (Hedin et al., 2011b). Many of the foster youth said that children need to be heard, involved in decision-making, told the reasons for their placement, and given somewhere to talk about their concerns (Schiller & de Wet, 2018).

In terms of placement, our studies provided a few examples where youth felt included in the process. Some youth either independently chose their families, initiated a move into a new home, or had a substantial role in the decision-making process (Burgess et al., 2010; Hedin et al., 2011b). One youth in the United Kingdom talked about how she secretly called her grandmother to get her and her sibling out of an unsafe situation. The two youth moved in with their grandmother prior to entering formal kinship care (Burgess et al., 2010). Ridley et al. (2016) found that several youth were included in the placement decision. One youth was taken to a number of potential living spaces and was given the agency to choose their placement (Ridley et al., 2016). However, this was not the norm, as many of those in traditional foster families had little to no agency in choosing (or knowing) the families prior to moving (Hedin et al., 2011b). There were various examples across studies that echoed this finding of youth feeling unsupported and like their feelings were not valued. For instance, Schiller and de Wet (2018) interviewed 29 adolescents in foster care, and several described being placed into care or experiencing placement changes with no explanation or no advance notice. Many youth said they wished that social workers would just talk to them. In interviews conducted by Rostill-Brookes et al. (2011), many youth described feeling confused and angry because no one discussed placement changes with them ahead of time. One youth told the interviewer about a time in which an unknown man arrived at her home at night and told her she would be leaving. Another youth talked about waking up one morning to find all her things packed up for her. A third youth described how his social worker picked him up from his current foster home before a new placement had been decided upon. He and his social worker drove around in the car waiting for more information until 7 pm when someone called to tell them where he would be living next (Rostill-Brookes et al., 2011). In interviews conducted by Biehal (2014), one child described how he wished to be adopted by his foster parents and how they had fought to keep him. However, since the child's birth mother objected, social workers refused to pursue adoption. Instead, he was moved back and forth between his mother and foster parents up until he was five years old. When interviewed at age 12, this child was still feeling insecure in his placement. In the interviews conducted by Schiller and de Wet (2018), several described wishing social workers would tell them when and why they were changing placement and that they could have a part in deciding where they would go. In cases related to housing, youth who are actively involved in making decisions about their own lives may end up having more buy-in, a stronger sense of belonging, and being more open to necessary changes.

Decisions at the Foster Home

Limited inclusion in decision-making was not exclusive to placement and placement changes.

"… Make sure that the foster parents do not speak on behalf of the child because often the foster child has a totally different opinion/view than the foster parents.[3]"

In many interviews, youth expressed a need for choices and the ability to contribute to family decisions, which would help them feel like accepted family members. These include simpler requests such as when to do chores, which furnishings are included in their bedrooms, or what color to paint their bedrooms (Hedin et al., 2011b; Mitchell & Kuczynski, 2010; Mitchell et al., 2010). Hedin et al. (2011b) found that when youth were given agency to make decisions about their daily routines, such as when to go to bed, they felt a stronger exchange of trust with their foster parents. Trust and negotiation were described by several youth in relation to their ability to participate in the decision-making process; more trust led to more negotiation and participation (Hedin et al., 2011a; Hedin et al., 2012). In other studies, youth were not given the agency to make these decisions or be involved in the decision-making process. For instance, Mitchell and Kuczynski (2010) described an interview with one youth who told of her first night in foster care. She said she was required to do the dishes within hours of being removed from her biological home. The youth asked if she could start chores the next day and was told that failure to complete the chores would lead to being cut off from friends and family members. Youth also had more substantial requests for a part in decision-making, such as choosing the type of food eaten for dinner, getting a part-time job, attending a concert with friends, or wanting to share their bedroom with siblings, (Dove & Powers, 2018; Hedin et al., 2011a; Hedin et al., 2012; Mitchell & Kuczynski, 2010; Rees et al., 2012). Some youth were able to achieve participation in the decision-making process about these larger requests, but only through negotiation and trust with their caregivers (Hedin et al., 2011a; Hedin et al., 2012). Other youth found this process difficult and agency was unattainable. One youth described being forbidden to sleep in his biological brother's bedroom where they could comfort each other (Mitchell & Kuczynski, 2010). When youth's feelings were dismissed, they felt less like accepted members of their families.

In the study by Dove and Powers (2018), several young Black women discussed their experiences surrounding culturally insensitive or culturally ignorant attitudes about Black hair. The young women described the importance of foster carers respecting them and their knowledge about their own hair, especially when foster parents were not Black themselves. Disrespect for Black young people and their hair care needs, contributes to significant losses, including loss of identity, belonging, and self-esteem. One child refused to look at pictures of herself because of how foster parents cared for her hair. She felt like her hair made her face look crooked. Young women recommended that foster carers educate themselves about Black hair and that they ask and listen to their foster children regarding what they need to care for their hair (Dove & Powers, 2018).

Decisions at School

Foster youth wish to be included in decisions about where they go to school. However, placement location, rather than youth choice, often determines what schools they will attend. (Burgund & Zegarac, 2016). Entering foster care and changing placements often involves changing schools. Although some youth wish to stay in schools where they already have friends, this is not always possible. Others are happy about the prospect of attending new schools and making new friends (Schwartz, 2010). Some youth have asked for the opportunity to visit different schools to learn about them before deciding where to go (Mitchell et al., 2010). When it is possible to give youth choices about where they go to school, this can help increase their sense of agency.

Options available to youth often depend on culture and customs. In the study by Burgund and Zegarac (2016), foster youth in Serbia felt like they had some choice about what schools they would attend. However, they also felt like the schools—and consequently their future professions—were ultimately chosen for them. Some youth said they would attend the school they were told to attend and would change professions later. One youth felt like the choice made for him was not reasonable and that it left him few options after graduation. Many youth in our studies recommended that they be included in conversations about school, specifically in which school they will attend (Mitchell et al., 2010; Schofield et al., 2012).

In addition to being included in decisions about where they go to school, youth express a desire to be included in decisions about what they learn at school (Hedin et al., 2011a). Many youth described receiving so much "support" that it actually hindered their progress. For example, in interviews with foster youth in Wales, one young woman who had been originally placed in an advanced coursework group, was moved to a lower group after entering foster care. She wished to remain in the advanced group but school officials said it would be too difficult for her and that she would not be able to cope (Mannay et al., 2017). In Serbia, youth were placed in less advanced schools because social workers felt the more advanced schools would be too difficult for them (Burgund & Zegarac, 2016).

"My decisions are not always considered in terms of schooling because sometimes I skip classes because I have to undergo diviner training, so my social worker does not consider this at all, forcing me to go to school.[4]"

Extracurricular activities have a positive impact on the youth's overall emotional well-being (Hedin et al., 2011a). Foster youth wish to be included in decisions about extracurricular activities at and during school, and some felt like their wishes were ignored by social workers. In one case, a child felt like their social worker forced them to attend school when it conflicted with a religious activity that was important to them (Schiller & de Wet, 2018). While the youth was not likely to be physically forced to attend anything, the authoritative position of the social worker may have led the youth to feeling like they were forced.

Other youth found happiness in being supported in the extracurricular choices. For example, several youth became excited when speaking to interviewers about their involvement in sports, art, dance, or writing (Sands et al., 2009). Finding enjoyment in activities might be helping these youth to feel a stronger sense of belonging and normalcy after moving away from their biological family's home. But being able to choose their activity might be helping these youth to feel stronger agency in their lives.

Decisions about Family Visits

Some youth develop a strong sense of belonging to their foster families, yet still desire to maintain relationships with their biological families (e.g., Holland, 2010). The desire to maintain contact with biological families varies among youth, but overall they want to play a role in making decisions about contact, including whether or not visitation occurred, frequency of contact, and the place/time of visits. Some youth were given agency to choose to engage in visitation with their biological families (Kiraly & Humphreys, 2013). However, in many studies we reviewed, youth described times when they requested visitation with their biological families, and those requests resulted in denial of visitation or failure by social workers to follow up with the youth and/or the biological families (Holland, 2010; Larkins et al., 2015).

"It took [the social worker] over a year to organize contact with my dad, and I asked at every [case] review, everything and in the end I took it upon myself to go and meet my dad. And then he [social worker] said 'Oh how did it go ... Now you can have unsupervised contact and sort it out yourself.[5]"

Reasons for lack of follow-up varied. Sometimes social workers do not fill out paperwork in time for visitation (Holland, 2010). Sometimes the reasons were never explained. Not all youth desire to see their birth parents. One youth explained how he was always given the option to contact his birth families, but always chose not to (Larkins et al., 2015). Other youth changed their mind after a few visits and decided to restrict visitation altogether (Kiraly & Humphreys, 2013). While these youth were given options about contact with birth families, other youth have struggled to make their opinions known or respected. Some social workers disbelieve youth when they say they would rather avoid visitation with their birth families. For example, rather than demonstrating value for youth concerns, social workers may question youth—sometimes repeatedly—when they express disinterest in visiting their birth parents (Christiansen et al., 2013). No matter the reason, not considering youth input when making decisions about visitation can leave the youth feeling like their thoughts and feelings about visitation do not matter.

In addition to being involved in decisions about whether or not visitation with family should occur, timing of visitation is also important to foster youth. One youth described feeling confident in their agency to change or cancel visitation appointments (Morrison et al., 2011). However, youth do not always get a say in the scheduling of family visits. Some youth are unaware of who makes visitation decisions, and are unsure of how to cancel or change appointment times (Morrison et al., 2011). In many of the studies we reviewed, youth insisted that adults, including social workers, need to value the perspectives of foster youth more. Rather than being pushed into family visits, youth wish to help decide if and when visitation should occur (Kiraly & Humphreys, 2013; Ridley et al., 2016; Schofield et al., 2012). Family visitation can be beneficial to some youth, but it can be disruptive for others. Having a say in visitation decisions is a relatively simple way to give youth the agency in their lives that they deserve.

Decisions about Legal Proceedings and Meetings

Being in the foster care system means that there will be consistent legal meetings and case reviews to ensure the child's needs are met properly. The content of these meetings directly impacts the lives of the youth and can lead to changes that are desirable or undesirable. Foster youth show an understanding of why the legal meetings are necessary and use these meetings to help identify members of the care team that can help them make desired changes, hear other perspectives of how their care is going, or let them vent about concerns (Pert et al., 2017; Schofield et al., 2012). Prior to the meetings, foster youth's thoughts and opinions are, at times, elicited. However, the youth were often left out of the decision of when and where the meetings occurred, who attended the meetings, and what was discussed at the meetings (Mannay et al., 2017; Pert et al., 2017; Schofield et al., 2012). Specifically, social workers would have case reviews at school—during school time—even though youth wished reviews would be held elsewhere, so they would have privacy from their peers (Mannay et al., 2017). In their study of foster youth participation in review meetings, Pölkki et al. (2012) found that although children were allowed to attend meetings with social workers, many children reported that they were not notified of the meetings in advance. In these cases, social workers and other adults had time to prepare, whereas youth were caught off guard and unprepared for meetings. This could explain why some adults mistakenly assume foster youth are not well-equipped to contribute to decisions. Similarly, children did not appreciate being excused so the adults could discuss them and their needs while they were not present. Other youth specifically stated that they did not wish to attend meetings, but their presence was required. Many felt like they could communicate what they wanted to their foster parents, who would then bring up concerns on their behalf.

The youth also described being left out of the decisions of who would attend the meetings. Some youth wanted their birth parents to be present, but were not given the opportunity to make that choice (Pert et al., 2017). In other cases, there were quite a few strangers that attended and left the youth feeling uncomfortable (Pert et al., 2017; Schofield et al., 2012). For instance, one youth described being asked about her sex life by, and in front of, complete strangers (Schofield et al., 2012). More generally, even when attending the meetings, some youth felt like their opinions were not taken into consideration during court proceedings (Block et al., 2010). Having an ability to express opinions and concerns in all aspects of review meetings is consistent with ensuring youth have agency in both their lives and in the decision-making process.

Youth Feelings about Decision-Making

Depending on several variables, youth may be more or less likely to communicate their concerns because of prior experiences in care. Relationships and trust with individuals on care teams, in the foster home, and at school can greatly affect foster youth's decisions about confiding with adults about their concerns. When youth feel trust with their caregivers, teachers, and social workers, they are much more likely to share their concerns and feelings about care. At times, youth feel uncomfortable expressing their wants and needs because of feeling unheard, fearing punishment or anger, or feeling overwhelmed, embarrassment, and confusion (Kuyini et al., 2009; Pert et al., 2017; Rostill-Brookes et al., 2011). For example, in the study by Rostill-Brookes et al. (2011), one youth did not want to discuss his placement concerns because he felt ignored in the past. In another study, a foster youth feared retaliation because they had previously been punished for voicing their concerns (Kuyini et al., 2009). This youth avoided expressing their needs and wants as much as possible. In other cases, youth did not comment due to previous arguments with social workers (Pert et al., 2017). Allowing youth a metaphorical seat at the table can help eliminate some of youth's negative emotions associated with their involvement. Youth appreciate discussions about their experiences in care (e.g., Hedin et al., 2011a). When youth are included in these discussions, they trust their caregivers more (Hedin et al., 2012). In fact, when children are given choices about their care, they express happiness about the choices and their decisions (Schofield et al., 2012).

When social workers are respectful of youth's agency to participate in their case plans, youth are more likely to feel supported and like valued members of their care teams. For instance, Social Work Practices (SWPs) organizations in the United Kingdom were pilot programs that focused on prioritizing relationships with youth (Ridley et al., 2016). Instead of utilizing social workers in the local government, SWPs contracted social workers from outside the government and assigned them to foster youth. Youth in care under these organizations felt like their social workers paid attention to their concerns. Social workers in SWPs reported more manageable caseloads compared to those working in other care sites with youth of similar demographics (Stanley et al., 2012). These smaller caseloads may have given them more time to solicit youth opinions and allowed them the opportunities to demonstrate openness to youth concerns. Another example was found in Hedin et al. (2012) wherein youth felt like they were all included in decisions made about them. Their foster parents asked them to communicate their needs so they could discuss them together and trusted the youth to know what they needed (Hedin et al., 2012). The development of trust in the fostering relationship, and the combination of inclusion and support, can help strengthen the feeling of belonging that can develop in the foster home.

"Let them be independent and don't treat them as kids, give them respect.[6]*"*

Variables in the Decision-Making Process

There were various differences among youth regarding how much they felt included in the decisions made about their lives. Systemic biases within the foster care system contribute to discrimination toward youth who are Black, female, younger, or those in certain placement types. An example of possible racism and sexism can be found in research by Diehl et al. (2011). In this study, males felt like they had greater control in the decision-making process compared to the amount of control girls expressed. In addition, White youth perceived more control compared to Black youth. Although the test on race and gender interaction approached statistical significance, results suggested that White males perceived having the most control whereas those who felt like they had the least control were Black females.

Other research showed that youth age is a potential barrier for inclusion in the care decisions (Barnes, 2012; Kiraly & Humphreys, 2013; Southwell & Fraser, 2010). Although the definition of younger versus older was different across studies, younger youth consistently reported feeling less involved in the decision-making process. For example, in the study by Kiraly and Humphreys (2013), for younger youth, the opportunity to see their biological families was generally decided by the care team (Kiraly & Humphreys, 2013). In the study by Barnes (2012), older youth felt like they were treated like children, even into their teen years. They felt like once the care team started making decisions on their behalf, they had difficulty seeing the youth as older and more capable of making their own choices (Barnes, 2012). Older children interviewed in the Southwell and Fraser (2010) study felt like they were more involved in decisions made about themselves compared to younger children—under 12 to 15. However, some still felt like they didn't have much of a place in the decision-making process. It is possible that control and autonomy was perceived differently across contexts. However, it is important to ensure that youth feel like the adults in their lives are paying attention to them and valuing their thoughts and feelings about their own lives.

Hedin et al. (2012) studied social bonds in foster youth across placement types and described how placement type was related to how much youth were involved in the decision-making process. Among the youth they interviewed, all who were in nonrelative kinship care and most who were in kinship care either chose their foster families or were active participants in the choosing of their foster families. None of the youth in traditional foster care were given a choice about their potential foster families, although some did initiate the process of leaving their biological families' homes. Once they moved into their new placements, all the youth felt like they had some say about what happened in their daily lives. This was most evident for youth in both traditional and nonrelative kinship care who felt like they had input in creating rules for their own behavior (Hedin et al., 2011b). The various ways in which youth interact with their foster families and care team can impact the amount of participation they have in the decision-making process. Ideally, foster youth are viewed as experts of their own lives and—at the very least—consulted when life decisions need to be made. This study was unique in their findings that youth were heavily involved in decisions made about themselves.

Youth Recommendations

In many of the studies we reviewed, researchers asked youth for recommendations they would give to child welfare workers. Foster youth continually described their amount of control and involvement in their own lives once entering the foster care system. Some felt like they had a say in their daily lives, could bring up concerns to their foster parents, and could participate effectively in legal meetings. However, other youth reported feeling unnoticed, unappreciated, ignored, or like they were treated unfairly. These perceptions are important to understand to ensure foster youth are appropriately supported during their time in care by acknowledging and responding to their concerns and wishes.

There were several recommendations by the foster youth that could help administrators understand the importance of foster youth involvement in decision-making. Youth generally expressed the need for social workers to allow them to participate in decisions made about themselves (Kiraly & Humphreys, 2013; Mitchell & Kuczynski, 2010; Pert et al., 2017; Rostill-Brookes et al., 2011; Selwyn et al., 2010). The type of involvement varied between youth, but there was also quite a bit of overlap. Mitchell et al. (2010) specifically asked youth for recommendations for social workers. These youth advised that social workers should ask children which schools they preferred to attend, whether or not they wished to visit their families, and if they needed anything from their old homes. In other research, many youth insisted that adults need to acknowledge foster youth's agency, not push them into family contact, and let them make choices for themselves (e.g., Kiraly & Humphreys, 2013).

Summary

The development of agency and belonging does not occur overnight. It takes work to build trust among foster youth, care teams, foster families, and biological families. As the trust builds, so does the sense of agency in the decision-making process and belonging within the foster family. As experts of their own lives, foster youth bring a wealth of resources and insider information to the conversation.

Notes

1 Age 14; Daly, 2009, p. 468.
2 Age 10–11; Mitchell et al., 2010, p. 182.
3 Age 16 years; Fylkesnes et al., 2021, p. 1994.
4 Age not given, range 12–19; Shiller & de Wet, 2018, p. 247.
5 Age 14–16; Larkins et al., 2015, p. 305.
6 Age 16 years; Fylkesnes et al., 2021, p. 1990.

References

Balsells, M. Á., Fuentes-Peláez, N., & Pastor, C. (2017). Listening to the voices of children in decision-making: A challenge for the child protection system in Spain. *Children and Youth Services Review, 79*, 418. 10.1016/j.childyouth.2017.06.055

Barnes, V. (2012). Social work and advocacy with young people: Rights and care in practice. *The British Journal of Social Work, 42*(7), 1275–1292. 10.1093/bjsw/bcr142

Biehal, N. (2014). A sense of belonging: Meanings of family and home in long-term foster care. *The British Journal of Social Work, 44*(4), 955. 10.1093/bjsw/bcs177

Block, S. D., Oran, H., Oran, D., Baumrind, N., & Goodman, G. S. (2010). Abused and neglected children in court: knowledge and attitudes. *Child Abuse & Neglect, 34*(9), 659–670. 10.1016/j.chiabu.2010.02.003

Botswana Bill of Child Rights. (2021). https://botswanalaws.com/alphabetical-list-of-statutes/children-s#Ch2804s77

Burgess, C., Rossvoll, F., Wallace, B., & Daniel, B. (2010). 'It's just like another home, just another family, so it's nae different' Children's voices in kinship care: a research study about the experience of children in kinship care in Scotland. *Child & Family Social Work, 15*(3), 297–306. http://dx.doi.org/10.1111/j.1365-2206.2009.00671.x

Burgund, A., & Zegarac, N. (2016). Perspectives of youth in care in Serbia. Child & *Adolescent Social Work Journal, 33*(2), 151–161. 10.1007/s10560-015-0413-5

Buys, N., Tilbury, C., Creed, P., & Crawford, M. (2011). Working with youth in-care: Implications for vocational rehabilitation practice. *Disability and Rehabilitation, 33*(13-14), 1125–1135. 10.3109/09638288.2010.521614

Christiansen, Ø., Havnen, K. J. S., Havik, T., & Anderssen, N. (2013). Cautious belonging: Relationships in long-term foster-care. *The British Journal of Social Work, 43*(4), 720–738. 10.1093/bjsw/bcr198

Daly, W. (2009). "Adding their flavour to the mix": Involving children and young people in care in research design. *Australian Social Work, 62*(4), 460–475. 10.1080/03124070903265732

Dansey, D., John, M., & Shbero, D. (2018). How children in foster care engage with loyalty conflict: Presenting a model of processes informing loyalty. *Adoption & Fostering, 42*(4), 354–368. 10.1177/0308575918798767

Diehl, D. C., Howse, R. B., & Trivette, C. M. (2011). Youth in foster care: Developmental assets and attitudes towards adoption and mentoring. *Child & Family Social Work, 16*(1), 81–92. 10.1111/j.1365-2206.2010.00716.x

Dove, L. M., & Powers, L. E. (2018). Exploring the complexity of hair and identity among African American female adolescents in foster care. *Children and Youth Services Review, 95*, 368–376. 10.1016/j.childyouth.2018.10.043

Fylkesnes, M., Larsen, M., Havnen, K., Christiansen, Ø., & Lehmann, S. (2021). Listening to advice from young people in foster care—from participation to belonging. *British Journal of Social Work, 51*, 1983–2000. 10.1093/bjsw/bcab138

Gayapersad, A., Ombok, C., Kamanda, A., Tarus, C., Ayuku, D., & Braitstein, P. (2019). The production and reproduction of kinship in charitable children's institutions in Uasin Gishu County, Kenya. *Child & Youth Care Forum, 48*, 797–828. 10.1007/s10566-019-09506-8

Hedin, L., Höjer, I., & Brunnberg, E. (2011a). Why one goes to school: what school means to young people entering foster care. *Child & Family Social Work, 16*(1), 43–51. 10.1111/j.1365-2206.2010.00706.x

Hedin, L., Höjer, I., & Brunnberg, E. (2011b). Settling into a new home as a teenager: About establishing social bonds in different types of foster families in Sweden. *Children and Youth Services Review, 33*(11), 2282–2289. 10.1016/j.childyouth.2011.07.016

Hedin, L., Höjer, I., & Brunnberg, E. (2012). Jokes and routines make everyday life a good life-on 'doing family' for young people in foster care in Sweden. *European Journal of Social Work*, *15*(5), 613–628. 10.1080/13691457.2011.579558

Holland, S. (2010). Looked after children and the ethic of care. *The British Journal of Social Work*, *40*(6), 1664–1680. 10.1093/bjsw/bcp086

International Federation of Social Workers. (2018). *Global social work statement of ethical principles*. https://www.ifsw.org/global-social-work-statement-of-ethical-principles/

Kiraly, M., & Humphreys, C. (2013). Perspectives from young people about family contact in kinship care: "Don't push us—listen more". *Australian Social Work*, *66*(3), 314–327. 10.1080/0312407x.2012.715658

Kuyini, A. B., Alhassan, A. R., Tollerud, I., Weld, H., & Haruna, I. (2009). Traditional kinship foster care in northern Ghana: The experiences and views of children, carers and adults in Tamale. *Child & Family Social Work*, *14*(4), 440–449. 10.1111/j.1365-2206.2009.00616.x

Larkins, C., Ridley, J., Farrelly, N., Austerberry, H., Bilson, A., Hussein, S., Manthorpe, J., & Stanley, N. (2015). Children's, young people's and parents' perspectives on contact: Findings from the evaluation of social work practices. *The British Journal of Social Work*, *45*(1), 296–312. 10.1093/bjsw/bct135

Mannay, D., Evans, R., Staples, E., Hallett, S., Roberts, L., Rees, A., & Andrews, D. (2017). The consequences of being labelled 'looked-after': Exploring the educational experiences of looked-after children and young people in Wales. *British Educational Research Journal*, *43*(4), 683–699. 10.1002/berj.3283

McLeod, A. (2006). Respect or empowerment?: Alternative understandings of 'listening' in childcare social work. *Adoption & Fostering*, *30*(4), 43–52. 10.1177/030857590603000407

Mitchell, M. B., & Kuczynski, L. (2010). Does anyone know what is going on? Examining children's lived experience of the transition into foster care. *Children and Youth Services Review*, *32*(3), 437–444. 10.1016/j.childyouth.2009.10.023

Mitchell, M. B., Kuczynski, L., Tubbs, C. Y., & Ross, C. (2010). We care about care: Advice by children in care for children in care, foster parents and child welfare workers about the transition into foster care. *Child & Family Social Work*, *15*(2), 176–185. 10.1111/j.1365-2206.2009.00657.x

Morrison, J., Mishna, F., Cook, C., & Aitken, G. (2011). Access visits: Perceptions of child protection workers, foster parents and children who are Crown wards. *Children and Youth Services Review*, *33*(9), 1476–1482. 10.1016/j.childyouth.2011.03.011

Office of the High Commissioner, Human Rights. (2021). *Status of ratification: Interactive dashboard* [data set]. United Nations. https://indicators.ohchr.org/

Pert, H., Diaz, C., & Thomas, N. (2017). Children's participation in LAC reviews: A study in one English local authority. *Child & Family Social Work*, *22*(S2), 1–10. 10.1111/cfs.12194

Pölkki, P., Vornanen, R., Pursiainen, M., & Riikonen, M. (2012). Children's participation in child-protection processes as experienced by foster children and social workers. *Child Care in Practice*, *18*(2), 107–125. 10.1080/13575279.2011.646954

Rees, A., Holland, S., & Pithouse, A. (2012). Food in foster families: Care, communication and conflict. *Children & Society*, *26*(2), 100–111. 10.1111/j.1099-0860.2010.00332.x

Ridley, J., Larkins, C., Farrelly, N., Hussein, S., Austerberry, H., Manthorpe, J., & Stanley, N. (2016). Investing in the relationship: Practitioners' relationships with looked-after children and care leavers in social work practices. *Child & Family Social Work*, *21*(1), 55–64. 10.1111/cfs.12109

Rostill-Brookes, H., Larkin, M., Toms, A., & Churchman, C. (2011). A shared experience of fragmentation: making sense of foster placement breakdown. *Clinical Child Psychology and Psychiatry, 16*(1), 103–127. 10.1177/1359104509352894

Sands, R. G., Goldberg-Glen, R. S., & Shin, H. (2009). The voices of grandchildren: A strengths-resilience perspective. *Child Welfare League of America, 88*(2), 25–45. https://www.jstor.org/stable/48623254

Schiller, U., & de Wet, G. (2018). Communication, indigenous culture and participatory decision making amongst foster adolescents. *Qualitative Social Work, 17*(2), 236–251. 10.1177/1473325016662329

Schofield, G., Beek, M., & Ward, E. (2012). Part of the family: Planning for permanence in long-term family foster care. *Children and Youth Services Review, 34*(1), 244–253. 10.1016/j.childyouth.2011.10.020

Schwartz, A. E. (2010). "Nobody Knows Me No More": Experiences of Loss Among African American Adolescents in Kinship and Non-Kinship Foster Care Placements. *Race and Social Problems, 2*(1), 31–49. http://doi.org/10.1007/s12552-010-9025-z

Selwyn, J., Saunders, H., & Farmer, E. (2010). The views of children and young people on being cared for by an independent foster-care provider. *The British Journal of Social Work, 40*(3), 696–713. 10.1093/bjsw/bcn117

Southwell, J., & Fraser, E. (2010). Young people's satisfaction with residential care: Identifying strengths and weaknesses in service delivery. *Child Welfare, 89*(2), 209–228. https://pubmed.ncbi.nlm.nih.gov/20857888/

Stanley, N., Austerberry, H., Bilson, A., Farrelly, N., Hargreaves, K., Hussein, S., Holingworth, K., Ingold, A., Larkins, C., Manthorpe, J., Ridley, J., & Strange, V. (2012). *Social work practices: Report of the national evaluation.* DfE. https://www.academia.edu/70003778/Social_Work_Practices_Report_of_the_National_Evaluation

The Child Protection Act. (1999). https://www.legislation.qld.gov.au/view/whole/html/inforce/current/act-1999-010

The Juvenile Justice (Care and Protection of Children) Act, 2015. (2020). https://kslsa.kar.nic.in/pdfs/jjb/jj_act.pdf

Three-Year Programme on Austrian Development Policy 2013-2015. (2012). https://www.entwicklung.at/fileadmin/user_upload/Dokumente/Publikationen/3_JP/Englisch/2013-2015_3-YP.pdf

Tindall-Biggins, C. (2020). *Heard least but matter most: Listening to youth voice to understand the process of youth empowerment* (Publication No. 2447553079) [Doctoral dissertation, Loyola University]. ProQuest Dissertations Publishing. https://www.proquest.com/dissertations-theses/heard-least-matter-most-listening-youth-voice/docview/2447553079/se-2

Chapter 4

Children's Relationships with Their Social Workers

"[She] looks at you and thinks, 'you're just a piece of paperwork'[1]"

Children in foster care generally must interact with social workers (Victor Staff, 2021). This chapter describes children's feelings, views, and expectations of their social workers. As this chapter is about youth relationships and interactions with social workers, it is important to also understand what factors can affect these relationships. Thus, the perspectives of social workers are included at the end of several subsections to provide a more comprehensive picture of the overall relationships and interactions among youth and social workers.

The Purpose of the Social Worker

In the United States, evaluations are often conducted to determine if social workers and children's needs are being met effectively (see e.g., Child Welfare Information Gateway, n.d.). Internationally, the UN Committee on the Rights of the Child reviews reports by countries that have ratified the convention to ensure that children's rights are being protected. At times, nongovernmental agencies, such as UNICEF, assist with this process (UNICEF, n.d.). Moreover, this is a topic covered in many of the studies in our systematic review. Researchers in Sweden, Serbia, Canada, and England asked youth multiple questions about youth experiences with social workers, including youth expectations and connectedness. Foster youth described the purpose of their social workers in diverse ways. Social workers tended to be viewed as the givers of tangible items (Burgund & Zegarac, 2016; Mitchell et al., 2010) or people with whom to develop personal relationships (Pert et al., 2017). Some youth felt social workers' purpose was to provide practical assistance in terms of scheduling contact with birth parents and for assisting with placement and accommodations (Larkins et al., 2015; Lindahl & Bruhn, 2017). Children interviewed in a study by Skoog et al., (2015) said they wanted social workers to go above and beyond to show they truly cared for them.

Children's feelings about social workers also varied. Some youth felt that being in care was good, and that social workers helped them with their well-being and getting their needs met, but they also felt like the social workers did

DOI: 10.4324/9781003309215-4

not have enough time for them personally (Burgund & Zegarac, 2016). Some youth described their social workers as friendly, funny, trustworthy, and helpful with family and personal problems (Aldgate, 2009; Lindahl & Bruhn, 2017; Ridley et al., 2016). Other youth felt like their social workers were horrible and only interested in enforcing rules (Lindahl & Bruhn, 2017). Still others were more neutral, saying they felt generally disconnected from social workers who were people who just sit and take notes (Lindahl & Bruhn, 2017; Ridley et al., 2016). In a study by Wissö et al. (2019), some youth did not have social workers because custody had been transferred to their foster parents, and their cases were considered closed. These youth described how they did not miss having social workers and how they felt more like other kids, since their social workers were no longer around.

Selwyn et al. (2010) reported on children's views about social workers from an independent fostering provider (IFP) in England. IFPs are agencies that employ social workers–and find and train potential caregivers–outside the government, for a fee. At the beginning of placements, youth expectations and feelings varied from negative to positive. Some children felt like the social workers required too many forms, some did not know the purpose of social workers, one described the social worker as bald and a fan of an incompetent sports team. Others expressed gratitude for the help they received from their social workers. After these children had spent time in care with the IFP, their descriptions were generally positive (e.g., describing social workers as kind, magic, and trustworthy). Likewise, youth appreciated when social workers helped them start desired extracurricular activities (i.e., football), improve at school, and mediated contact with birth siblings.

Relationships

Personal relationships between social workers and foster youth can lead to better outcomes for the youth. For instance, in many of the studies we reviewed, foster children had more positive feelings about their social workers when they had personal relationships with them (Larkins et al., 2015; Lindahl & Bruhn, 2017; Pert et al., 2017; Pölkki et al., 2012; Ridley et al., 2016). Youth needed their social workers to be "official" and to handle their bureaucratic needs; but they also wanted close friend-type relationships (Lindahl & Bruhn, 2017).

Although supportive relationships were defined in several ways, one consistency was having social workers who care and who listen (Barnes, 2012; Larkins et al., 2015; Lindahl & Bruhn, 2017; Pölkki et al., 2012; Ridley et al., 2016; see Chapter 1 for more information about procedural justice). In the following paragraphs, we will discuss youth's perceptions of personal relationships with their social workers.

"They should above all try to build a good relationship, like a relationship between friends. This is important to being able to open up.[2]*"*

One way that social workers showed they cared was by engaging with the youth in a more friend-like way. Aldgate (2009) found that children in Scotland appreciated a "child-centered" approach (i.e., meeting one on one, playing games, being consistent in their appointments). Children also appreciated various types of communication from social workers, like receiving letters, texts, and emails (Pölkki et al., 2012). Foster youth appreciated going out to engage in activities together (i.e., bowling, laser tag) or being able to talk and be open with their social worker (Lindahl & Bruhn, 2017). When the youth and social worker were able to engage in real conversations on topics that the youth were interested in (i.e., certain shows, movies, or books), the youth felt like they could count on their social workers (Ridley et al., 2016).

In research in England (Larkins et al., 2015), children described how they valued having their social worker present when they went to see their biological families, respecting their decision to not see biological family members, or providing support if/when visitation was desired. Some youth stated that their social workers listened to them and helped them deal with the negative emotions associated with being in care. One youth felt supported when they were missing their biological family members, and another appreciated that the social worker was available to hear her vent. Youth felt cared for when social workers expressed interest in their lives and talked about how they could help make things better (Larkins et al., 2015). Ridley et al. (2016) and Hedin (2014) found similar outcomes. For example, some youth described their social worker as being funny and able to improve their mood whenever they were upset, some described social workers helping them cope with stressful events in their lives. Another youth described reciprocal contact wherein the social worker would reach out to the youth at nearly the same rate as the youth would reach out to the social worker.

Although there were many youth who felt cared for and supported by their social workers, there were other youth who did not (Burgess et al., 2010;

Holland, 2010; Larkins et al., 2015; Lindahl & Bruhn, 2017; Ridley et al., 2016). Negative relationships were described as having social workers who were disrespectful, did not include the youth in decisions about their own lives, or failed to communicate effectively or in a timely manner (Barnes, 2012; Ridley et al., 2016). Fargas-Malet and McSherry (2018) found similar concerns when children in Ireland described feeling that social workers did not spend enough time getting to know them. Youth noted that frequent changes in social workers made it difficult to develop and maintain relationships with them (Skoog et al., 2015). Social workers aim to be supportive for the youth on their caseloads, and turnover is one barrier to developing that caring and trusting relationship.

Although the current systematic review and meta-analysis focus was on youth voices, in many of the studies we reviewed, social workers were also interviewed. While the ultimate goal for social workers that oversee foster youth cases is reunification with biological families (Victor Staff, 2021), or finding a long-term alternative placement, social workers have several other responsibilities during the youth's time in care. The following are examples of how social workers view their roles in the system and their relationships with foster youth. Some social workers felt like they knew what was best for foster youth. Thus, they made decisions *for and about* youth, especially when such decisions were related to issues such as health, safety, and well-being (Barnes, 2012). As an example, several social workers expressed how review meetings can be embarrassing or painful to listen to, so they often scheduled these meetings while the youth were in school[3] (Pölkki et al., 2012). Some social workers described foster children as invisible, explaining that they worked more with biological parents rather than the youth themselves (Pölkki et al., 2012). Other social workers noted that their roles during supervised visits with biological parents were to model behavior to parents, provide tangible items (food, toys, or activities), and to redirect painful conversations initiated by parents, which limited their time to interact directly with youth (Morrison et al., 2011).

Tangible Support

Youth expected social workers to be caring and emotionally supportive, but many described a good social worker as one who provided tangible support, as well. In research in the United Kingdom, youth expressed appreciation for social workers who were fast and efficient with paperwork, helped them procure necessary equipment, provided the opportunity to tour potential new placements, and helped them decorate their new rooms (Ridley et al., 2016). In another study in England, youth felt their social workers were supportive when they went above and beyond to arrange family member–birth parents and siblings–and friend visits. For example, social workers dealt with difficult schedules, made sure accommodation costs were covered for visits, brought family members to youth in their own vehicles, or were present during visitation to ensure youth's maximum comfort (Larkins et al., 2015). Although social workers promised tangible support, few youth felt that their social workers actually followed through with those promises (see e.g., Larkins et al., 2015; Southwell & Fraser, 2010). In the study by Larkins et al. (2015), some youth described a lack of support around visits with family members and friends. That is, social workers *said* multiple times that they would arrange contact (across many years in one case). However, youth experienced extended delays before seeing loved ones and some never got to see their families at all.

Although in some cases youth see their social workers as ineffective in providing necessary tangible support, those opinions may change over time. This is evident in the study by Selwyn et al. (2010), which was described earlier in this chapter. They found that after one year, the youth were less likely to view their social workers negatively, and none described disliking their social workers. In fact, many of the youth described how the social workers cared for them, initiated contact with birth families, assisted in educational pursuits, or helped facilitate vacations (Selwyn et al., 2010).

"I talk to my worker. She comes round to see how I'm doing. It's all about me. We play games and that's what helps me talk.[4]*"*

Generally, youth described that support from their social workers was positive and easy to access (Aldgate, 2009; Hedin, 2014; Ridley et al., 2016; Selwyn et al., 2010). It is possible that in the cases wherein social workers were described as unable to provide tangible support, the youth just needed to give the social workers a bit more time to demonstrate what they could accomplish.

Availability

Social workers often have large caseloads that make it difficult to spend time with foster youth ways that meet youth's expectations. For instance, many youth in the studies we reviewed expected social workers to be available all the time, either in the form of physical presence or responsiveness (e.g., Lindahl &

Bruhn, 2017; Ridley et al., 2016; Skoog et al., 2015). Some children felt their social workers purposefully avoided them (i.e., by scheduling visits while they were at school; Aldgate, 2009) or were not present enough (Burgund & Zegarac, 2016; Lindahl & Bruhn, 2017; Skoog et al., 2015; Southwell & Fraser, 2010). Conversely, youth viewed their social workers as trustworthy when they felt the social workers were present and available (Lindahl & Bruhn, 2017). Further, youth perceived relationships as positive when they felt like the social workers spent enough time with them (although no definition of "enough" was provided by either youth or researchers; Ridley et al., 2016).

Responsiveness was something that came up frequently as a concern for foster youth (Barnes, 2012; Fargas-Malet & McSherry, 2018; Skoog et al., 2015; Southwell & Fraser, 2010). For example, youth in Sweden said that, although social workers promised to contact them frequently, this was not happening, and getting in contact was generally difficult (Skoog et al., 2015).

"You're like just one in a hundred for them. They can't manage really listening much and it really seems like they are stressed the whole time and really don't have time.[5]*"*

Frequency alone was not the only issue related to responsiveness in social workers. Youth in the United Kingdom valued having access to their social workers outside of typical 9–5 working hours (Ridley et al., 2016). One youth discussed getting help over the weekend when their living situation was in flux. Another discussed the ease of sending a quick text if something needed to be resolved, but not necessarily urgently (Ridley et al., 2016). Trust, responsiveness, and availability appear to be intertwined and necessary for foster youth to feel supported by their social worker.

Caseloads

Youth who understood caseloads viewed caseload size as an important factor in the development of support and trust between themselves and their social workers. Some children said that they understood they were competing for attention with many other children[6] (Skoog et al., 2015). Researchers suggested that large caseloads meant that social workers only had time to help youth with bare essentials, leaving no time for help with school or job placement (Buys et al., 2011).

As we mentioned earlier in this chapter, some of the studies we reviewed included interviews with both the foster youth and social workers. In addition, while not part of our initial systematic review, we found several publications and reports on social workers' perspectives and needs. The following includes information from these interviews and reports, to supplement information gathered from the foster youth themselves.

Time issues were echoed by social workers across studies. Thus, many social workers noted that their time was spread thinly across cases because of their large caseloads, giving them less time to spend on each case (e.g., Barnes, 2012; Buys et al., 2011; Ridley et al., 2016). Several social workers said youth expected more from them than what they could actually provide (Brown et al., 2019; Rostill-Brookes et al., 2011). For example, social workers felt each child wanted all the time spent on them and not anyone else. In addition, social workers felt youth wanted them to go "above and beyond," which would mean working overtime and being accessible by phone day and night (Brown et al., 2019). Other social workers described having more administrative duties and less time to spend face-to-face with the youth (Barnes, 2012). Of interest, a pilot program in the United Kingdom was designed to facilitate social workers' abilities to provide more consistent and responsive care for foster youth. In this program, social workers had caseloads of 15–18 families, social workers felt they were more available to youth and their families. They felt this helped them communicate more effectively and build higher quality relationships with youth (Ridley et al., 2016).

The Office of the Chief Social Worker of Child, Youth and Family (2014) interviewed 98 social workers in New Zealand which helps contextualize the caseloads of social workers. They found that caseloads ranged from a single foster youth to more than 27 (the bulk of respondents, 57%, had more than 27 youth on their caseload). Other international studies found similar information about actual caseload size. For instance, social workers' caseloads included 22–25 youth (Singapore; Ministry of Social and Family Development, 2021), 1–74 youth (England; Beer, 2016), 8–76 youth (United States; Yamatani et al., 2009), 20–45 youth (United States; Steen, 2020), or 25–30 youth (Sweden; Marttila et al., 2012).

Our review of studies indicate that the actual size of the social worker's caseloads were generally much higher than what many studies identified for best practices. In further examination of caseload size recommendations, we found limited information, and at the time of writing, some web pages referenced in journal articles were no longer available. The number of recommended cases per best practices was 8–18 youth (Office of the Chief

Social Worker of Child, Youth and Family, 2014), 15 youth (Council on Accreditation as cited in Yamatani et al., 2009), 12–15 youth (Hughes & Lay, 2012) and "reasonable," which does not indicate size, but instead describes a caseload that allows the practitioner to effectively do their job (National Association of Social Workers, 2013). Generally, smaller caseloads are recommended as best practices across studies.

Turnover

Youth often mentioned social worker turnover in their interviews, including how turnover affected their ability to develop relationships and trust. Many youth changed social workers frequently; some even changed during the course of individual studies. This led many of the youth to feel disconnected from their social workers (Buys et al., 2011; Holland, 2010; Lindahl & Bruhn, 2017).

"I think it's sad that the officer is going to quit. … It will take time for me to trust the new officer and to let her into my life. … It takes time to open up to someone new.[7]"

In a study involving eight youth in the United Kingdom, only one did not change social workers during the year of data collection and was the only youth who felt close to her social worker (Holland, 2010). Children appreciated it when they had the same social worker for an extended period because it helped them build relationships with them (Pölkki et al., 2012). These relationships were mediated by time and trust. As trust developed, so was the youth's openness (Lindahl & Bruhn, 2017).

The following information is not from our systematic review. However, in an effort to create a more complete understanding of the social worker/foster youth relationship, we have included research on turnover from social workers themselves. Social workers indicated a variety of factors that affect their abilities to do their jobs effectively, including caseload size and secondary trauma, both of which contribute to exhaustion and decreased morale

(California Child Welfare Co-Investment Partnership, 2017). For example, their responsibilities can be so overwhelming that social workers end up caring more for their clients than themselves. These problems can intensify over time and lead to burnout, and eventually turnover (Lane, 2021). Some social workers discussed how turnover negatively impacted the foster youth on their caseload (although it was not discussed how youth were affected; Buys et al., 2011). In a study of social workers who were part of a caseload reduction project in the United States, after their caseloads were reduced, social workers had more time for biological and foster parents, foster youth, and their own self-care (Steen, 2020). All of these benefits led to higher job satisfaction and lower turnover for social workers, and increased safety and well-being for the foster youth (Steen, 2020).

Communication

One key to building a strong relationship is communication. Many youth wished social workers would communicate with them so they would know what to expect (e.g., Morrison et al., 2011; Pölkki et al., 2012; Rostill-Brookes et al., 2011). In their study of foster youth's participation in case reviews in Finland, Pert et al. (2017) found that only two of eight youth (25%) said their social workers asked them about their needs or wants before reviews. However, none of the other children's social workers talked with them in preparation of their reviews. Similarly, there was limited communication between foster youth and social workers prior to visits with biological family members. For instance, children in Canada described communication with social workers about family visits (Morrison et al., 2011). A few of the children said their social workers talked with them before visitation and then again afterward, but many said that no one talked with them about their visits at all (Morrison et al., 2011). Some youth described a lack of clarity in social workers' communication. In addition youth varied in their perceptions of social workers' willingness to communicate with them. For example, in a survey of 5,873 foster youth in the United States, nearly 17% felt like their social workers were unwilling to put in extra effort to explain things in a way they could understand (Dolan et al., 2011). However, this was not always the case. During in-depth interviews with foster youth in Finland, youth specifically stated that they could depend upon their social workers to answer any questions they had (Pölkki et al., 2012).

It is important for social workers to communicate with youth and get input from them regarding decisions to be made about their care (see Chapter 3). This is true from the start of placement throughout their time in the foster care system. Our review indicated that some foster youth felt supported while others felt unheard, ignored, or left out of the decision-making process, altogether. For example, in their study of youth perceptions of the transition process in Sweden (Wissö et al., 2019), some youth felt like their social workers did not pay attention to their wishes about placement and instead tried to convince them to do something that they did not want to do. But foster youth desired to participate in decisions on a day-to-day basis as well. As an example, youth surveyed in Sweden said they did not like it when social workers made decisions for them without consulting them (Lindahl & Bruhn, 2017). Youth in Canada reported that their social workers did not explain why family visits had to be supervised (Morrison et al., 2011). Further, several youth stated that they did not like it when social workers took notes about them during visits (Lindahl & Bruhn, 2017; Morrison et al., 2011). When social workers and foster youth engage in open dialogue, youth feel more trust in the decisions made about and for them, and feel less confused about the system and their role within it (e.g., Lindahl & Bruhn, 2017).

Youth need social workers to communicate and include them in the decision-making process. Additionally it is important for social workers to pay attention to youth and view their concerns as credible so that children will trust and confide in them. For example, in two of the studies we reviewed, children said they kept quiet about problems with their biological and foster carers because social workers did not take their concerns seriously (Pölkki et al., 2012; Skoog et al., 2015). Morerover, children expressed frustration and surprise that the social workers could not see the problems they experienced while living with biological parents. For instance, one young woman described how during social worker visits, her biological parents were on their best behavior, so her concerns regarding her safety and well-being were not taken seriously (Pölkki et al., 2012). Examples like the ones above reaffirm those prior experiences, which contributes to continued victimization.

Youth across studies noted that active listening is important in creating and maintaining good relationships (e.g., Ridley et al., 2016).

"He stops what he's saying and listens to what I have to [say], like if I had a problem and he was talking about something else he, he'd stop and then he'd listen to what I was saying and so he, he obviously cares, he listens.[8]"

Some foster youth said that their social workers would sometimes listen, and other times they felt like the social workers were not listening at all (Dolan et al., 2011). The following is not from our systematic review, but helps to outline the different perspectives of communication between social workers and foster youth. Sinclair (1998) wrote "while social workers may think they are listening, young people do not feel as though they are heard" (p. 139). McLeod (2006) found similar disparities in their study of foster youth's perspectives on social workers' ability to listen. Social workers felt that they were excellent at listening, communicating, and supporting youth, whereas most of the foster youth described feeling exactly the opposite. Moreover, they found conflicting definitions, from youth and adults, of what listening entailed. For example, foster youth defined listening as action and follow through with requests, while adults defined listening as being empathetic and understanding youth's emotions (McLeod, 2006). These differences can lead to communication errors and misunderstandings that can take a significant toll on the overall well-being of the youth in general and their relationship with their caseworkers. However, the opposite is also true. When social workers and foster youth communicate well, trust is developed and the youth are happier.

Recommendations by and for Foster Youth

Foster youth made a variety of recommendations for social workers. These included engaging in open communication, ensuring confidentiality, being more organized, and making more frequent contacts (Pölkki et al., 2012; Selwyn et al., 2010; Skoog et al., 2015). Of interest, Swedish foster youth interviewed by Skoog et al. (2015) specifically asked that social workers talk more about what youth do well and less about what they do wrong or don't do well. Some of the most comprehensive advice came from youth in a study in Canada conducted by Mitchell et al. (2010). Children suggested that social workers be more open about themselves by describing themselves and their roles. Many of their recommendations centered on ways social workers could help children transition into foster care. Social workers could help make children feel more comfortable during transition into foster care by listening to their concerns, helping to alleviate these concerns as much as possible, going with them to meet their new foster parents, and telling them what to expect in care. Youth also recommended that when a social worker is moving a child to a new home, they should talk to the child about the upcoming move, explain what to expect during the process, describe what the foster family is like, and tell them if there are pets at the new home. Furthermore, if the social worker was able to drive a child to the new home, they could discuss these things along the way. One youth specifically mentioned that having a prior foster youth accompany the social worker could help mediate the process to help answer any questions that the new foster youth might have.

Youth said there are things that social workers could ask themselves to better understand what youth need when they learn that they must enter foster care. Youth in Mitchell et al.'s (2010) study suggested that social workers consider the following:

- Do children need to rush to leave their current homes?
- Can the family spend one last day together?
- Can they give children time to work through their emotions, pack, or say goodbyes?
- Do the children want to know why they are being placed in care?
- Are there significant items children need beyond basic necessities?

The studies we reviewed contained a wealth of information regarding youth's perceptions about how social workers can improve in their relationships while working with foster youth and the importance of following through with promises made to youth. Given that social workers may be the only stable person in that child's life (even if it's on a temporary basis for a short period of time), it is particularly important that social workers engage in the types of behaviors recommended above to build those trusting, supportive relationships.

Summary

Negative relationships with social workers resulted from youth feeling disrespected and not listened to. Positive relationships occurred when social workers spent time with youth and made efforts to get to know them. Youth felt like heavy caseloads made it difficult for social workers to spend enough time with them (Barnes, 2012), For example, some youth reported only seeing social workers around the time of case reviews (Pert et al., 2017). Heavy caseloads, limited support and high volumes of paperwork can make social workers' jobs especially difficult (Buys et al., 2011). It is important we find ways to support social workers so they can be more effective in aiding and advocating for foster youth. Fortunately, as described above, foster youth provided recommendations for social workers to improve relationships with those on their caseload.

Notes

1 Age 17; Brown et al., 2019, p. 224.
2 Age not given, range 14–19; Lindahl & Bruhn, 2017, p. 1420.
3 This is inconsistent with what many foster youth have said. Foster youth often wish to be involved in their review meetings (see Chapter 3).
4 Age not given, range 8–16; Aldgate, 2009, p. 54.
5 Age not given, range 8–18; Skoog et al., 2015, p. 1899.
6 The studies did not indicate how the foster youth knew that the social workers had other children on their caseloads. It is potentially problematic if this is a conversation occurring between youth and their social workers.

7 Age 17–19; Lindahl & Bruhn, 2017, p. 1420.
8 Age 10; Ridley et al., 2016, p. 61.

References

Aldgate, J. (2009). Living in kinship care: A child-centered view. *Adoption & Fostering*, *33*(3), 51–63. 10.1177/030857590903300306

Barnes, V. (2012). Social work and advocacy with young people: Rights and care in practice. *The British Journal of Social Work*, *42*(7), 1275–1292. 10.1093/bjsw/bcr142

Beer, O. W. J. (2016). *Predictors of and causes of stress among social workers: A national survey* [Master's thesis, University of Plymouth, UK]. ResearchGate. https://www. researchgate.net/profile/Oliver-Beer/publication/308612639_Predictors_of_and_ Causes_of_Stress_Among_Social_Workers_A_National_Survey/links/ 580f97be08aee15d49120f61/Predictors-of-and-Causes-of-Stress-Among-Social- Workers-A-National-Survey.pdf

Brown, R., Alderson, H., Kaner, E., McGovern, R., & Lingam, R. (2019). 'There are carers, and then there are carers who actually care'; Conceptualizations of care among looked after children and care leavers, social workers and carers. *Child Abuse & Neglect*, *92*, 219–229. 10.1016/j.chiabu.2019.03.018

Burgess, C., Rossvoll, F., Wallace, B., & Daniel, B. (2010). 'It's just like another home, just another family, so it's nae different' Children's voices in kinship care: A research study about the experience of children in kinship care in Scotland. *Child & Family Social Work*, *15*(3), 297–306. 10.1111/j.1365-2206.2009.00671.x

Burgund, A., & Zegarac, N. (2016). Perspectives of youth in care in Serbia. *Child & Adolescent Social Work Journal*, *33*(2), 151–161. 10.1007/s10560-015-0413-5

Buys, N., Tilbury, C., Creed, P., & Crawford, M. (2011). Working with youth in-care: Implications for vocational rehabilitation practice. *Disability and Rehabilitation*, *33*(13-14), 1125–1135. 10.3109/09638288.2010.521614

California Child Welfare Co-Investment Partnership. (2017). *Balancing head & heart: California's child welfare workforce.* insights, volume XIV, Winter 2017. https:// www.courts.ca.gov/documents/BTB24-4B-6.pdf

Child Welfare Information Gateway. (n.d.). *Caseload, workload, and time studies.* https://www.childwelfare.gov.

Dolan, M., Smith, K., Casanueva, C., & Ringeisen, H. (2011). *NSCAW II baseline report: Caseworker characteristics, child welfare services, and experiences of children placed in out-of-home care* (Report No. 2011-27e). National Survey of Child and Adolescent Well-Being. https://www.acf.hhs.gov/sites/default/files/documents/opre/ nscaw2_cw.pdf

Fargas-Malet, M., & McSherry, D. (2018). The mental health and help-seeking behavior of children and young people in care in Northern Ireland: Making services accessible and engaging. *The British Journal of Social Work*, *48*(3), 578–595. 10. 1093/bjsw/bcx062

Hedin, L. (2014). A sense of belonging in a changeable everyday life - a follow-up study of young people in kinship, network, and traditional foster families. *Child & Family Social Work*, *19*(2), 165–173. 10.1111/j.1365-2206.2012.00887.x

Holland, S. (2010). Looked after children and the ethic of care. *The British Journal of Social Work*, *40*(6), 1664–1680. 10.1093/bjsw/bcp086

Hughes, S., & Lay, S. (2012). *Direct service workers' recommendations for child welfare financing and system reform.* Child Welfare League of America. https://www.cwla. org/wp-content/uploads/2014/05/DirectServiceWEB.pdf

Lane, A. (2021). *Social workers' perspective on burnout: Causes and effective interventions* [Master's thesis, California State University, Sacramento] (28495567). ProQuest Dissertations Publishing. http://proxy.lib.csus.edu/login?url=https://www.proquest.com/dissertations-theses/social-workers-perspective-on-burnout-causes/docview/2597764684/se-2?accountid=10358

Larkins, C., Ridley, J., Farrelly, N., Austerberry, H., Bilson, A., Hussein, S., Manthorpe, J., & Stanley, N. (2015). Children's, young people's and parents' perspectives on contact: Findings from the evaluation of social work practices. *The British Journal of Social Work, 45*(1), 296–312. 10.1093/bjsw/bct135

Lindahl, R., & Bruhn, A. (2017). Foster children's experiences and expectations concerning the child-welfare officer role–prerequisites and obstacles for close and trustful relationships. *Child & Family Social Work, 22*(4), 1415–1422. 10.1111/cfs.12362

Marttila, A., Johansson, E., Whitehead, M., & Burström, B. (2012). Dilemmas in providing resilience-enhancing social services to long-term social assistance clients: A qualitative study of Swedish social workers. *BMC Public Health, 12*, 517. 10.1186/1471-2458-12-517

McLeod, A. (2006). Respect or empowerment?: Alternative understandings of 'listening' in childcare social work. *Adoption & Fostering, 30*(4), 43–52. 10.1177/030857590603000407

Ministry of Social and Family Development. (2021). *Average number of cases per social worker in the past five years.* https://www.msf.gov.sg/media-room/Pages/Average-Number-of-Cases-Per-Social-Worker-in-the-Past-Five-Years.aspx

Mitchell, M. B., Kuczynski, L., Tubbs, C. Y., & Ross, C. (2010). We care about care: Advice by children in care for children in care, foster parents and child welfare workers about the transition into foster care. *Child & Family Social Work, 15*(2), 176–185. 10.1111/j.1365-2206.2009.00657.x

Morrison, J., Mishna, F., Cook, C., & Aitken, G. (2011). Access visits: Perceptions of child protection workers, foster parents and children who are Crown wards. *Children and Youth Services Review, 33*(9), 1476–1482. 10.1016/j.childyouth.2011.03.011

National Association of Social Workers. (2013). *NASW Standards for Social Work Case Management.* https://www.socialworkers.org/LinkClick.aspx?fileticket=acrzqmEfhlo%3D&portalid=0

Office of the Chief Social Worker of Child, Youth and Family. (2014). *Workload and Casework Review: Qualitative Review of Social Worker Caseload, Casework and Workload Management.* https://www.socialserviceworkforce.org/system/files/resource/files/workload-and-casework-review.pdf

Pert, H., Diaz, C., & Thomas, N. (2017). Children's participation in LAC reviews: A study in one English local authority. *Child & Family Social Work, 22*(S2), 1–10. 10.1111/cfs.12194

Pölkki, P., Vornanen, R., Pursiainen, M., & Riikonen, M. (2012). Children's participation in child-protection processes as experienced by foster children and social workers. *Child Care in Practice, 18*(2), 107–125. 10.1080/13575279.2011.646954

Ridley, J., Larkins, C., Farrelly, N., Hussein, S., Austerberry, H., Manthorpe, J., & Stanley, N. (2016). Investing in the relationship: Practitioners' relationships with looked-after children and care leavers in social work practices. *Child & Family Social Work, 21*(1), 55–64. 10.1111/cfs.12109

Rostill-Brookes, H., Larkin, M., Toms, A., & Churchman, C. (2011). A shared experience of fragmentation: making sense of foster placement breakdown. *Clinical Child Psychology and Psychiatry, 16*(1), 103–127. 10.1177/1359104509352894

Selwyn, J., Saunders, H., & Farmer, E. (2010). The views of children and young people on being cared for by an independent foster-care provider. *The British Journal of Social Work*, *40*(3), 696–713. 10.1093/bjsw/bcn117

Sinclair, R. (1998). Involving children in planning their care. *Child & Family Social Work*, *3*(2), 137–142. 10.1046/j.1365-2206.1998.00081.x

Skoog, V., Khoo, E., & Nygren, L. (2015). Disconnection and dislocation: Relationships and belonging in unstable foster and institutional care. *The British Journal of Social Work*, *45*(6), 1888–1904. 10.1093/bjsw/bcu033

Southwell, J., & Fraser, E. (2010). Young people's satisfaction with residential care: Identifying strengths and weaknesses in service delivery. *Child Welfare*, *89*(2), 209–228. https://pubmed.ncbi.nlm.nih.gov/20857888/

Steen, J. (2020). Case manager perceptions of the effects of caseload level reduction in a child welfare agency. *Journal of Family Strengths*, *20*(2), 1–15. https://digitalcommons. library.tmc.edu/jfs/vol20/iss2/2?utm_source=digitalcommons.library.tmc.edu%2Fjfs %2Fvol20%2Fiss2%2F2&utm_medium=PDF&utm_campaign=PDFCoverPages

UNICEF. (n.d.). *Implementing and monitoring the Convention on the Rights of the Child*. https://www.unicef.org/child-rights-convention/implementing-monitoring

Victor Staff. (2021, March 16). Celebrating the foster care social worker. *Victor*. https://blog.victor.org/ffa/the-full-impact-of-social-workers-in-foster-care#:~:text= Social%20Work%20in%20Child%20Welfare&text=Our%20goal%20is%20always %20to,for%20children%20and%20foster%20parents.

Wissö, T., Johansson, H., & Höjer, I. (2019). What is a family? Constructions of family and parenting after a custody transfer from birth parents to foster parents. *Child & Family Social Work*, *24*(1), 9–16. 10.1111/cfs.12475

Yamatani, H., Engel, R., & Spjeldnes, S. (2009). Child welfare worker caseload: What's just right? *Social Work*, *54*(4), 361–368. 10.1093/sw/54.4.361

Chapter 5

Contact with Birth Families

"You don't even know what [mom] looks like anymore[1]"

It has long been determined that maintaining relationships with birth parents and birth siblings is important for some foster youth, but not all (Fawley-King et al., 2017; Kiraly & Humphreys, 2013; Mateos et al., 2012; Schofield et al., 2012). While foster youth, at times, can be placed with their siblings, this is not always the case. Because foster youth vary in their desires to keep in contact with birth families, their participation in decision making is imperative to their success in the system. Contact with birth families can lead to youth feeling supported (Lundström & Sallnäs, 2012), but can also lead to reduced cohesion with foster families (Fernandez, 2009), problems with mental or emotional health (Fawley-King et al., 2017), or feeling split between two families (Christiansen et al., 2013). Research recommends supporting foster youth who want to maintain relationships with their birth families (Kiraly & Humphreys, 2013; Larkins et al., 2015; Mitchell et al., 2010). Several states in the United States include access to contact with birth families as part of foster youth's rights (National Conference of State Legislatures, 2019).

> *"When I'm sad, I just want to see my mom.[2]"*

Contact with Birth Parents

Several researchers in our systematic review noted that few or none of the children had contact with *all* biological family members, but most had contact with at least one (Burgund & Zegarac, 2016; Hedin et al., 2011; Hedin et al., 2012; Lundström & Sallnäs, 2012; Mateos et al., 2012; Schwartz, 2010). In their study of loss experienced by 18 Black children in kinship and

DOI: 10.4324/9781003309215-5

nonkinship care in the United States, Schwartz (2010) found that children in kinship care saw their birth mothers more frequently than children in traditional foster care. Conversely, being in care did not change the amount of time children spent with their birth fathers because they did not see their birth fathers often before they entered care. The lack of contact with birth fathers seemed to be a pattern across several studies. To provide a picture of the youth contact with birth families during the time of our studies, we conducted a meta-analysis on whether youth had contact with their birth mothers and fathers (see Appendix A).

The meta-analysis indicated that youth were much more likely to have contact with their birth mothers than their birth fathers (we will discuss youth's feelings about contact later in the chapter). Most youth had contact with at least one of their birth parents, but it ranged between regular informal visits to just occasional phone or email contact (Hedin et al., 2011; Lundström & Sallnäs, 2012; Mateos et al., 2012). McMahon and Curtin (2013) noted that youth who had been in foster care for 4 or more years were more likely to have limited contact with birth families than those in care for 1–3 years. For some of those that did have consistent contact, the experience was described as negative. For instance, biological parents were aggressive, they were late or failed to show up, or did not show youth affection (Mateos et al., 2012). However, some youth liked being able to see them (Mateos et al., 2012). In fact, youth were more likely to describe their experiences as positive if they were informal and took place with additional people with whom the youth felt comfortable (Kiraly & Humphreys, 2013).

While contact is important, our research also found that this topic is more complicated than just contact or no contact. There are many factors surrounding contact or visitation that must be considered. These include type, frequency, satisfaction with contact, but also the desire from both sides to have contact and foster youth's involvement in the decisions made about contact. The following gives an in-depth description of youth's experiences and, for some, the complications of contact with birth families.

Children had mixed views about the amount and quality of contact and personal connection with birth parents. Nearly all foster youth studied by Hedin et al. (2011) in Sweden expressed feeling sad and missing their biological families. However these feelings seem to be more common for those in traditional foster families rather than kinship. Similar feelings were described by foster youth across studies. Children felt rejected when birth parents did not want to see them, frequently canceled meetings, or did not ask how they were doing (Ahmed, 2015; Biehal, 2014; Kiraly & Humphreys, 2013; Mateos et al., 2012; Morrison et al., 2011). Some youth expressed feelings of loss, resentment, or distrust due to previous experiences (e.g., maltreatment, lack of care, suicidal ideation, drug/alcohol abuse) and did not want to see their parents (Ahmed, 2015; Aldgate, 2009; Kiraly & Humphreys,

2013; Schwartz, 2010; Skoog et al., 2015). Some expressed feeling unloved by their birth parents (Dansey et al., 2018; Ellingsen et al., 2011).

Many children felt like their birth parents were unreliable and contact was difficult or painful. Some youth felt loyal to their birth parents, some felt loyalty to their foster parents, and some felt loyalty to both. Thus, some youth felt guilty because they were emotionally divided between their birth parents and foster carers (Burgess et al., 2010; Christiansen et al., 2013; Dansey et al., 2018; Ellingsen et al., 2011; Fargas-Malet & McSherry, 2018). For some who did not see their birth parents, thinking of them led to feelings of sadness, rejection, and abandonment (Downie et al., 2009) whereas others were content with a lack of contact (Downie et al., 2009). Youth in several studies described feeling emotional distress around contact with birth parents. Therefore, this should be examined further to find effective ways to ensure foster youth's emotional needs are being met.

There were varying findings about how contact with birth families seemed to affect relationships between foster youth and their foster carers. Three studies of foster youth in Serbia, Spain, and the United Kingdom all found that the quality of the relationship, and amount of contact between youth and their birth parents, predicted their adjustment to foster care. That is, those who had conflict or no contact with biological parents had more positive opinions about their foster parents and more negative opinions about their birth parents (Burgund & Zegarac, 2016; Farmer et al., 2013; Martinez et al., 2016). However, some youth found strong relationships with both their foster and birth families.

"We get along great because foster mom thinks my mom is a very great parent and my mom thinks it's awesome that she comes over for barbeques.[3]"

Children who had consistent and frequent contact with their birth parents tended to consider their birth parents as part of their close support network (Farmer et al., 2013), appreciated the cooperation between the family members (Hedin, 2014; Morrison et al., 2011), and felt like they belonged to two families (Christiansen et al., 2013; Schofield et al., 2012). For example, one youth was positive about his circumstances because he spent time with both his foster and biological families, playing games as a family or all having dinner together (Hedin et al., 2012). It should be noted, however, only a few youth (across those five studies) described this level of cooperation between their biological and foster families.

In other cases, youth were less connected to their foster carers than they were with their birth parents (Biehal, 2014; Burgess et al., 2010). Some of those who had at least some connection with birth parents still felt ambivalence toward them. That is, they felt embarrassment, loyalty, and frustration, with birth parents, while still viewing them as important members of their social network (Biehal, 2014). Other children considered birth parents to be a part of their lives, even when they had little physical contact with them (Wissö et al., 2019). A few youth only listed their biological family members when defining their families (Ellingsen et al., 2011). A couple youth expressed strong tendencies toward *not* caring about their birth parents, and that merged with a lack of caring toward their foster parents too (Dansey et al., 2018). Generally, when describing relationships with biological and foster families, youth who had stronger bonds with biological parents tended to have weaker bonds and relationships with their foster families (Ellingsen et al., 2011; Fernandez, 2009). Conversely, youth with strong relationships with their foster families tended to have weaker relationships with birth parents (Ellingsen et al., 2011).

Contact with birth parents was not always positive. One youth expressed anger about her birth mother's lack of care. When confronting her birth mother, she said, "You're not my mother, because a mother is attached to you and be there [sic] for you, not kick you out" (Holland, 2010, p. 1674). In their study of 452 foster youth and their contact with parents in the United States, McWey and Cui (2017) found many relationships between problem behavior and amount of maternal contact. Youth who saw their biological mothers monthly or never were more withdrawn or depressed than those youth who saw their biological mothers at least weekly. Youth that never saw their biological mothers were more aggressive or delinquent than those youth who saw their biological mothers at least weekly. There was no difference in youth behaviors based on the amount of contact with biological fathers (the authors do not speculate as to why this may be the case; McWey & Cui, 2017).

Children had a variety of experiences regarding visits with biological families. In their study of foster children and visitation in Canada, Morrison et al. (2011) interviewed 24 children, most of whom felt the visits were beneficial. Other youth wanted to see their families more often, some liked having breaks between visits, and some just wanted to check on their families and make sure they were okay (Morrison et al., 2011). Some children without contact were generally satisfied with their lack of contact (Hunt et al., 2010). In their study of 169 Australian youth and their satisfaction in residential care, Southwell and Fraser (2010) noted that 52% of youth wished they could spend more time with their families. However, compared to younger children (12 and under), older children (16–17) were happy with the amount of contact they had with their birth families (Southwell & Fraser, 2010). Some children wished to return home to their birth families, although a few understood that this was likely not possible, or expected to move back home to help care for their biological parents when they were older (Morrison et al., 2011; Selwyn et al., 2010).

Youth's histories with their biological families, and the amount and quality of visitation, affected their desire to spend time with birth parents. Some children wanted to see their birth parents more frequently, whether their experiences with them were positive or traumatic (Ahmed, 2015; Aldgate, 2009; Bamba & Haight, 2009; Schwartz, 2010). In their longitudinal study of 59 foster children's well-being in Australia, Fernandez (2009) found that most youth had contact with their birth mothers at least every few months and many wanted to see them more frequently. Many youth saw their birth fathers at least quarterly and most wanted to see them more frequently. A sibling group of three in England were not in contact with their father and all three wished to know him or find a way to contact him (Hunt et al., 2010).

"I wish I could see my real dad.[4]"

Older youth were more likely to be satisfied with the frequency and length of contact than younger youth (Larkins et al., 2015). Regardless of frequency of contact, some children enjoyed their contact and others did not (Schwartz, 2010).

Some youth said it was problematic to spend time with their birth parents. Some of these youth knew that contact with birth parents would occur randomly in the community and found ways to cope with seeing their birth parents even when general contact was not desired (Burgess et al., 2010). Still some children wanted to forget their birth families completely and said that contact with their birth parents did more harm than good (Dansey et al., 2018; Skoog et al., 2015). For example, one youth described how her mother attempted to ruin her placement so she would have to go back home. Another stated that after each visit, it was increasingly more difficult to leave (Skoog et al., 2015). A youth in a different study stayed away from their birth parents because the parents had attempted to illegally take them away in the past (Downie et al., 2009). Children's experiences, emotions, and satisfaction about contact with their birth parents were varied depending upon their relationships with birth and foster families, experiences before and after removal into foster care, and satisfaction with the type, length, and frequency of contact.

Siblings

The following describes the intricacies surrounding contact with siblings, both those who are placed together and those who are separated. Across the studies we reviewed, many foster youth had siblings. However, their bond, relationship, and amount of contact varied. This depended partly on placement. For example, while some children were placed with their birth siblings, this was not the case for many—leading to other issues of contact and visitation. In their research of sibling relations in Austria, Sting (2013) found that when siblings lived together in foster care, they reported a special bond that developed because of sharing two families. One pair described each other as trustworthy, understanding, and supportive (Sting, 2013). These sibling relationships were especially important for children who had infrequent or no contact with their biological families. Some sibling groups said that being able to fight and make fun of their siblings gave them a sense of normalcy. Children interviewed by Holland (2010) and Downie et al. (2009) echoed this bond.

"… The best thing about living with my Nan would have to be that we're all together [all the siblings] … we're not in foster care or all split up all over the place …[5]"

Of interest, some youth were carers in addition to being in care. They looked after their younger siblings and sought to protect them, especially if the siblings were still living with birth parents (Holland, 2010).

When children are not placed with all their siblings, this creates a built-in barrier to keeping in contact with each other (Aldgate, 2009; Fernandez, 2009). In the studies we reviewed, some youth reported frequent contact with siblings (Fernandez, 2009; Schwartz, 2010), whereas others said contact was rare (Lundström & Sallnäs, 2012). The type of placement sometimes affected the likelihood of contact with siblings. For instance, it was more likely for youth in residential placement versus typical foster or kinship care to lose contact with siblings (Lundström & Sallnäs, 2012). In research by Schwartz (2010) in the United States, a third of youth in kinship care said there was no disruption in their contact with birth siblings. However, youth who were not in kinship foster care reported decreased contact with birth siblings after being placed in care. That is, for youth not in kinship care who did not live with their siblings, none saw their siblings more often than weekly. For some of these children, barriers, such as the need for special approval from the child welfare system, made contact with siblings more difficult. As a result, children described secretly seeking out their siblings by arranging to run into them at school or at a store. If youth saw siblings by happenstance, they either talked with them but did not tell their foster carers, or they ignored them to avoid getting in trouble for not going through the proper channels for approval (Schwartz, 2010).

Factors influencing the desire for more or less contact with siblings included time in care, type of care, and frequency of current contact. For example, across all studies we reviewed, many youth who did not have regular contact with their siblings desired more contact. Two studies we reviewed (in Sweden and Australia) indicated that the majority of youth wanted more contact with their siblings, a couple wanted less contact, and the remainder were okay with the current amount of contact (Fernandez, 2009; Lundström & Sallnäs, 2012). Lundström and Sallnäs (2012) found that the longer youth were in care, the more they wished to have increased contact with their siblings. Also, girls were more likely than boys, and those in foster care were more likely than those in residential care, to wish for more contact with their siblings. No matter the living situation, youth expressed that consistent contact with siblings (those not living with them) would make their lives better (Mateos et al., 2012).

The heightened emotions related to creating and maintaining sibling relationships was found to be a recurring theme across studies. For instance, youth expressed the importance of siblings and how hard it was when they were separated from them (Kiraly & Humphreys, 2013). However, at times, youth seemed to have competing feelings regarding their relationships with their siblings.

"It's difficult to be with a sister, but intolerable to be without her.[6]"

For example, some youth who were separated from their siblings defined the relationships as depressing or meaningless (Wojciak, 2017). Sibling groups in Austria had more difficulty getting along when personal space was not available, verbal interactions involved discomforting topics, or boundaries were either not explicit or not respected (Sting, 2013). Similarly, Leichtentritt (2013) found that youth in Israel reported difficulties in sibling relationships. Their siblings were reminders of the other family members that they missed. In addition, when placed with siblings, youth said they lacked privacy and fought with each other frequently. Further, the youth felt they were blamed for things the sibling did, bullied, or inappropriately compared to their siblings. These situations led the youth to feel annoyed or betrayed by their siblings.

However, those same youth also reported needing siblings and appreciating the emotional connection with them. Siblings helped youth feel a sense of home and were a reminder of good times from before placement. Siblings placed together felt they had someone else to care for and protect, they had someone to confide in, and they felt cared about, protected, and respected. In addition, youth placed with their siblings felt less isolated (Leichtentritt, 2013). Some youth were unable to describe their relationships as positive or negative, but instead as a combination of the two (Wojciak, 2017). To maintain their own personal mental health, a few youth tended to push siblings away because they felt they would be separated again. One youth said it was more difficult to be separated and reunited for a brief period than to remain separated.

Across studies, there were youth who felt incredibly positive about their siblings. Wojciak (2017) explained that a majority of the 197 youth they interviewed in the United States were separated from living with their siblings. These youth felt their siblings were supportive and necessary for survival, which helped them stave off loneliness. Other youth described their siblings as important, someone they can depend on, a lifelong friend, and a model for the future. Youth often discussed the strong love and joy they felt toward and from their siblings, and how the siblings helped them to have hope (Wojciak, 2017). Many studies showed the importance of both contact and the maintenance of the relationships between foster youth and their siblings.

Summary and Youth Recommendations

The amount of contact with birth families varies for youth in foster care. What is really important to consider, though, is how much contact foster youth *want* to have with their birth families. As with all other topics covered in this book, it is imperative that children's feelings and experiences be taken into account when making decisions about contact with birth families. Further, although it may seem counterintuitive, social workers should be respectful of youth's wishes, and not second-guess youth who say they do not wish to see their families. We understand, however, that many elements influence how much contact foster youth have with birth parents, and youth's desires cannot be the only factors when making such decisions.

Amount and quality of contact with birth families can affect youth well-being. Some youth yearned for more effort and emotional connection to be displayed by their biological parents during visitations (Mateos et al., 2012). One youth described how their biological parents engaged them in conversation during visitations, but never showed them any affection. Inconsistent or intermittent contact with siblings can make it difficult for youth to maintain sibling relationships and increase heartache children feel when they must separate from siblings again. Additionally, lack of contact with biological fathers, parents failing to show up for visits, abuse occurring during visits, and spending time with parents who do not show love or affection can reopen old wounds and impair healing. However, positive experiences and consistent contact can keep relationships alive and facilitate reuniting with birth families after rehabilitation.

Notes

1 Age not given, range 11–14; Schwartz, 2010, p. 39.
2 Age not given, range 11–14; Schwartz, 2010, p. 38.
3 Age not given, range 8–12; Morrison et al., 2011, p. 1479.
4 Age not given, range 5–14; Hunt et al., 2010, p. 87.
5 Age 15; Downie et al., 2009, p. 15.
6 Age 11, Leichtentritt, 2013, p. 766.

References

Ahmed, K., Windsor, L., & Scott, S. (2015). In their own words: Abused children's perceptions of care provided by their birth parents and foster carers. *Adoption & Fostering*, *39*(1), 21–37. 10.1177/0308575914565068

Aldgate, J. (2009). Living in kinship care: A child-centered view. *Adoption & Fostering*, *33*(3), 51–63. 10.1177/030857590903300306

Bamba, S., & Haight, W. (2009). Maltreated children's emerging well-being in Japanese state care. *Children and Youth Services Review*, *31*(7), 797–806. 10.1016/j.childyouth.2009.02.006

Biehal, N. (2014). A sense of belonging: Meanings of family and home in long-term foster care. *The British Journal of Social Work*, *44*(4), 955. 10.1093/bjsw/bcs177

Burgess, C., Rossvoll, F., Wallace, B., & Daniel, B. (2010). 'It's just like another home, just another family, so it's nae different' Children's voices in kinship care: A research study about the experience of children in kinship care in Scotland. *Child & Family Social Work*, *15*(3), 297–306. 10.1111/j.1365-2206.2009.00671.x

Burgund, A., & Zegarac, N. (2016). Perspectives of youth in care in Serbia. *Child & Adolescent Social Work Journal*, *33*(2), 151–161. 10.1007/s10560-015-0413-5

Christiansen, Ø., Havnen, K. J. S., Havik, T., & Anderssen, N. (2013). Cautious belonging: Relationships in long-term foster-care. *The British Journal of Social Work*, *43*(4), 720–738. 10.1093/bjsw/bcr198

Dansey, D., John, M., & Shbero, D. (2018). How children in foster care engage with loyalty conflict: Presenting a model of processes informing loyalty. *Adoption & Fostering, 42*(4), 354–368. 10.1177/0308575918798767

Downie, J. M., Hay, D. A., Horner, B. J., Wichmann, H., & Hislop, A. L. (2009). Children living with their grandparents: Resilience and wellbeing. *International Journal of Social Welfare, 19*(1), 8–22. 10.1111/j.1468-2397.2009.00654.x

Ellingsen, I. T., Shemmings, D., & Størksen, I. (2011). The concept of 'family' among Norwegian adolescents in long-term foster care. *Child and Adolescent Social Work Journal, 28*(4), 301–318. 10.1007/s10560-011-0234-0

Fargas-Malet, M., & McSherry, D. (2018). The mental health and help-seeking behavior of children and young people in care in Northern Ireland: Making services accessible and engaging. *The British Journal of Social Work, 48*(3), 578–595. 10.1093/bjsw/bcx062

Farmer, E., Selwyn, J., & Meakings, S. (2013). 'Other children say you're not normal because you don't live with your parents'. Children's views of living with informal kinship carers: Social networks, stigma and attachment to carers. *Child & Family Social Work, 18*(1), 25–34. 10.1111/cfs.12030

Fawley-King, K., Trask, E. V., Zhang, J., & Aarons, G. A. (2017). The impact of changing neighborhoods, switching schools, and experiencing relationship disruption on children's adjustment to a new placement in foster care. *Child Abuse & Neglect, 63*, 141–150. 10.1016/j.chiabu.2016.11.016

Fernandez, E. (2009). Children's wellbeing in care: Evidence from a longitudinal study of outcomes. *Children and Youth Services Review, 31*(10), 1092–1100. 10.1016/j.childyouth.2009.07.010

Hedin, L., Höjer, I., & Brunnberg, E. (2011). Settling into a new home as a teenager: About establishing social bonds in different types of foster families in Sweden. *Children and Youth Services Review, 33*(11), 2282–2289. 10.1016/j.childyouth.2011.07.016

Hedin, L., Höjer, I., & Brunnberg, E. (2012). Jokes and routines make everyday life a good life-on 'doing family' for young people in foster care in Sweden. *European Journal of Social Work, 15*(5), 613–628. 10.1080/13691457.2011.579558

Hedin, L (2014). A sense of belonging in a changeable everyday life – a follow-up study of young people in kinship, network, and traditional foster families. *Child & Family Social Work, 19*(2), 165–173. http://dx.doi.org/10.1111/j.1365-2206.2012.00887.x

Holland, S. (2010). Looked after children and the ethic of care. *The British Journal of Social Work, 40*(6), 1664–1680. 10.1093/bjsw/bcp086

Hunt, J., Waterhouse, S., & Lutman, E. (2010). Parental contact for children placed in kinship care through care proceedings. *Child and Family Law Quarterly, 22*, 71–92. https://ssrn.com/abstract=1939941

Kiraly, M., & Humphreys, C. (2013). Perspectives from young people about family contact in kinship care: "Don't push us—listen more". *Australian Social Work, 66*(3), 314–327. 10.1080/0312407x.2012.715658

Larkins, C., Ridley, J., Farrelly, N., Austerberry, H., Bilson, A., Hussein, S., Manthorpe, J., & Stanley, N. (2015). Children's, young people's and parents' perspectives on contact: Findings from the evaluation of social work practices. *The British Journal of Social Work, 45*(1), 296–312. 10.1093/bjsw/bct135

Leichtentritt, J. (2013). "It is difficult to be here with my sister but intolerable to be without her": Intact sibling placement in residential care. *Children and Youth Services Review, 35*(5), 762–770. 10.1016/j.childyouth.2013.01.022

Lundström, T., & Sallnäs, M. (2012). Sibling contact among Swedish children in foster and residential care-out of home care in a family service system. *Children and Youth Services Review, 34*(2), 396–402. 10.1016/j.childyouth.2011.11.008

Martínez, M. D. S., Fuentes, M. J., Bernedo, I. M., & García-Martín, M. A. (2016). Contact visits between foster children and their birth family: The views of foster children, foster parents and social workers. *Child & Family Social Work*, *21*(4), 473–483. 10.1111/cfs.12163

Mateos, A., Balsells, M. À., Molina, M. C., & Fuentes-Peláez, N. (2012). The perception adolescents in kinship foster care have of their own needs. *Revista de Cercetare si Interventie Sociala*, *38*, 25–41. http://hdl.handle.net/2445/103325

McMahon, C., & Curtin, C. (2013). The social networks of young people in Ireland with experience of long-term foster care: some lessons for policy and practice. *Child & Family Social Work*, *18*(3), 329–340. 10.1111/j.1365-2206.2012.00849.x

McWey, L. M., & Cui, M. (2017). Parent–child contact for youth in foster care: Research to inform practice. *Family Relations*, *66*(4), 684–695. 10.1111/fare.12276

Mitchell, M. B., Kuczynski, L., Tubbs, C. Y., & Ross, C. (2010). We care about care: Advice by children in care for children in care, foster parents and child welfare workers about the transition into foster care. *Child & Family Social Work*, *15*(2), 176–185. 10.1111/j.1365-2206.2009.00657.x

Morrison, J., Mishna, F., Cook, C., & Aitken, G. (2011). Access visits: Perceptions of child protection workers, foster parents and children who are Crown wards.*Children and Youth Services Review*, *33*(9), 1476–1482. 10.1016/j.childyouth.2011.03.011

National Conference of State Legislatures. (2019). *Foster care bill of rights*. https://www.ncsl.org/research/human-services/foster-care-bill-of-rights.aspx

Schofield, G., Beek, M., & Ward, E. (2012). Part of the family: Planning for permanence in long-term family foster care. *Children and Youth Services Review*, *34*(1), 244–253. 10.1016/j.childyouth.2011.10.020

Schwartz, A. E. (2010). "Nobody knows me no more": Experiences of loss among African American adolescents in kinship and non-kinship foster care placements. *Race and Social Problems*, *2*(1), 31–49. 10.1007/s12552-010-9025-z

Selwyn, J., Saunders, H., & Farmer, E. (2010). The views of children and young people on being cared for by an independent foster-care provider. *The British Journal of Social Work*, *40*(3), 696–713. 10.1093/bjsw/bcn117

Skoog, V., Khoo, E., & Nygren, L. (2015). Disconnection and dislocation: Relationships and belonging in unstable foster and institutional care. *The British Journal of Social Work*, *45*(6), 1888–1904. 10.1093/bjsw/bcu033

Southwell, J., & Fraser, E. (2010). Young people's satisfaction with residential care: Identifying strengths and weaknesses in service delivery. *Child Welfare*, *89*(2), 209–228. https://pubmed.ncbi.nlm.nih.gov/20857888/

Sting, S. (2013). Sibling relations in alternative child care results of a study on sibling relations in SOS Children's Villages in Austria. *Kriminologija & Socijalna Integracija*, *21*(1), 119–128. https://www.proquest.com/scholarly-journals/sibling-relations-alternative-child-care-results/docview/1450029344/se-2?accountid=10358

Wissö, T., Johansson, H., & Höjer, I. (2019). What is a family? Constructions of family and parenting after a custody transfer from birth parents to foster parents.*Child & Family Social Work*, *24*(1), 9–16. 10.1111/cfs.12475

Wojciak, A. S. (2017). 'It's complicated.' Exploring the meaning of sibling relationships of youth in foster care. *Child & Family Social Work*, *22*(3), 1283–1291. 10.1111/cfs.12345

Chapter 6

Differences between Foster and Birth Families

"These [parents] are mine, even though we're not blood related[1]"

The relationships that foster youth develop during placement can affect their overall well-being. Foster parents and siblings can provide valuable sources of support or can be problematic for foster youth. The sections ahead begin with a description of the various qualities of foster youth's relationships with their foster parents and siblings, and end with a discussion of the differences youth find between their foster and birth parents.

Foster Families

The relationships that foster youth develop with their foster families are as important as they are impactful. The foster youth reported a range of positive and negative sustained interactions with various foster family members that may have been significant in shaping their futures.

Foster Parents/Caregivers

Many foster youth described close relationships with carers (see e.g., Fernandez, 2009; Southwell & Fraser, 2010). For example, Fernandez (2009) found that 98% of youth reported good relationships with their foster mothers and 90% reported good relationships with their foster fathers. Closeness and good relationships were often defined by open communication (Clarkson et al., 2017; Malinga-Musamba, 2015). Youth interviewed in the United Kingdom said that they felt close with caregivers who were accepting of conflicting opinions, ideas, and perspectives (Clarkson et al., 2017). Many youth said they felt trust, caring, and mutual respect with caregivers when they were able to talk openly with them (see e.g., Clarkson et al., 2017; Hedin, 2014; Hedin et al., 2011b; Mitchell & Kuczynski, 2010). Cultural respect was also important (see Chapter 10 for more on cultural responsiveness). When interviewing Black girls about hair care, Dove and Powers (2018) discovered that when foster carers–regardless of race–learned about how to do the girls' hair, their relationships improved.

DOI: 10.4324/9781003309215-6

In addition to open communication, close relationships often depended upon youth feeling like they were treated well, cared about, and understood (Southwell & Fraser, 2010). According to Skoog et al. (2015), children wanted their foster caregivers to treat them like everyone else in the family. They wanted caregivers who would care about their needs, but they also needed foster parents to genuinely care about them personally, like they cared about other family members. Caregivers' encouragement, feedback, and confirmation (through praise and recognition of hard work) were also important to most of the youth in terms of their overall sense of well-being (Kelly et al., 2019). There were many examples of positive relationship qualities between foster youth and their caregivers. Youth considered their foster parents to be part of their support networks and identified them as their key sources of practical support, social support, and advice (Farmer et al., 2013; McMahon & Curtin, 2013). Youth also appreciated when their caregivers supported continuous contact with their birth families (Schwartz, 2010). Of interest, among youth interviewed in the United States, girls rated their relationships with caregivers stronger than boys did. However, the researchers did not suggest any reasons for this difference (Farineau et al., 2013). Generally, the relationship between foster youth and caregiver was affected most by trust, openness, and communication.

Strong close relationships between foster caregivers and youth were beneficial in many ways. Youth who had close relationships with their caregivers reported feeling less scared and more comfortable than they did when they first moved into the new placements (Mitchell et al., 2010). Fernandez (2009) found that with youth in Australia, the stronger the relationship between foster mothers and foster youth, the more likely youth were to go to them when needing reassurance. The stronger the relationship between foster fathers and foster youth, the more likely youth were to be inclusive with peers and less likely to engage in fighting. Furthermore, when youth trusted their foster carers, they sometimes thought of them as potential adoptive parents (Lorthridge et al., 2018). Strong relationships with caregivers also affected school performance. For instance, in three of the studies we reviewed, good relationships with foster carers predicted better concentration at school (Fernandez, 2009; Lorthridge et al., 2018; Pears et al., 2012). In addition, when girls felt supported by caregivers, their aggression against peers decreased as they transitioned from elementary school to middle school (Pears et al., 2012).

Foster youth also experienced difficult relationships with foster caregivers. Some felt like they had built a relationship, even though it was not necessarily defined as a good one (Skoog et al., 2015). Youth interviewed by Mateos et al. (2012) noted that when the age gap was larger (as in those living with grandparents) they were often misunderstood or communication in general was lacking.

"They [foster parents] are very old so often they don't understand me.[2]"

Although this was not always the case, youth in the Mateos et al. study also reported that they enjoyed living with their extended family members and were okay with the boundaries set and changes that were made by their foster caregivers. Several other children described the unfair and uncompassionate expectations that their caregivers placed on them, and how it initially strained their relationships (Mitchell & Kuczynski, 2010). In their study of orphaned children in Kenya, Skovdal (2010) found children often had to care for the people who were supposed to be caring for them. The youth shared that their foster caregivers were too sick to take care of themselves and could only provide a roof and a place to sleep. Children sometimes felt like their current caregivers had more difficult lives because they were providing foster care. These youth often helped care for their foster caregivers and support their families (Skovdal, 2010). Others were unsure of where they stood regarding their relationship. For example, a few of the youth stated that they were rarely told by foster parents or social workers if they were doing well or not in their placement (i.e., if they were being "good"; Burgund & Zegarac, 2016). More serious concerns arose in a study conducted in the Netherlands by Euser et al. (2014). In this study, 81 out of 315 foster youth experienced abuse while in care. Of the youth who experienced physical abuse, around two-thirds of youth were abused by caregivers or staff, depending on their living situations. The remaining youth were abused by other family members, residents, teachers, or strangers (Euser et al., 2014). Although problematic and needing attention, it is important to note that reports of abuse were less common than reports of strong, positive relationships between foster youth and their caregivers.

Many children interviewed provided recommendations for new foster children about how to build relationships with foster carers. Children recommended that newly fostered children should get to know their foster carer. This led to understanding each other's likes and dislikes and the foster carer was more likely to provide the things that the child preferred (Mitchell et al., 2010). As an example, as trust grew between one child and her foster mother, so did her enjoyment of trying new foods (Rees et al., 2012).

Foster youth emphasized that closeness with foster parents was important. For instance, in one study, all but one child indicated that they were closer (or equally close) to their foster family than they were with birth parents (Hunt et al., 2010). Many youth wanted to maintain these relationships with carers, even once they left the placement. However, these children usually had to arrange this contact themselves. Many used social media to connect with former foster caregivers (Skoog et al., 2015). Overall, foster youth seemed to desire a strong, positive relationship with their foster carers.

Some of the youth appreciated discipline and rules given by their foster carers (Ahmed et al., 2015; Burgess et al., 2010; Hedin et al., 2011a; Hedin et al., 2011b). Other studies found that children did not like being told what to do or having their caregivers watching and monitoring their behavior (Selwyn et al., 2010; Traube et al., 2012). However, youth did not like it when their foster parents implemented vague or unrealistic rules, were excessively angry or coercive, or engaged in physical or emotional abuse (Ahmed et al., 2015; Brown et al., 2019; Kuyini et al., 2009; Traube et al., 2012). Other studies found that some foster parents would threaten to give children back as a means of punishment (Ahmed et al., 2015; Biehal, 2014).

"She said that she should just 'wash her hands of that fostering bit.[3]"

Mazzone et al. (2019) reported other types of punishments that included withholding money, access to activities, or access to phones–although many youth described these as being ineffective. For those in kinship care with their grandparents, youth in Australia felt that grandparents were purposefully strict in efforts to avoid mistakes they had made in the past. These youth said their grandparents unnecessarily used physical punishment, were distrustful, and unrealistic in their expectations (Downie et al., 2009). In response to what they felt were unreasonable rules and/or discipline, youth in traditional foster care in Sweden (versus kinship care) reported purposefully breaking rules imposed upon them (Hedin et al., 2011b).

Some caregivers were viewed as being uncaring. For example, during interviews with children in Canada, one child discussed being required to do chores within a couple of hours of their arrival, after they had just been removed from their birth parents' care. When they refused to do the dishes, the foster parents sent them to their room and temporarily grounded them from visiting friends and birth parents (Mitchell & Kuczynski, 2010). Some youth viewed their caregivers as fulfilling an obligation or benefiting economically, rather than being genuine in their carer relationship (Brown et al., 2019; Malinga-Musamba, 2015). For example, Malinga-Musamba (2015) interviewed youth in Botswana who felt that they were being cared for only because of their government stipends. Some Black girls in the United States felt their foster parents made no efforts to understand their culture and the importance of Black hair care (Dove & Powers, 2018). These girls felt like their foster parents did not care about them and what was important to them. Kalverboer et al. (2017) found that youth living in residential campuses in the Netherlands described feeling neglected and lonely rather than supported and cared for. Kelly et al. (2019) found that this lack of caring contributed to youth's lack of well-being and difficulty coping. Similarly, Burgund and Zegarac (2016) found that children in residential care in Serbia did not feel a close connection with their carers. Further, in a study of foster youth in the United States, youth in traditional foster care had significantly closer relationships with caregivers compared to youth in group homes (Farineau et al., 2013).

Although some youth felt uncared for, others described their caregivers in a more neutral or positive way. These youth felt their caregivers were kind and their role was to provide a house, just not a home (Kalverboer et al., 2017; Mateos et al., 2012). However, the importance of being, or feeling, cared for was strong for many of the youth across studies. Ways that the foster families affected youth's perception of caring included providing tangible support, emotional support, affection, concern, reliability, commitment, and trust or by involving them in joint activities (Ahmed et al., 2015; Aldgate, 2009; Brown et al., 2019; Downie et al., 2009; Hedin et al., 2011a; Hedin, 2014; Holland, 2010; Kalverboer et al., 2017; Mateos et al., 2012; Southwell & Fraser, 2010). Feeling cared for also led youth to describe themselves as having adjusted to foster care (Ellingsen et al., 2011) and the importance of maintaining their foster relationships throughout their life span (Christiansen et al., 2013). For some youth, time influenced their relationships with foster caregivers. For example, Hedin (2014) found that after one year, most of the children were living with the same foster family and those children had developed stronger relationships with their foster parents than those who moved more often. Additionally, children who felt a higher quality relationship with their caregivers were more likely to report that their lives would have been worse if they had stayed with their birth families (Dunn et al., 2010). Generally, foster youth felt that their foster parents truly cared about them.

Foster Siblings

Relationships with carers were important for many of the foster youth, but in some cases, placement meant living with other children while in care. The relationships youth have with their foster siblings are important. Fernandez (2009) and Southwell and Fraser (2010) found that 86% and 75%, respectively, of youth reported having good relationships with their foster siblings. This was echoed in other studies (Hedin et al., 2011b; Kelly et al., 2019). Many youth developed strong bonds as friends, or role model/mentor type relationships (Hedin et al., 2011b). Some children built relationships with foster siblings and maintained these relationships after changing placement (Wissö et al., 2019).

> *"... We [former foster siblings] have a special connection, and we can talk on the phone and we chat, share photos on Facebook, and so on. You could say that they are like sisters to me.*[4]*"*

Sometimes adults were not available to offer needed emotional and physical support. Thus, children counted on each other for emotional support (e.g., Hedin et al., 2011b; Kelly et al., 2019), relied on each other for learning new skills (Emond, 2010), or helped each other in their studies (Emond, 2010). In a study of sibling groups in Austria, one sibling group sought out another sibling group to help them cope when their birth father was sent to jail (Sting, 2013). When bullied or mistreated by peers, younger children could often rely on older foster siblings to protect them (Emond, 2010).

Whereas many children described their foster siblings as friends, other youth felt like they did not fit in with foster siblings because they were treated differently from the family's biological or other foster children (Ward, 2009). For example, one youth in Sweden described being singled out by the biological children for being a foster child. This led to a lack of trust with their foster parents and the other foster siblings (Hedin et al., 2011b). Youth in Botswana reported that other children in the home were given special treatment that they themselves did not receive and that they were required to do more work than the other kids (Malinga-Musamba, 2015). It is unclear what is meant by "other children." In another study in Ghana, Kuyini et al., (2009) found that 25% of children reported getting fewer school materials, clothes, or money for educational expenses compared to biological children in the family. Other youth reported that they were made to do chores while the other children played (Kuyini et al., 2009). Children interviewed in the United Kingdom felt foster parents were more strict with them compared to the biological children. This made them feel unloved and unwanted (Ahmed et al., 2015). Whether foster sibling relationships were viewed as positive or negative, living with other children in care affected the lives of foster youth.

Differences between Foster and Birth Parents

Several youth across studies described differences between their birth and foster parents. In many ways, the differences were positive. Many youth said their foster homes had better access to basic needs, such as having a clean and safe home, clean clothing, and access to regular showers (Aldgate, 2009; Burgess et al., 2010; Downie et al., 2009; Rees et al., 2012).

"… It's like better cause you can eat whenever you need and you get a shower every day.[5]"

Sometimes differences between foster and birth parents were negative. For example, in their study on hair care for Black girls, Dove and Powers (2018) found that foster parents did not understand the cultural significance of Black girls' hair and did not provide for their hair care needs, whereas biological parents did. For some youth, the differences were emotional, such as being allowed to escape the negative experiences from their past (Downie et al., 2009). Further some youth described being loved by their foster families, but being unloved by their biological parents (Biehal, 2014; Selwyn et al., 2010). Still other youth focused on tangible differences wherein they were more able to buy things and engage in more activities than when living with their birth parents (Burgess et al., 2010). Many youth described themselves as being better off and liking the foster care situation more than they did living with their biological families (e.g., Aldgate 2009; Hedin et al., 2011b; Mateos et al., 2012).

For some youth, it is difficult to define or describe differences between foster and birth parents. For instance, Baker et al., (2013) interviewed foster youth in the United States and concluded that foster parents were much less likely than biological parents to psychologically abuse the youth in their care. In their study of contact visits between foster youth and their birth parents in

Spain, Martinez et al. (2016) found that foster parents showed more warmth and communication compared to the biological parents. Conversely, they also found that foster parents showed more rejection and criticism compared to biological parents.

Summary

Generally, youth described their experiences living with foster parents as different from living with biological parents. These differences were not always positive, and they were not always negative. Foster care is intended to be a solution for abused and neglected children who cannot safely live with their biological parents. Sometimes it meets this need, but sometimes it does not. When we pay attention to children's perspectives about their experiences, we are better equipped to meet the needs that foster care is meant to fulfill.

Notes

1 Age 17; Clarkson et al., 2017, p. 43.
2 Age not given, range 12–16; Mateos et al., 2012, p. 34.
3 Age 13; Ahmed et al., 2015; p. 31.
4 Age 15; Wissö et al., 2019, p. 14.
5 Age 12; Burgess et al., 2010, p. 303.

References

Ahmed, K., Windsor, L., & Scott, S. (2015). In their own words: Abused children's perceptions of care provided by their birth parents and foster carers. *Adoption & Fostering, 39*(1), 21–37. 10.1177/0308575914565068

Aldgate, J. (2009). Living in kinship care: A child-centered view. *Adoption & Fostering, 33*(3), 51–63. 10.1177/030857590903300306

Baker, A. J. L., Brassard, M. R., Schneiderman, M. S., & Donnelly, L. J. (2013). Foster children's report of psychological maltreatment experiences. *Journal of Public Child Welfare, 7*(3), 235–252. 10.1080/15548732.2013.779624

Biehal, N. (2014). A sense of belonging: Meanings of family and home in long-term foster care. *The British Journal of Social Work, 44*(4), 955. 10.1093/bjsw/bcs177

Brown, R., Alderson, H., Kaner, E., McGovern, R., & Lingam, R. (2019). 'There are carers, and then there are carers who actually care'; Conceptualizations of care among looked after children and care leavers, social workers and carers. *Child Abuse & Neglect, 92*, 219–229. 10.1016/j.chiabu.2019.03.018

Burgess, C., Rossvoll, F., Wallace, B., & Daniel, B. (2010). 'It's just like another home, just another family, so it's nae different' Children's voices in kinship care: A research study about the experience of children in kinship care in Scotland. *Child & Family Social Work, 15*(3), 297–306. 10.1111/j.1365-2206.2009.00671.x

Burgund, A., & Zegarac, N. (2016). Perspectives of youth in care in Serbia. *Child & Adolescent Social Work Journal, 33*(2), 151–161. 10.1007/s10560-015-0413-5

Christiansen, Ø., Havnen, K. J. S., Havik, T., & Anderssen, N. (2013). Cautious belonging: Relationships in long-term foster-care. *The British Journal of Social Work, 43*(4), 720–738. 10.1093/bjsw/bcr198

Clarkson, H., Dallos, R., Stedmon, J., & Hennessy, C. (2017). Exploring the relationship: Joint narratives of foster carers and young people. *Adoption & Fostering, 41*(1), 35–51. 10.1177/0308575916681711

Dove, L. M., & Powers, L. E. (2018). Exploring the complexity of hair and identity among African American female adolescents in foster care. *Children and Youth Services Review, 95,* 368–376. 10.1016/j.childyouth.2018.10.043

Downie, J. M., Hay, D. A., Horner, B. J., Wichmann, H., & Hislop, A. L. (2009). Children living with their grandparents: Resilience and wellbeing.*International Journal of Social Welfare, 19*(1), 8–22. 10.1111/j.1468-2397.2009.00654.x

Dunn, D. M., Culhane, S. E., & Taussig, H. N. (2010). Children's appraisals of their experiences in out-of-home care. *Children and Youth Services Review, 32*(10), 1324–1330. 10.1016/j.childyouth.2010.05.001

Ellingsen, I. T., Shemmings, D., & Størksen, I. (2011). The concept of 'family' among Norwegian adolescents in long-term foster care. *Child and Adolescent Social Work Journal, 28*(4), 301–318. 10.1007/s10560-011-0234-0

Emond, R. (2010). Caring as a moral, practical and powerful endeavour: Peer care in a Cambodian orphanage. *The British Journal of Social Work, 40*(1), 63–81. 10.1093/bjsw/bcn102

Euser, S., Alink, L. R. A., Tharner, A., van Ijzendoorn, M. H., & Bakermans-Kranenburg, M. J. (2014). Out of home placement to promote safety? The prevalence of physical abuse in residential and foster care. *Children and Youth Services Review, 37,* 64–70. 10.1016/j.childyouth.2013.12.002

Farineau, H. M., Wojciak, A. S., & McWey, L. M. (2013). You matter to me: important relationships and self-esteem of adolescents in foster care. *Child & Family Social Work, 18*(2), 129–138. 10.1111/j.1365-2206.2011.00808.x

Farmer, E., Selwyn, J., & Meakings, S. (2013). 'Other children say you're not normal because you don't live with your parents'. Children's views of living with informal kinship carers: Social networks, stigma and attachment to carers. *Child & Family Social Work, 18*(1), 25–34. 10.1111/cfs.12030

Fernandez, E. (2009). Children's wellbeing in care: Evidence from a longitudinal study of outcomes. *Children and Youth Services Review, 31*(10), 1092–1100. 10.1016/j.childyouth.2009.07.010

Hedin, L. (2014). A sense of belonging in a changeable everyday life - a follow-up study of young people in kinship, network, and traditional foster families. *Child & Family Social Work, 19*(2), 165–173. 10.1111/j.1365-2206.2012.00887.x

Hedin, L., Höjer, I., & Brunnberg, E. (2011a). Why one goes to school: what school means to young people entering foster care. *Child & Family Social Work, 16*(1), 43–51. 10.1111/j.1365-2206.2010.00706.x

Hedin, L., Höjer, I., & Brunnberg, E. (2011b). Settling into a new home as a teenager: About establishing social bonds in different types of foster families in Sweden. *Children and Youth Services Review, 33*(11), 2282–2289. 10.1016/j.childyouth.2011.07.016

Holland, S. (2010). Looked after children and the ethic of care. *The British Journal of Social Work, 40*(6), 1664–1680. 10.1093/bjsw/bcp086

Hunt, J., Waterhouse, S., & Lutman, E. (2010). Parental contact for children placed in kinship care through care proceedings. *Child and Family Law Quarterly, 22,* 71–92. https://ssrn.com/abstract=1939941

Kalverboer, M., Zijlstra, E., van Os, C., Zevulun, D., ten Brummelaar, M., & Beltman, D. (2017). Unaccompanied minors in the Netherlands and the care facility in which they flourish best. *Child & Family Social Work, 22*(2), 587–596. 10.1111/cfs.12272

Kelly, C., Anthony, E. K., & Krysik, J. (2019). "How am I doing?" Narratives of youth living in congregate care on their social-emotional well-being. *Children and Youth Services Review, 103*, 255–263. 10.1016/j.childyouth.2019.06.001

Kuyini, A. B., Alhassan, A. R., Tollerud, I., Weld, H., & Haruna, I. (2009). Traditional kinship foster care in northern Ghana: The experiences and views of children, carers and adults in Tamale. *Child & Family Social Work, 14*(4), 440–449. 10.1111/j.1365-2206.2009.00616.x

Lorthridge, J., Evans, M., Heaton, L., Stevens, A., & Phillips, L. (2018). Strengthening family connections and support for youth in foster care who identify as LGBTQ: Findings from the PII-RISE evaluation. *Child Welfare, 96*(1), 53–78. https://www.jstor.org/stable/48628035

Malinga-Musamba, T. (2015). The nature of relationships between orphans and their kinship carers in Botswana. *Child & Family Social Work, 20*(3), 257–266. 10.1111/cfs.12121

Martínez, M. D. S., Fuentes, M. J., Bernedo, I. M., & García-Martín, M. A. (2016). Contact visits between foster children and their birth family: The views of foster children, foster parents and social workers. *Child & Family Social Work, 21*(4), 473–483. 10.1111/cfs.12163

Mateos, A., Balsells, M. À., Molina, M. C., & Fuentes-Peláez, N. (2012). The perception adolescents in kinship foster care have of their own needs. *Revista de Cercetare si Interventie Sociala, 38*, 25–41. http://hdl.handle.net/2445/103325

Mazzone, A., Nocentini, A., & Menesini, E. (2019). Bullying in residential care for children: Qualitative findings from five European countries. *Children and Youth Services Review, 100*, 451–460. 10.1016/j.childyouth.2019.03.025

McMahon, C., & Curtin, C. (2013). The social networks of young people in Ireland with experience of long-term foster care: some lessons for policy and practice. *Child & Family Social Work, 18*(3), 329–340. 10.1111/j.1365-2206.2012.00849.x

Mitchell, M. B., & Kuczynski, L. (2010). Does anyone know what is going on? Examining children's lived experience of the transition into foster care. *Children and Youth Services Review, 32*(3), 437–444. 10.1016/j.childyouth.2009.10.023

Mitchell, M. B., Kuczynski, L., Tubbs, C. Y., & Ross, C. (2010). We care about care: Advice by children in care for children in care, foster parents and child welfare workers about the transition into foster care. *Child & Family Social Work, 15*(2), 176–185. 10.1111/j.1365-2206.2009.00657.x

Pears, K. C., Kim, H. K., & Leve, L. D. (2012). Girls in foster care: Risk and promotive factors for school adjustment across the transition to middle school. *Children and Youth Services Review, 34*(1), 234–243. 10.1016/j.childyouth.2011.10.005

Rees, A., Holland, S., & Pithouse, A. (2012). Food in foster families: Care, communication and conflict. *Children & Society, 26*(2), 100–111. 10.1111/j.1099-0860.2010.00332.x

Schwartz, A. E. (2010). "Nobody knows me no more": Experiences of loss among African American adolescents in kinship and non-kinship foster care placements. *Race and Social Problems, 2*(1), 31–49. 10.1007/s12552-010-9025-z

Selwyn, J., Saunders, H., & Farmer, E. (2010). The views of children and young people on being cared for by an independent foster-care provider. *The British Journal of Social Work, 40*(3), 696–713. 10.1093/bjsw/bcn117

Skoog, V., Khoo, E., & Nygren, L. (2015). Disconnection and dislocation: Relationships and belonging in unstable foster and institutional care. *The British Journal of Social Work, 45*(6), 1888–1904. 10.1093/bjsw/bcu033

Skovdal, M. (2010). Children caring for their "caregivers": Exploring the caring arrangements in households affected by AIDS in Western Kenya. *AIDS Care, 22*(1), 96–103. 10.1080/09540120903016537

Southwell, J., & Fraser, E. (2010). Young people's satisfaction with residential care: Identifying strengths and weaknesses in service delivery. *Child Welfare, 89*(2), 209–228. https://pubmed.ncbi.nlm.nih.gov/20857888/

Sting, S. (2013). Sibling relations in alternative child care results of a study on sibling relations in SOS Children's Villages in Austria. *Kriminologija & Socijalna Integracija, 21*(1), 119-128. https://www.proquest.com/scholarly-journals/sibling-relations-alternative-child-care-results/docview/1450029344/se-2?accountid=10358

Traube, D. E., James, S., Zhang, J., & Landsverk, J. (2012). A national study of risk and protective factors for substance use among youth in the child welfare system. *Addictive Behaviors, 37*(5), 641–650. 10.1016/j.addbeh.2012.01.015

Ward, H. (2009). Patterns of instability: Moves within the care system, their reasons, contexts and consequences. *Children and Youth Services Review, 31*(10), 1113–1118. 10.1016/j.childyouth.2009.07.009

Wissö, T., Johansson, H., & Höjer, I. (2019). What is a family? Constructions of family and parenting after a custody transfer from birth parents to foster parents. *Child & Family Social Work, 24*(1), 9–16. 10.1111/cfs.12475

Chapter 7

Children's Experiences of Transitions into and during Foster Care Placement

"It's like you're being kidnapped[1]"

Every foster child experiences transitions into and out of placement, and those experiences range from positive to negative. For some foster youth, placement changes while in care are more common. Youth interpret these transitions differently based on their individual situations. In this chapter, we will discuss youth transitions into, within, and out of foster care.

Transitions into Foster Care

Youth entering foster care often do so because of negative experiences in the home (i.e., abuse, neglect, or parental death; California Child Welfare Indicators Project, 2022; Skovdal, 2010). However, some children are sent to foster care for reasons other than abuse. For instance, in Ghana, children may be sent to foster care by their parents to keep extended families together, help families practice old traditions, or to give children the opportunity to attend school (Kuyini et al., 2009). In many cases, even when leaving abusive or neglectful homes, children experience difficulty adjusting and feeling positive about the change (Dansey et al., 2018; Mitchell & Kuczynski, 2010).

Many youth do not fully understand the reasons for placement and report not being told much (if anything) about why they were removed from their homes (Aldgate, 2009; Balsells et al., 2017; Burgund & Zegarac, 2016; Downie et al., 2009; Farmer et al., 2013; Pölkki et al., 2012). The studies we reviewed include children from Spain, Scotland, Finland, Canada, and Serbia who share similar experiences and feelings about placement. Although some children were too young to remember why they were placed into foster care, several reported feeling like adults lied to them about why they were in placement, where they were going, and how long they would be there (Aldgate, 2009; Balsells et al., 2017; Pölkki et al., 2012).

DOI: 10.4324/9781003309215-7

"I would have liked to have been told that instead of telling me that I was going to go play, that they would have told me that they were going to separate me from my mother.²"

Some youth described shock and the inability to fully comprehend what was happening, and two said being placed in care felt like they were being kidnapped (Mitchell & Kuczynski, 2010). Many children expressed confusion, fear, loss, loneliness, and feeling unwelcome, when first entering foster care (Dansey et al., 2018; Mitchell & Kuczynski, 2010; Schwartz, 2010; Ward, 2009). However, other children said that while they did not receive much information about their new placements in advance, they also felt that they could trust in what the system decided for them (Burgund & Zegarac, 2016).

For some youth, entering care meant moving to new neighborhoods and losing old friends (Aldgate, 2009; McMahon & Curtin, 2013; Mitchell & Kuczynski, 2010). In addition, many children had to adapt to new household environments. For example, while some children experienced more privacy because of entering care, many children experienced a loss of privacy because of overcrowding and having to share bedrooms (Aldgate, 2009). This led to disruptions in sleeping patterns. Some children moving from rural to urban areas disliked the unfamiliar sounds of the city, whereas those moving from urban to rural areas said the neighborhood was boring and it was difficult to see or make new friends (Aldgate, 2009). Other children in Canada described feeling afraid because they did not know where they would sleep or had to ask for things they were not used to asking for (Mitchell & Kuczynski, 2010).

Transitions into care were easier for some youth than others. Youth felt that transition into care went more smoothly when transitions were gradual (Burgess et al., 2010; Schwartz, 2010), they already knew or had met their foster carers (Hedin et al., 2011b; Hedin et al., 2012; Schwartz, 2010), they moved within the same (or nearby) neighborhoods (Burgess et al., 2010; McMahon & Curtin, 2013; Mitchell & Kuczynski, 2010), or foster and birth families worked together with little to no rivalry (Ellingsen et al. 2011). Youth described ways in which foster families helped them adjust to their transition

(Mitchell et al., 2010; Mitchell & Kuczynski, 2010). For example, youth felt it was helpful when foster parents were open about their past and why they were living together (Pölkki et al., 2012). In addition, many youth found comfort if their foster family had a pet, or when they brought a favorite stuffed animal–especially one that had sentimental value from one of their birth parents. One child recommended keeping busy and distracted until their first visitation with their biological families–which he stated could take a couple of months (Mitchell et al., 2010).

Several youth made recommendations for adults and social workers to help children transition smoothly into care (Mitchell et al., 2010; Pölkki et al., 2012). For instance, children said that foster parents should take time to get to know them, take them out for something like buying clothes or ice cream, allow access to music to help them sleep better at night, and give them basic information about the household and household rules. Other children said that talking to other foster children and getting support from them during transition would help them cope. Youth also wanted social workers to listen to them during transition into care, not to minimize their feelings, and help them work through their fears and anxiety. They wanted to know ahead of time if there were pets and to be shown around so they knew where things were (Mitchell et al., 2010). Other children said adults should give them more information about why they were in placement, tell them what the placement process entailed for the future, explain social workers' roles, and tell them when/if they can live with their biological families again (Pölkki et al., 2012). Transitioning into care is not easy for many youth, but with the right support, the move can be less difficult.

Transition Differences Across Types of Placement

Moving from living with their birth parents to living in care seemed more difficult for some youth than others, especially when considering the type of placement. Further, children in different types of placements have different experiences with relationships and placement loss. For example, Schwartz (2010) questioned foster youth in the United States about their perceptions of loss related to their placement into care. Children in traditional foster care experienced more relationship and placement loss compared to children in kinship care and were more emotionally affected by these losses. In Sweden, 17 youth in kinship and traditional foster care talked about their transitions into care (Hedin et al., 2011b). Although all 17 youth interviewed reported having difficulty adjusting, those in traditional foster care had the most challenging time with the transition. Youth mentioned losing contact with siblings, living with strangers, and not feeling at home as some reasons why the transition into traditional foster care was difficult for them.

"They [foster parents] still feel like strangers.[3]"

Across the studies we reviewed, youth in kinship care typically had more positive experiences and attitudes about being in care than in other types of care (e.g., Fawley-King et al., 2017; Hedin et al., 2011b; Schwartz, 2010). Youth described the transition as less jarring because they were moved into familiar households (Aldgate, 2009; Schwartz, 2010). Downie et al. (2009) found that youth in kinship care in Australia appreciated the effort their grandparents made to keep family connections intact after placement. More specifically, grandparents often took in youth *and* their siblings, so they could all stay together (Downie et al., 2009).

However, while unique benefits exist for those in kinship care, there are unique challenges as well. Some of these challenges are specific to living with grandparents or older carers. These challenges were similar across studies conducted in the United States, Australia, and various European countries. Some children who moved in with grandparents felt there was a large generation gap and that their grandparents did not understand what it was like to be young (Aldgate, 2009; Mateos et al., 2012). For example, one youth described the generation gap between her foster parent and herself as being a barrier to effective hair care strategies (Dove & Powers, 2018). The generational difference in what constitutes "good" or appropriate hair left the youth feeling unsure of how to manage her own hair. In another study, one youth said that living with grandparents was boring (Farmer et al., 2013). For youth interviewed in the United Kingdom, the number of children's close relationships decreased as their caregivers got older (Farmer et al., 2013). Some youth said their carers were distressed and fatigued, which sometimes meant that youth had to do household chores that their carers could not do themselves (Downie et al., 2009; Farmer et al., 2013; Skovdal, 2010). Youth sometimes worried that the grandparents would become sick or no longer be able to care for them (Burgess et al., 2010; Downie et al., 2009). While youth described several concerns while living in kinship or traditional foster care, more youth described problems living in residential care.

Youth in residential care often experienced a much different household structure than those in kinship or traditional foster care. For example, Kalverboer et al. (2017) evaluated interviews with children living in foster care across the Netherlands. Children in residential care always prepared their own food, but children in foster homes were not required to do this. Moreover, the youth in residential care discussed specific problems related to making their own food. For instance, they did not have access to appropriate cooking utensils, they lacked money for ingredients, or kitchens were dirty and often unavailable when they wanted to cook. Because of these problems, youth did not enjoy eating, had to eat food that was unfamiliar to them, and often resorted to ready-made food. In addition, compared to those living with foster families, youth in residential care were far less positive about their living conditions, daily routines, physical care, safety, overall atmosphere, and stability. During interviews, these youth frequently stated that residential care facilities should be closed (Kalverboer et al., 2017). In a different study in Finland, some of the children were placed in residential facilities temporarily, until they could be moved into foster homes. These youth described feeling confused because there was no timeline for changing placements and no way to know what to expect (Pölkki et al., 2012).

Some experiences and environments in residential care were more extreme. Compared to youth living in foster or kinship care, youth in such environments were more likely to believe that their lives would have been better if they stayed with their biological families (Dunn et al., 2010). This may be because youth in residential care are often surrounded by other residents who engage in violence and drug/alcohol abuse (Kalverboer et al., 2017). Further, compared to youth in traditional foster care, these youth often lacked support and help in times of distress, had inadequate role models, felt disrespected, had a reduced social network, lacked contact with peers, and had poor access to education (Kalverboer et al., 2017). Youth in residential care in Serbia experienced more emotional problems (i.e., depression, anxiety, and problem behaviors) than those in foster care (Damnjanovic et al., 2011). Their overall quality of life, as measured by the Pediatric Quality of Life Scale (PedsQL–a self-report questionnaire), was significantly lower compared to traditional foster youth.

In a study of charitable residential institutions in Kenya (Gayapersad et al., 2019) children described their experiences there as vastly different from traditional families. Children felt like they had no say in decisions made about their own lives. They had to follow strict Christian value-based rules, which children were afraid of breaking, lest they be expelled. For example, boys were circumcised, and all children's heads were shaved. In addition, children could not socialize outside of the home, practice their religions, speak their own languages, or engage in their cultural traditions.

Placement Changes

Many youth, when asked, said that they wanted to remain in their current foster home or that a single, long-term placement was the ideal situation (see e.g., Fernandez, 2009; Selwyn et al., 2010; Southwell & Fraser, 2010). In fact, when foster youth stay with the same caregivers for longer periods, they feel happier and show fewer depressive symptoms (Bulat, 2010; Selwyn et al., 2010; Southwell & Fraser, 2010). However, transitions from one placement to another can occur frequently while in care (Annie E. Casey Foundation, 2023; Skoog et al., 2015). As of 2021, 35% of foster youth in the United States experience more than two placement changes per year (Annie E. Casey Foundation, 2023).

Placement changes lead to unique problems and experiences that youth with consistent placements do not typically experience. For instance, youth who experienced placement changes in Sweden and the United Kingdom said they were nervous about moving and that it was difficult to adjust to the new home's structure, learn a new set of rules, or get used to different smells (Rostill-Brookes et al., 2011; Schofield et al., 2012; Skoog et al., 2015). In the study by Selwyn et al. (2010) 119 of 160 (74%) youth stayed with the same foster carers for the duration of the study (one year) and 41 (26%) changed placements at least once. Those with placement changes described themselves as less happy, and their overall views were more negative than those without placement changes. Reasons for their negative opinions included being yelled at, feeling like foster parents did not have time for them, disliking particular members of the foster family, feeling lost and confused because of the family's religious beliefs, not liking the cooking, being the only sibling of their gender, or feeling like they were always getting in trouble.

Many youth blame the adults in their last foster home as the reason for placement change, but some blame their own bad behavior (Selwyn et al., 2010). For example, in the Selwyn study, one youth said they assaulted another child, and others said they changed placements because they ran away or asked to leave (p. 706). Regardless, placement change is difficult for children no matter the cause of the disruption, even when the initial placement is in a negative environment (Skoog et al., 2015). Many youth who change placements have to relive the experiences of leaving their friends and neighborhoods (McMahon & Curtin, 2013; Schwartz, 2010; Skoog et al., 2015), and feeling fear or uncertainty of where they will go (Barnes, 2012; Rostill-Brookes et al., 2011). One youth in the United Kingdom woke up one morning and her bags had been packed for her; no one talked about the placement change until a government employee arrived to take her to her new home (Rostill-Brookes et al., 2011). Another youth described the nearly constant moves between family members' homes–in some circumstances overhearing the caregiver telling another family member that he was not wanted anymore (Ward, 2009). Furthermore, when youth experienced several placement changes, they were more likely to be impatient and demanding with their caregivers (Fernandez, 2009). This could be because multiple placements decreased children's abilities to connect with their foster families or because the difficulty connecting increased the likelihood of placement change (Fernandez, 2009).

Sometimes youth felt they needed to settle down quickly because they were not sure how long they would be in care would last or even how long they would stay in their current placement (Aldgate, 2009; Dansey et al., 2018).

"When you live in a foster family ... you always have a feeling like I won't be here that long because maybe they'll only want me a half year or so.[4]"

Some youth described difficulty in focusing on other aspects of life (like school work), feeling angry, being distrustful, and having a harder time making and keeping friends when they were not sure of where they would be living from one day to the next (Buys et al., 2011). Youth repeatedly brought up the importance of maintaining friendships and how moving made this process more difficult or impossible. For instance, some youth stated that their caregivers did not encourage them to maintain contact with old friends after moving, while others felt displaced because they had no contact with friends anymore (Kelly et al., 2019; McMahon & Curtin, 2013). Their friends had helped them feel a sense of belonging, and moving took that away from them (Kelly et al., 2019). Some youth who were able to remain in their same placement described that it was difficult seeing *other* kids come and go (Ward, 2009). Contrary to what many youth said in other studies, one youth in Japan was more interested in staying in residential care–rather than moving to a foster home–so he could remain with the friends he made in care (Bamba & Haight, 2009).

Children who had to adapt multiple times to different placements brought up concerns about their own mental health and emotional well-being (Bulat, 2010; Skoog et al., 2015). Bulat (2010) assessed depressive symptoms in youth who were in foster care or residential care in the Republic of Croatia across a 5-year interval. At the beginning, youth in residential care exhibited more depressive symptoms compared to youth in foster care. At the end of 5 years, there was no significant difference between the groups, and overall, depressive symptoms decreased. Researchers attributed this to stability in placement. Similarly, Southwell and Fraser (2010) found that children in Australia with four or fewer placements were significantly happier in care compared to children with more than five placements. For more on mental health and well-being, see Chapter 9.

Placement changes were stressful experiences for many youth in care, but were more likely to occur for some youth than others. Youth in kinship care experienced significantly fewer placements compared to youth in regular foster care (Schwartz, 2010). Children in kinship care reported positive feelings about moving from foster care to kinship care, although one child said she was sad to leave a foster mother who was nice. Girls in detention centers experienced issues with transitions that youth in other placement types did not. For example, some youth could not leave the detention centers because their foster carers did not pick them up, or it was difficult to make arrangements for them even once they had completed their sentences. Sometimes their exit out of the detention center was delayed, which meant the girls had to unpack and request their belongings again. Other times this meant the girls had difficulty meeting their own basic needs, such as showering (Flores et al., 2018). Placement changes lead to inconsistency in care, relationship strain, and disruptions in friendships, routines, and even school (see Chapter 8 for more about foster youth experiences in school, including how school transitions affect youth).

Transitions Out of Care

Sometimes youth transition out of care to be reunified with their biological parents. This transition can be difficult for children, especially if they are not involved in the decision-making process (see Chapter 3 for further discussions about youth's involvement in the decision-making process). Across the studies we reviewed, the best example of this is in the study by Balsells et al. (2017). The researchers interviewed foster children in Spain who had been reunited with their biological parents or who were in the process of reunification. Of interest, some children were never told of the plan to reunify and only found out on the day they left foster care. For children who had been told, many did not fully understand what was happening because they had limited information or were minimally involved in the decision-making process. Children who were not involved in the reunification planning described feeling discomfort and sadness, and in some cases feeling like they betrayed their foster carers by leaving to live with their biological parents (Balsells et al., 2017). For some children, returning to live with biological parents is especially difficult because they move from foster care to their biological families and back to foster care again– sometimes repeatedly (Pölkki et al., 2012).

Some children wish to be reunited with their biological families whereas others do not. This often depends on what their lives were like before moving into foster care, their interactions with biological families during care, and their relationships with foster carers (see e.g., Dansey et al., 2018). Some youth who have returned to live with biological parents remain in contact with their foster carers. One youth who had returned to his birth parent as planned, discussed remaining close to his foster carer (Hedin, 2014).

Some youth transition out of care because they have reached an age where they are no longer eligible for foster care. The prospect of aging out of care can be frightening for youth. Many youth stated that their biggest concern about the future was what would happen to their lives when they aged out of the foster care system (Mateos et al., 2012). Across studies, youth often described feeling fear, loss, and shock at the thought of leaving care (Buys et al., 2011; Gayapersad et al., 2019; Rostill-Brookes et al., 2011; Sting, 2013). This suggests that the foster care system could better prepare youth for what may occur when they age out of the system and provide additional support as they approach transitioning out of care. These concerns are eased for youth who expect to stay with foster carers for at least some time after they age out (e.g., Christiansen et al., 2013). Indeed, some youth do not leave care immediately when they age out.

"They [foster parents] tell me I can stay until I'm 40 but then I have to move out.[5]"

Because of this, although outside the scope of our systematic review, we included the perspectives of care leavers about their experiences leaving the foster care system (Gayapersad et al., 2019; Holland, 2010). Although eligible to leave, several youth in charitable institutions in Kenya remained at their placement after they turned 18. Others returned to the institution in a mentorship capacity. One former foster youth expressed that leaving the institution was the most difficult part of being in care (Gayapersad et al., 2019). Care leavers in the United Kingdom said they kept in touch with their foster families because they felt close to them (Holland, 2010).

Summary and Youth Recommendations

Youth stated that their biggest concern about the future was about what would happen to their lives when they aged out of the foster care system (Mateos et al., 2012). This suggests that the foster care system could better prepare youth for what may occur when they age out of the system and provide additional support as they approach transitioning out of care.

Typically, transitions into care can be difficult for youth, even for those who understand the reasons for their placements. Foster youth experience several types of placements: into foster care, within foster care, and out of foster care, and these transitions can be difficult. Even for youth who do not experience placement change, witnessing the transitions of their foster siblings is painful. Unfortunately, during all of these transitions many children are not given adequate information about what is happening and why.

Children in the studies we reviewed described wanting to be involved in the decision-making process regarding their placements. However, in addition to being excluded from the decision-making process, some children are not given any warning about impending changes in their lives. This only serves to increase children's distress when they have already been traumatized, and has the potential to negatively affect their acclimation to and success while in care. This uncertainty children experience makes it difficult for them to trust and build meaningful relationships with adults, foster families, and friends. Foster care is meant to create a safe place where children can grow up and thrive. By increasing communication with children during the foster care placement and transition process, we increase the ability for children to thrive.

Notes

1 Age 12–13 years; Mitchell & Kuczynski, 2010, p. 440.
2 Age 12–17; Balsells et al., 2017, p. 79.
3 Age not given, range 13–16; Hedin et al., 2011b, p. 2288.
4 Age not given, range 8–18; Skoog et al., 2015, p. 1900.
5 Age not given, range 13–18; Christiansen et al., 2013, p. 731.

References

Aldgate, J. (2009). Living in kinship care: A child-centered view. *Adoption & Fostering*, *33*(3), 51–63. 10.1177/030857590903300306

Annie E. Casey Foundation. (2023, May 30). *Child welfare and foster care statistics*. https://www.aecf.org/blog/child-welfare-and-foster-care-statistics

Balsells, M. Á., Fuentes-Peláez, N., & Pastor, C. (2017). Listening to the voices of children in decision-making: A challenge for the child protection system in Spain. *Children and Youth Services Review*, *79*, 418. 10.1016/j.childyouth.2017.06.055

Bamba, S., & Haight, W. (2009). Maltreated children's emerging well-being in Japanese state care. *Children and Youth Services Review*, *31*(7), 797–806. 10.1016/j.childyouth.2009.02.006

Barnes, V. (2012). Social work and advocacy with young people: Rights and care in practice. *The British Journal of Social Work*, *42*(7), 1275–1292. 10.1093/bjsw/bcr142

Bulat, L. R. (2010). A longitudinal study of depressiveness in children in public care. *International Journal of Social Welfare*, *19*(4), 412–423. 10.1111/j.1468-2397.2009.00698.x

Burgess, C., Rossvoll, F., Wallace, B., & Daniel, B. (2010). 'It's just like another home, just another family, so it's nae different' Children's voices in kinship care: A research study about the experience of children in kinship care in Scotland. *Child & Family Social Work*, *15*(3), 297–306. 10.1111/j.1365-2206.2009.00671.x

Burgund, A., & Zegarac, N. (2016). Perspectives of youth in care in Serbia. *Child & Adolescent Social Work Journal*, *33*(2), 151–161. 10.1007/s10560-015-0413-5

Buys, N., Tilbury, C., Creed, P., & Crawford, M. (2011). Working with youth in-care: Implications for vocational rehabilitation practice. *Disability and Rehabilitation*, *33*(13-14), 1125–1135. 10.3109/09638288.2010.521614

California Child Welfare Indicators Project. (2022). *Child maltreatment allegations/ child count (Version 7554C759) [Data set]*. https://ccwip.berkeley.edu/childwelfare/ reports/Allegation/MTSG/r/ab636/s

Christiansen, Ø., Havnen, K. J. S., Havik, T., & Anderssen, N. (2013). Cautious belonging: Relationships in long-term foster-care. *The British Journal of Social Work*, *43*(4), 720–738. 10.1093/bjsw/bcr198

Damnjanovic, M., Lakic, A., Stevanovic, D., & Jovanovic, A. (2011). Effects of mental health on quality of life in children and adolescents living in residential and foster care: A cross-sectional study. *Epidemiology and Psychiatric Sciences*, *20*(3), 257–262. 10.1017/s2045796011000291

Dansey, D., John, M., & Shbero, D. (2018). How children in foster care engage with loyalty conflict: Presenting a model of processes informing loyalty. *Adoption & Fostering*, *42*(4), 354–368. 10.1177/0308575918798767

Dove, L. M., & Powers, L. E. (2018). Exploring the complexity of hair and identity among African American female adolescents in foster care. *Children and Youth Services Review*, *95*, 368–376. 10.1016/j.childyouth.2018.10.043

Downie, J. M., Hay, D. A., Horner, B. J., Wichmann, H., & Hislop, A. L. (2009). Children living with their grandparents: Resilience and wellbeing. *International Journal of Social Welfare*, *19*(1), 8–22. 10.1111/j.1468-2397.2009.00654.x

Dunn, D. M., Culhane, S. E., & Taussig, H. N. (2010). Children's appraisals of their experiences in out-of-home care. *Children and Youth Services Review*, *32*(10), 1324–1330. 10.1016/j.childyouth.2010.05.001

Ellingsen, I. T., Shemmings, D., & Størksen, I. (2011). The concept of 'family' among Norwegian adolescents in long-term foster care. *Child and Adolescent Social Work Journal*, *28*(4), 301–318. 10.1007/s10560-011-0234-0

Farmer, E., Selwyn, J., & Meakings, S. (2013). 'Other children say you're not normal because you don't live with your parents'. Children's views of living with informal kinship carers: Social networks, stigma and attachment to carers. *Child & Family Social Work*, *18*(1), 25–34. 10.1111/cfs.12030

Fawley-King, K., Trask, E. V., Zhang, J., & Aarons, G. A. (2017). The impact of changing neighborhoods, switching schools, and experiencing relationship disruption on children's adjustment to a new placement in foster care. *Child Abuse & Neglect*, *63*, 141–150. 10.1016/j.chiabu.2016.11.016

Fernandez, E. (2009). Children's wellbeing in care: Evidence from a longitudinal study of outcomes. *Children and Youth Services Review*, *31*(10), 1092–1100. 10.1016/ j.childyouth.2009.07.010

Flores, J., Hawes, J., Westbrooks, A., & Henderson, C. (2018). Crossover youth and gender: What are the challenges of girls involved in both the foster care and juvenile justice systems? *Children and Youth Services Review*, *91*, 149–155. 10.1016/ j.childyouth.2018.05.031

Gayapersad, A., Ombok, C., Kamanda, A., Tarus, C., Ayuku, D., & Braitstein, P. (2019). The production and reproduction of kinship in charitable children's institutions in Uasin Gishu County, Kenya. *Child & Youth Care Forum*, *48*, 797–828. 10.1007/s10566-019-09506-8

Hedin, L., Höjer, I., & Brunnberg, E. (2012). Jokes and routines make everyday life a good life—on 'doing family' for young people in foster care in Sweden. *European Journal of Social Work*, *15*(5), 613–628. http://dx.doi.org/10.1080/13691457. 2011.579558

Hedin, L. (2014). A sense of belonging in a changeable everyday life - A follow-up study of young people in kinship, network, and traditional foster families. *Child & Family Social Work, 19*(2), 165–173. 10.1111/j.1365-2206.2012.00887.x

Hedin, L., Höjer, I., & Brunnberg, E. (2011). Settling into a new home as a teenager: About establishing social bonds in different types of foster families in Sweden. *Children and Youth Services Review, 33*(11), 2282–2289. 10.1016/j.childyouth.2011.07.016

Holland, S. (2010). Looked after children and the ethic of care. *The British Journal of Social Work, 40*(6), 1664–1680. 10.1093/bjsw/bcp086

Kalverboer, M., Zijlstra, E., van Os, C., Zevulun, D., ten Brummelaar, M., & Beltman, D. (2017). Unaccompanied minors in the Netherlands and the care facility in which they flourish best. *Child & Family Social Work, 22*(2), 587–596. 10.1111/cfs.12272

Kelly, C., Anthony, E. K., & Krysik, J. (2019). "How am I doing?" Narratives of youth living in congregate care on their social-emotional well-being. *Children and Youth Services Review, 103*, 255–263. 10.1016/j.childyouth.2019.06.001

Kuyini, A. B., Alhassan, A. R., Tollerud, I., Weld, H., & Haruna, I. (2009). Traditional kinship foster care in northern Ghana: The experiences and views of children, carers and adults in Tamale. *Child & Family Social Work, 14*(4), 440–449. 10.1111/j.1365-2206.2009.00616.x

Mateos, A., Balsells, M. À., Molina, M. C., & Fuentes-Peláez, N. (2012). The perception adolescents in kinship foster care have of their own needs. *Revista de Cercetare si Interventie Sociala, 38*, 25–41. http://hdl.handle.net/2445/103325

McMahon, C., & Curtin, C. (2013). The social networks of young people in Ireland with experience of long-term foster care: Some lessons for policy and practice. *Child & Family Social Work, 18*(3), 329–340. 10.1111/j.1365-2206.2012.00849.x

Mitchell, M. B., & Kuczynski, L. (2010). Does anyone know what is going on? Examining children's lived experience of the transition into foster care. *Children and Youth Services Review, 32*(3), 437–444. 10.1016/j.childyouth.2009.10.023

Mitchell, M. B., Kuczynski, L., Tubbs, C. Y., & Ross, C. (2010). We care about care: Advice by children in care for children in care, foster parents and child welfare workers about the transition into foster care. *Child & Family Social Work, 15*(2), 176–185. 10.1111/j.1365-2206.2009.00657.x

Pölkki, P., Vornanen, R., Pursiainen, M., & Riikonen, M. (2012). Children's participation in child-protection processes as experienced by foster children and social workers. *Child Care in Practice, 18*(2), 107–125. 10.1080/13575279.2011.646954

Rostill-Brookes, H., Larkin, M., Toms, A., & Churchman, C. (2011). A shared experience of fragmentation: Making sense of foster placement breakdown. *Clinical Child Psychology and Psychiatry, 16*(1), 103–127. 10.1177/1359104509352894

Schofield, G., Beek, M., & Ward, E. (2012). Part of the family: Planning for permanence in long-term family foster care. *Children and Youth Services Review, 34*(1), 244–253. 10.1016/j.childyouth.2011.10.020

Schwartz, A. E. (2010). "Nobody knows me no more": Experiences of loss among African American adolescents in kinship and non-kinship foster care placements. *Race and Social Problems, 2*(1), 31–49. 10.1007/s12552-010-9025-z

Selwyn, J., Saunders, H., & Farmer, E. (2010). The views of children and young people on being cared for by an independent foster-care provider. *The British Journal of Social Work, 40*(3), 696–713. 10.1093/bjsw/bcn117

Skoog, V., Khoo, E., & Nygren, L. (2015). Disconnection and dislocation: Relationships and belonging in unstable foster and institutional care. *The British Journal of Social Work, 45*(6), 1888–1904. 10.1093/bjsw/bcu033

Skovdal, M. (2010). Children caring for their "caregivers": Exploring the caring arrangements in households affected by AIDS in Western Kenya. *AIDS Care, 22*(1), 96–103. 10.1080/09540120903016537

Southwell, J., & Fraser, E. (2010). Young people's satisfaction with residential care: Identifying strengths and weaknesses in service delivery. *Child Welfare, 89*(2), 209–228. https://pubmed.ncbi.nlm.nih.gov/20857888/

Sting, S. (2013). Sibling relations in alternative child care results of a study on sibling relations in SOS *Children's Villages in Austria. Kriminologija & Socijalna Integracija, 21*(1), 119–128. https://www.proquest.com/scholarly-journals/sibling-relations-alternative-child-care-results/docview/1450029344/se-2?accountid=10358

Ward, H. (2009). Patterns of instability: Moves within the care system, their reasons, contexts and consequences. *Children and Youth Services Review, 31*(10), 1113–1118. 10.1016/j.childyouth.2009.07.009

Chapter 8

Challenges and Benefits of Being in Care

"I've never had it so easy, I get twice as much [food] and I don't have to fight for it![1]"

Foster care is meant to benefit youth and provide them with safe and nurturing home environments where they can grow and thrive. Typically youth enter into foster care because of adverse or traumatic events, such as child maltreatment or the death of a parent. Indeed foster care may be the only solution for children who do not have safe places to live. However, even when youth benefit from being in foster care, there are still challenges they experience. Being removed from home and placed into care can be traumatizing, even when home is an unsafe place to live. For example, as we have described elsewhere in this book, children do not always understand why they are being placed into foster care. In addition, changing homes can mean changing neighborhoods, schools, and friends, causing children to lose what existing support networks they have. In this chapter, we discuss the challenges of being in foster care along with the benefits, as they are described by youth in the studies we reviewed.

Challenges with Being in Foster Care

Many youth described challenges they experienced while in foster care. Some of these, we discuss in other chapters (e.g., adapting to unfamiliar environments in Chapter 7, missing biological family members in Chapter 5, and being treated differently from other children in Chapter 10). Other challenges include lack of resources, feeling like they had become caregivers of sorts to others in the house, difficulty building relationships with adults, transitioning to new schools, and difficulty in relationships with peers and friends (Dunn et al., 2010; Emond, 2010; Farmer et al., 2013). We will describe these next, along with ways that youth found to mitigate some of these challenges.

Lack of Resources

Foster care youth reported lack of access to resources relating to basic needs (e.g., shelter and food) and mental health services. Across some

DOI: 10.4324/9781003309215-8

villages in Kenya (Sala, 2009), nearly all orphaned children reported having inadequate clothing, and most did not have enough food (either because their carers did not provide food, carers were not home, or because there was not enough money for food). Some children worked to earn money, some boys skipped school to look for food, and all girls and most boys reported overcrowding and a lack of space. Some of the children slept on the floor, shared a single blanket, or only had access to bug infested bedding (blankets, mattresses, mats, etc.; Sala, 2009). Children interviewed in Ghana (Kuyini et al., 2009) described being afraid to ask for things they needed (either because they feared how their foster parents would react or because they felt there was not enough money). Youth in Ireland found it difficult to access resources they needed for their mental health (Fargas-Malet & McSherry, 2018). There were long waiting lists, services were too far away, it was difficult for youth to get needed referrals, there were delays in treatment, and information about where and how to access services was generally lacking.

Caring for Others

In terms of feeling like caregivers for others, youth living with grandparents in kinship care often felt more responsibility for family and household dynamics (e.g., Downie et al., 2009).

> *"I sometimes do the cooking, washing up, cleaning the house and the washing of the clothes … generally helping her out with stuff.[2]"*

These youth tried to give their grandparents more space and breaks and did their best not to complain. They also understood financial constraints, and helped more with daily household tasks and chores. One youth in Australia chose to care for his grandmother rather than socialize, since she was in poor health and needed help around the house (Farmer et al., 2013). In other cases, youth were responsible for younger children in the household. For instance, older children in Cambodia helped teach the younger children how to do chores and be contributing members of the household (Emond, 2010).

Relationships with Adults

Building relationships with adults was difficult for some youth. Sometimes, youth felt that the type of placement influenced their relationships with adults. For example, children preferred kinship care over foster care because they did not always feel loved in foster care (e.g., Burgess et al., 2010). Youth in Japan described how it was difficult to trust adults because of previous abusive experiences at birth homes (Bamba & Haight, 2009). Gayapersad et al. (2019) found that in the residential, dorm-style living areas in Kenya, emotional bonding was difficult as the carers were not living there full-time (they were considered the aunties and uncles rather than the parents or grandparents). These carers tended to develop stronger relationships with some, but not all, resulting in some youth feeling like they were treated unfairly compared to other children in the home (Gayapersad et al., 2019). There were additional examples of children saying they were treated differently from other children in the home. For instance, youth in kinship care in Botswana told interviewers that the children who were well liked by the caregivers did fewer chores (Malinga-Musamba, 2015). Children in Ghana described physical abuse or being yelled at for mistakes (Kuyini et al., 2009). They also felt like their freedoms were restricted or they did not have as many privileges compared to foster parents' biological children. Crossover youth in the United States (youth who are part of both the juvenile justice system and the foster care system), felt like they were viewed as criminals, even when they were engaging in good behavior (Flores et al., 2018). In addition, they were more likely to be rearrested for minor offenses (fighting with other kids or being accused of minor crimes). As such, a few of these youth decided it was better to run away than to be rearrested (Flores et al., 2018).

School

School can also be a negative place for youth for reasons such as placement instability or simply because they are in foster care. Placement instability can make it difficult for youth to develop meaningful relationships with teachers and friends (Buys et al., 2011; Fawley-King et al., 2017), puts youth behind in their schoolwork (Buys et al., 2011; Julianelle, 2008), and ultimately hinders youth's ability to develop meaning, belonging, and purpose at school.

*"Chang[ing] foster placements ... makes you worry about that and not worry about anything else like your schoolwork ... and then you fall behind.*³*"*

Youth in our studies talked about falling behind, experiencing bullying, lacking friends, feeling bored and miserable at school, and being discriminated against by school staff (Buys et al., 2011; Mateos et al., 2012; Schiller & de Wet, 2018; Selwyn et al., 2010). In their study of Serbian foster youth perspectives, Burgund and Zegarac (2016) noted that some children were unhappy because their caregivers determined which schools they would attend, and youth wished they could choose for themselves.

Relationships with adults at school were especially difficult when youth felt that they were discriminated against or treated differently by these adults (Mateos et al., 2012; Schiller & de Wet, 2018). For instance, sometimes youth felt judged based on the behavior of their biological parents. In addition, some youth did not want to discuss their living arrangements, because school staff asked too many intrusive questions. Other youth felt adults perceived them negatively once it was revealed they were in foster care (Buys et al., 2011). One youth in Scotland refused to tell her peers, even close friends, about being in foster care. However, when other children started bullying her for being in foster care, it became clear to her that the teacher had said something about it to other students (Madigan et al., 2013). Some youth felt like adults at school treated them unfairly. One youth in the United Kingdom said staff reported all tardiness to the police, even when she was only a bit late. She felt like school staff did not care that she was hurting and upset because she was in foster care and could not see her brother and sister (Brown et al., 2019).

Type of placement also affected youth's perspectives of school. This may be because youth in kinship care change schools less frequently compared to youth in other types of care (Casey Family Programs, 2018). In their research with foster youth in the United States, Schwartz (2010) found that only half of the youth in kinship care changed schools as a result of initial placement or placement change, whereas all of the youth in nonkinship care youth changed schools. Many of the nonkinship care youth expressed fear about transitioning to new schools. They worried about a lack of diversity, schedules or routines, liking their teachers, or making new friends. Conversely, kinship care youth found changing schools to be okay and did not define the change as a loss. Of the youth in kinship care who changed schools, some went to schools where they already knew other children and teachers, which may have helped them cope with the change. School is a key place for youth in general to find a sense of confidence and belonging. Developing these positive perspectives of school can be much more difficult for youth in care. Being in foster care, especially for youth who experience placement disruption, can make it more difficult for youth to make friends and find this confidence and belonging.

Peers and Friends

Making new friends can be difficult, especially when changing schools (Hedin et al., 2011b; Hedin, 2014). In the studies we reviewed, some children described wanting to make new friends and assumed doing so would be easy (Burgund & Zegarac, 2016; Selwyn et al., 2010), whereas others felt like making new friends would be scary (Selwyn et al., 2010). However, many foster youth were eventually successful in finding peers in school and in community spaces (Aldgate, 2009; Hedin et al., 2011b; Hedin, 2014). Some youth who lived in rural areas could only make friends at school rather than in their neighborhoods. These youth tried to spend as much time with their friends at school and tended to feel lonelier once they got home (Hedin et al., 2011b).

Maintaining friendships after initial placement or placement change was also difficult for some youth (Burgund & Zegarac, 2016; Kelly et al., 2019; McMahon & Curtin, 2013). For example, 90% of youth interviewed by McMahon and Curtin (2013) lost access to their friends after moving and could not engage in the same social activities as they did before. Moreover, the likelihood of continuing activities and socialization with peers decreased with each subsequent move, and the longer youth were in placement, the less likely they were to maintain friendships with old friends. Type of placement is also related to how well youth maintain friendships. For instance, Schwartz (2010) found that compared to those in kinship care, youth who were not in kinship care saw their friends less frequently or not at all after placement and most described that change as a loss. Of interest, youth interviewed by Hedin et al. (2011b) stayed connected with old friends through the internet and with their phones. Since that study's publication, social media has likely made it easier for foster youth to keep in contact with their friends though future studies should examine this. Keeping old friends and making new ones is important, especially for youth who have been removed from their families and youth who experience placement instability. For more information about placement changes, see Chapter 7.

Mitigating Challenges with Foster Care

Challenges like the ones mentioned above make it difficult for youth to develop a sense of belonging and consistency while they are in foster care (see Chapter 9 for more in depth discussions about youth's sense of belonging). However, social networks of peers and adults seemed to help youth deal with these challenges. Children who did not feel comfortable talking about their experiences with adults, found it helpful to talk to friends, especially if those friends understood what they were going through (Downie et al., 2009; Kelly et al., 2019; Pölkki et al., 2012). For example, youth in residential care saw their peers in the group home as part of their support network because they had similar experiences, whereas other friends sometimes had difficulty understanding what it was like to live in foster care (Kelly et al., 2019). Some children attended formal support groups and found them to be helpful, and those who did not attend support groups thought it would be good to join one (Burgess et al., 2010).

Benefits of Being in Foster Care

While there are several challenges associated with being in care, youth also found foster care to be beneficial because of experiences of abuse and neglect in their biological families or because foster care gave them access to things they did not have in their biological families. For instance, foster care meant that youth's basic needs were met, they had access to education, they made new friends, and they engaged in new activities (Downie et al., 2009; Dunn et al., 2010; Emond, 2010; Gayapersad et al., 2019; Hedin et al., 2011a; Kelly et al., 2019; Kuyini et al., 2009; Mitchell et al., 2010; Morrison et al., 2011; Schiller & de Wet, 2018).

"Yeah, I used to be absent from school a lot, you know, and I didn't do well in school, didn't do homework and stuff. Now, living like this, it feels almost fun to go to school all day.[4]*"*

Moreover, youth frequently described how much they appreciated how their foster carers provided privacy; emotional and disability-specific support; structure in their daily routines; and safe, clean, and harmonious households (Burgess et al., 2010; Dunn et al., 2010; Farmer et al., 2013; Gayapersad et al., 2019; Hedin et al., 2011b; Hedin et al., 2012; Mateos et al., 2012; Southwell & Fraser, 2010). Some youth felt that the ritual of consistent family mealtimes allowed for opportunities to talk about their days, and they enjoyed sharing the routines of preparation and clean up (Rees et al., 2012). Each of these experiences influenced youth's perception of care in a positive way, and led youth to feel happier than in their biological homes (Dunn et al., 2010). Youth also described specific benefits related to school and relationships with peers and friends. We will describe these next, along with some recommendations by and for foster youth.

School

School can be a positive place for youth to develop feelings of meaning, belonging, and purpose (Buys et al., 2011; Hedin et al., 2011a; Mariano & Going, 2011). Foster care youth in the United Kingdom reported being happy with school, and this satisfaction increased over time (Selwyn et al., 2010). In their study of youth in Sweden, Hedin et al. (2011a) found that before entering care, some children rarely attended school or were failing all their classes. One child had missed a full year of school before entering care. Another child tried skipping classes after she entered into care but quickly changed her behavior because her foster family enforced rules about attending school. She reported doing better and feeling better while at school. Some children reported having fun at school, which was a new experience for them (Hedin et al., 2011a).

Youth across studies talked about their positive experiences in school and how attending school gave them a sense of purpose and a way to better their own lives (Hedin et al., 2011a; Hedin, 2014). Many youth had to change schools because of entering care. Those who felt that changing schools was a positive experience described getting a fresh start or better educational support, finding a sense of belonging, and shifting their perception of school from negative to positive (Buys et al., 2011; Hedin et al., 2011a). These changes were related to better academic performance, increased self-confidence, and better outlooks for the future (Hedin et al., 2011a). Of interest, youth in Wales described their school experiences differently depending on their age. Younger youth described school as a place where they socialized or as somewhere they were made to work, and some older youth described school as a place where they could find support from peers and adults (Mannay et al., 2017). Research outside the scope of our review has shown that relationships with peers and adults at school along with opportunities for growth are positively related to youth's sense of well-being (Gadermann et al., 2016; Konu et al., 2002). For more about youth well-being, see Chapter 9.

Peers and Friends

As previously described in the challenges section, making and keeping friends is especially important to youth. For some youth, making new friends was key in helping them find benefits of being placed into the foster care system. After moving to new schools, youth seemed to experience more positive relationships with peers (Hedin et al., 2011b; Hedin, 2014). Many children felt close to their friends and felt like they could confide in them (Burgess et al., 2010). Those with close friends felt better about being in foster care (Dansey et al., 2018), felt like they belonged, and did better academically (Hedin, 2014). A few of the youth did not change schools when they were placed into foster care. Some of these youth discussed making new friends anyway because their interests had changed after moving into foster care (Hedin et al., 2011b). Friendships seemed to help youth adjust to being in care.

Youth Recommendations

Across the studies we reviewed, children and youth gave recommendations for other foster youth about how to deal with being in care, and many of these recommendations involved friends. Youth suggested that other children stay connected with old friends by texting, make as many new friends as possible, and to get out and do stuff with friends (Mitchell et al., 2010).

"Make as many friends as possible.[5]"

Foster youth reported feeling closer to friends than other members of their support networks (McMahon & Curtin, 2013). Youth described their friends as their biggest source of information and advice, practical support, and emotional support and recommended that foster youth actively seek out relationships with friends.

Summary

Many youth described challenges they experienced while in foster care. However, others described the benefits of being in foster care and said they felt happier and safer in care than they had with their biological families. Some ways that adults can help youth develop and cultivate this sense of self is to be respectful of children's cultures, help them stay connected with their communities, treat them like they do children who are not in care, and encourage children to pursue their goals and education.

Notes

1 Age not given, range 9–16; Rees et al., 2012, p. 104.
2 Age 12; Farmer et al., 2013, p. 29.
3 Age not given, range 13–18; Buys et al., 2011, p. 1128.
4 Age not given, range 13–16; Hedin et al., 2011a, p. 47.
5 Age 12–13; Mitchell et al., 2010, p. 179.

References

Aldgate, J. (2009). Living in kinship care: A child-centered view. *Adoption & Fostering*, *33*(3), 51–63. 10.1177/030857590903300306

Bamba, S., & Haight, W. (2009). Maltreated children's emerging well-being in Japanese state care. *Children and Youth Services Review*, *31*(7), 797–806. 10.1016/j.childyouth.2009.02.006

Brown, R., Alderson, H., Kaner, E., McGovern, R., & Lingam, R. (2019). 'There are carers, and then there are carers who actually care'; Conceptualizations of care among looked after children and care leavers, social workers and carers. *Child Abuse & Neglect*, *92*, 219–229. 10.1016/j.chiabu.2019.03.018

Burgess, C., Rossvoll, F., Wallace, B., & Daniel, B. (2010). 'It's just like another home, just another family, so it's nae different' Children's voices in kinship care: A research study about the experience of children in kinship care in Scotland. *Child & Family Social Work*, *15*(3), 297–306. 10.1111/j.1365-2206.2009.00671.x

Burgund, A., & Zegarac, N. (2016). Perspectives of youth in care in Serbia. *Child & Adolescent Social Work Journal*, *33*(2), 151–161. 10.1007/s10560-015-0413-5

Buys, N., Tilbury, C., Creed, P., & Crawford, M. (2011). Working with youth in-care: Implications for vocational rehabilitation practice. *Disability and Rehabilitation*, *33*(13–14), 1125–1135. 10.3109/09638288.2010.521614

Casey Family Programs. (2018). *What impacts placement stability?* https://www.casey.org/placement-stability-impacts/

Dansey, D., John, M., & Shbero, D. (2018). How children in foster care engage with loyalty conflict: Presenting a model of processes informing loyalty. *Adoption & Fostering*, *42*(4), 354–368. 10.1177/0308575918798767

Downie, J. M., Hay, D. A., Horner, B. J., Wichmann, H., & Hislop, A. L. (2009). Children living with their grandparents: Resilience and wellbeing. *International Journal of Social Welfare*, *19*(1), 8–22. 10.1111/j.1468-2397.2009.00654.x

Dunn, D. M., Culhane, S. E., & Taussig, H. N. (2010). Children's appraisals of their experiences in out-of-home care. *Children and Youth Services Review*, *32*(10), 1324–1330. 10.1016/j.childyouth.2010.05.001

Emond, R. (2010). Caring as a moral, practical and powerful endeavour: Peer care in a Cambodian orphanage. *The British Journal of Social Work*, *40*(1), 63–81. 10.1093/bjsw/bcn102

Fargas-Malet, M., & McSherry, D. (2018). The mental health and help-seeking behavior of children and young people in care in Northern Ireland: Making services accessible and engaging. *The British Journal of Social Work*, *48*(3), 578–595. 10.1093/bjsw/bcx062

Farmer, E., Selwyn, J., & Meakings, S. (2013). 'Other children say you're not normal because you don't live with your parents'. Children's views of living with informal kinship carers: Social networks, stigma and attachment to carers. *Child & Family Social Work, 18*(1), 25–34. 10.1111/cfs.12030

Fawley-King, K., Trask, E. V., Zhang, J., & Aarons, G. A. (2017). The impact of changing neighborhoods, switching schools, and experiencing relationship disruption on children's adjustment to a new placement in foster care. *Child Abuse & Neglect, 63*, 141–150. 10.1016/j.chiabu.2016.11.016

Flores, J., Hawes, J., Westbrooks, A., & Henderson, C. (2018). Crossover youth and gender: What are the challenges of girls involved in both the foster care and juvenile justice systems? *Children and Youth Services Review, 91*, 149–155. 10.1016/j.childyouth.2018.05.031

Gadermann, A. M., Guhn, M., Schonert-Reichl, K. A., Hymel, S., Thomson, K., & Hertzman, C. (2016). A population-based study of children's well-being and health: The relative importance of social relationships, health-related activities, and income. *Journal of Happiness Studies, 17*, 1847–1872. 10.1007/s10902-015-9673-1

Gayapersad, A., Ombok, C., Kamanda, A., Tarus, C., Ayuku, D., & Braitstein, P. (2019). The production and reproduction of kinship in charitable children's institutions in Uasin Gishu County, Kenya. *Child & Youth Care Forum, 48*, 797–828. 10.1007/s10566-019-09506-8

Hedin, L. (2014). A sense of belonging in a changeable everyday life - A follow-up study of young people in kinship, network, and traditional foster families. *Child & Family Social Work, 19*(2), 165–173. 10.1111/j.1365-2206.2012.00887.x

Hedin, L., Höjer, I., & Brunnberg, E. (2011a). Why one goes to school: What school means to young people entering foster care. *Child & Family Social Work, 16*(1), 43–51. 10.1111/j.1365-2206.2010.00706.x

Hedin, L., Höjer, I., & Brunnberg, E. (2011b). Settling into a new home as a teenager: About establishing social bonds in different types of foster families in Sweden. *Children and Youth Services Review, 33*(11), 2282–2289. 10.1016/j.childyouth.2011.07.016

Hedin, L., Höjer, I., & Brunnberg, E. (2012). Jokes and routines make everyday life a good life-on 'doing family' for young people in foster care in Sweden. *European Journal of Social Work, 15*(5), 613–628. 10.1080/13691457.2011.579558

Julianelle, P. (2008). *The McKinney-Vento Act and children and youth awaiting foster care placement: Strategies for improving educational outcomes through school stability*. National Association for the Education of Homeless Children and Youth.

Kelly, C., Anthony, E. K., & Krysik, J. (2019). "How am I doing?" Narratives of youth living in congregate care on their social-emotional well-being. *Children and Youth Services Review, 103*, 255–263. 10.1016/j.childyouth.2019.06.001

Konu, A. I., Lintonen, T. P., & Rimpelä, M. K. (2002). Factors associated with schoolchildren's general subjective well-being. *Health Education Research, 17*(2), 155–165. 10.1093/her/17.2.155

Kuyini, A. B., Alhassan, A. R., Tollerud, I., Weld, H., & Haruna, I. (2009). Traditional kinship foster care in northern Ghana: The experiences and views of children, carers and adults in Tamale. *Child & Family Social Work, 14*(4), 440–449. 10.1111/j.1365-2206.2009.00616.x

Madigan, S., Quayle, E., Cossar, J., & Paton, K. (2013). Feeling the same or feeling different? An analysis of the experiences of young people in foster care. *Adoption & Fostering, 37*(4), 389–403. 10.1177/0308575913508719

Malinga-Musamba, T. (2015). The nature of relationships between orphans and their kinship carers in Botswana. *Child & Family Social Work, 20*(3), 257–266. 10.1111/cfs.12121

Mannay, D., Evans, R., Staples, E., Hallett, S., Roberts, L., Rees, A., & Andrews, D. (2017). The consequences of being labelled 'looked-after': Exploring the educational experiences of looked-after children and young people in Wales. *British Educational Research Journal, 43*(4), 683–699. 10.1002/berj.3283

Mariano, J. M., Going, J. (2011). Youth purpose and positive youth development. In R. M. Lerner, J. V. Lerner, & J. B. Benson (Eds.). *Advances in child development and behavior* (Vol. 42, pp. 39–68). Academic Press. 10.1016/B978-0-12-386492-5. 00003-8

Mateos, A., Balsells, M. À., Molina, M. C., & Fuentes-Peláez, N. (2012). The perception adolescents in kinship foster care have of their own needs. *Revista de Cercetare si Interventie Sociala, 38*, 25–41. http://hdl.handle.net/2445/103325

McMahon, C., & Curtin, C. (2013). The social networks of young people in Ireland with experience of long-term foster care: some lessons for policy and practice. *Child & Family Social Work, 18*(3), 329–340. 10.1111/j.1365-2206.2012.00849.x

Mitchell, M. B., Kuczynski, L., Tubbs, C. Y., & Ross, C. (2010). We care about care: Advice by children in care for children in care, foster parents and child welfare workers about the transition into foster care. *Child & Family Social Work, 15*(2), 176–185. 10.1111/j.1365-2206.2009.00657.x

Morrison, J., Mishna, F., Cook, C., & Aitken, G. (2011). Access visits: Perceptions of child protection workers, foster parents and children who are Crown wards. *Children and Youth Services Review, 33*(9), 1476–1482. 10.1016/j.childyouth.2011. 03.011

Pölkki, P., Vornanen, R., Pursiainen, M., & Riikonen, M. (2012). Children's participation in child-protection processes as experienced by foster children and social workers. *Child Care in Practice, 18*(2), 107–125. 10.1080/13575279.2011. 646954

Rees, A., Holland, S., & Pithouse, A. (2012). Food in foster families: Care, communication and conflict. *Children & Society, 26*(2), 100–111. 10.1111/j.1099-0860.2010.00332.x

Sala, M. A. (2009). The quality of food, clothing and shelter provided to orphaned children under foster care in Kibera slums in Kenya. *East African Journal of Public Health, 6*(3), 312–316. https://pubmed.ncbi.nlm.nih.gov/20803926/

Schiller, U., & de Wet, G. (2018). Communication, indigenous culture and participatory decision making amongst foster adolescents. *Qualitative Social Work, 17*(2), 236–251. 10.1177/1473325016662329

Schwartz, A. E. (2010). "Nobody knows me no more": Experiences of loss among African American adolescents in kinship and non-kinship foster care placements. *Race and Social Problems, 2*(1), 31–49. 10.1007/s12552-010-9025-z

Selwyn, J., Saunders, H., & Farmer, E. (2010). The views of children and young people on being cared for by an independent foster-care provider. *The British Journal of Social Work, 40*(3), 696–713. 10.1093/bjsw/bcn117

Southwell, J., & Fraser, E. (2010). Young people's satisfaction with residential care: Identifying strengths and weaknesses in service delivery. *Child Welfare, 89*(2), 209–228. https://pubmed.ncbi.nlm.nih.gov/20857888/

Chapter 9

Mental Health, Well-Being, and Belonging

"If I am very sad, I write it all down and after that I burn it[1]"

This chapter will focus on two different, but related topics important for youth in foster care. In the first section, we will discuss mental health and well-being. Then we will describe belonging, its importance, and how foster youth develop this sense of belonging to their foster families.

Mental Health and Well-Being

Although many researchers use the terms mental-health and well-being, it is important to note that they were defined in various ways in the papers we reviewed. For example, some researchers used terms from psychological assessments (not diagnostic tools), some used words taken directly from youth interviews, and others identified themes and phrases based on their qualitative analyses of youth interviews. In the studies we reviewed, terms referring to mental health and well-being included: avoidance, withdrawal, somatic complaints (e.g., headaches, stomach pain), social problems, social involvement, sociability, lack of trust, troublesome thoughts, attention problems, status at school, delinquent behaviors, aggressive behaviors, stress, anger, loneliness, sadness, depressive symptoms, feeling anxious, suicidal ideology, self-harming, internalizing and externalizing symptoms, lack of confidence, high or low self-esteem, self-confidence, self-sufficiency, satisfaction, happiness, social and emotional well-being, ability to overcome adversity, self and emotion regulation (or dysregulation), sleep problems, pride, healthy decision making, balance, perseverance, and serenity (Bulat, 2010; Buys et al., 2011; Damnjanovic et al., 2011; Downie et al., 2009; Fargas-Malet & McSherry, 2018; Fawley-King et al., 2017; Kelly et al., 2019; Lundström & Sallnäs, 2012; Mota & Matos, 2015). To our knowledge, none of the studies noted above used clinical diagnoses of mental health problems in their analyses. For the purposes of this chapter, we will use the term well-being to describe the psychological and socioemotional factors encompassing the issues described above.

When youth are removed from their biological families and placed into foster care, they may feel sadness (and many other feelings). They may also

DOI: 10.4324/9781003309215-9

be processing troubling or traumatic experiences that led them to be placed into foster care (e.g., maltreatment). Many of the studies we reviewed noted youth's feelings and later the researchers pathologized them as diagnoses. In two of the studies that focused on well-being, researchers used either surveys which measured depressive symptoms or interviewed youth who made reference to feeling sad or depressed. In each case, the researchers then discussed this as "depression"–which is a clinical term–pathologizing their emotions (Bulat 2010; Buys et al., 2011). However, there is a vast difference between feeling sadness and being diagnosed with depression.

Additionally, there are cultural differences in how mental health and well-being are defined and how they are understood or experienced (i.e., youth in rural Japan are likely to describe feelings of depression differently than Indigenous youth in Australia). Furthermore, as researchers in the United States, our descriptions of mental health and well-being are from a specific lens that may not encompass the unique perspectives of youth included in all the studies that we reviewed. There is a potential for misinterpretation when dealing with such a personal, and subjective theme. However, it is important to note that we carefully screened all papers to identify social and emotional well-being described by youth themselves–and noted different ways researchers interpreted these descriptions. Then we separated and examined any studies that used quantitative, standardized clinical assessments to measure mental health symptoms. In the following sections, we will first discuss youth psychological and socioemotional well-being. Then, we will discuss the closely related topic of belonging.

Psychological and Socioemotional Well-Being

There are several studies in which youth generally reported improved well-being because they were in foster care. For example, children reported increased ability to focus at school (Buys et al., 2011); more self-sufficiency, self-control, self-esteem, and perseverance (Mota & Matos, 2015); along with general improvement in mental health and well-being due to being in care (Fargas-Malet & McSherry, 2018; Mota & Matos, 2015). Children also reported factors which negatively affected their well-being (i.e, placement changes, placement type, contact–or lack of contact–with biological family members, and stigma about being in foster care). We discuss these in the paragraphs below.

In several studies, youth reported that frequent placement changes negatively affected their well-being across multiple domains (Buys et al., 2011; Fargas-Malet & McSherry, 2018; Hedin, 2014; Lundström & Sallnäs, 2012; Rostill-Brookes et al., 2011; Skoog et al., 2015).

"Just my home life. Like I would have distractions ... and you know, I don't want to go to school and deal with it. It was just affecting my school work as well. Like I would go to school, I couldn't focus, I couldn't do my work. I would say definitely over this last year ... my behaviour wasn't good anymore.[2]"

Some youth told researchers that they were constantly losing friends and often felt confused and alone in new homes (Skoog et al., 2015). Others sometimes distanced themselves from their foster carers, even when the relationships were positive, for fear of having to pack up and leave again (Rostill-Brookes et al., 2011). Additionally, in the Buys et al. (2011) study, youth who had experienced multiple placements reported problems forming relationships with others, inability to trust others, anger management issues, low self-confidence, depression, stress, trouble adjusting to school, poor study habits, and difficulty with future career planning.

Placement type was related to youth feelings of well-being. For instance, youth in residential care reported more feelings of sadness, anxiety, or reduced well-being compared to those in foster or kinship care (Bulat, 2010; Damnjanovic, 2011; Fargas-Malet & McSherry, 2018; Hedin, 2014). In a study of youth in care in Sweden, those living in residential care compared to foster homes, experienced significantly more psychosomatic symptoms than youth in foster homes (i.e., "headache, stomach pain, sleeping problems, and stress"; Lundström & Sallnäs, 2012, p. 400). Fawley-King et al. (2017) surveyed youth in kinship care and traditional foster care. Youth in kinship care reported liking their foster families significantly more than youth in traditional foster care. In a 5-year longitudinal study, Bulat (2010) found that for some youth, depression symptoms decreased over time in care. She surveyed youth living in residential homes and those living in traditional foster families. At the beginning of their time in care, youth in residential homes had more depressive symptoms compared to youth in foster families. However, on a positive note these differences had disappeared after five years. The author attributed this change to children becoming more accustomed to being in care.

Other factors besides placement, such as sex, gender, age, separation from siblings, and relationships with adults, are related to foster youth's well-being. In the study by Lundström and Sallnäs (2012; described above), girls compared to boys, and older children compared to younger children, experienced significantly more headaches, stomach pain, stress, and sleep problems. In the studies we reviewed, findings about separation from siblings were sometimes contradictory. This could be because some studies were qualitative and some were quantitative. In the quantitative study by Fawley King et al. (2017), being separated from at least one sibling was associated with decreased loneliness and social dissatisfaction. Conversely in the qualitative study by Wojciak (2017), children expressed sadness and despair over separation from siblings. This is just one illustration of the influence foster care can have on youth and their relationships with family members. Relationships with adults can also affect youth well-being. For instance, when adults treated them differently because they were in care, youth in Australia reported feeling anxious, feeling depressed, having low self-esteem, and having difficulty focusing in school (Buys et al., 2011). However, in their research in Portugal, Mota and Matos (2015) found that good relationships with school staff and teachers were positively correlated with youth well-being and happiness.

Mental Health

While there is good reason to avoid pathologizing everyday emotions, there is a time and place to recognize when youth are in need of professional mental health support. In the study by Fargas-Malet and McSherry (2018) half of the 25 youth surveyed said that they had felt seriously depressed at some point in their lives (e.g., they had thought about suicide or engaged in self-harm) and four said they were still experiencing mental health problems. Youth expressed difficulty seeking help because of poor relationships with or trouble finding practitioners, or because of the stigma associated with seeking mental health services. Some youth found it hard to reach out to *anyone* about their mental health issues citing embarrassment, guilt, or fear of opening up.

Only three of the studies we reviewed used quantitative, standardized (well-established) clinical assessments to measure well-being, including depressive and anxiety symptoms (Bulat 2010; Damnjanovic et al., 2011; Farmer et al., 2013). In their longitudinal study, Bulat (2010) used seven standardized clinical assessments (six of which were given to foster youth directly) to measure depression symptoms, anxiety symptoms, and other well-being related problems in different ways. This methodology strengthened their findings because it gave the researchers the ability to compare several data points across various measurements over time. Children with more depressive symptoms had more somatic symptoms, social difficulties, thinking problems, aggressive behaviors, attention disorders, and daily stress. They also had worse self-image, self-esteem, and social support than youth with fewer depressive symptoms.

In a study in Serbia, nearly half of youth interviewed about their quality of life were currently experiencing depressive symptoms and a third were considered to have an unspecified anxiety disorder (as determined by cut-off scores on depression and anxiety questionnaires; Damnjanovic et al., 2011). Compared with youth in foster care in this study, the youth in residential care were significantly more likely to report depressive and anxiety symptoms as well as emotional and behavioral difficulties. Similarly, in a study of youth in the United Kingdom, many scored high on emotional and behavioral difficulties questionnaires (although these were rated by caregivers, not by the youth; Farmer et al., 2013). This is concerning because, for youth in care, increased anxiety symptoms and depressive symptoms are associated with perceived lower quality of life and smaller inner circles[3] (Damnjanovic et al., 2011; Farmer et al., 2013). These studies highlight the need for consistent and reliable mental health services for foster youth. Later in this chapter, we discuss mental health services for foster youth and the challenges associated with providing youth with such services. Of note, many researchers addressed this need by providing youth with mental health resources as part of the follow-up to their studies.

Coping

Youth responded to stressful situations, changes to their well-being, and difficulties in their relationships in various ways (see Bulat, 2010; Downie et al., 2009; Jansen & Haavind, 2011; Kelly et al., 2019 for examples of how youth coped with stressors associated with being in foster care). Some coping methods are often considered to be more productive (e.g., talking to friends, listening to music) whereas others are considered to be less productive (e.g., ignoring emotions, using drugs). At times, children felt unable to cope and instead turned to emotional outbursts, running away, or physical altercations with other children and/or adults (e.g., Bulat, 2010; Jansen & Haavind, 2011). Even when youth felt like they could cope, they still felt overwhelmed and defeated at times. Hedin (2014) discussed two youth who reported feeling depressed. Sometimes they felt like they could handle their emotions, and sometimes they felt like they would die or that their lives were ruined.

Ideally, mental health care would help youth cope with stressors related to being in foster care. However, mental health services were not always available, accessible, or beneficial. In some cases, there were often long waiting lists for therapists, or services were a long distance away; when children did receive therapy, high staff turnover made treatment more difficult. Because of this turnover, youth frequently had to retell and re-experience their stories, which is often counterproductive to the goals of therapy (Fargas-Malet & McSherry, 2018).

"... the social worker ended up sending me to three different counsellors and I keep explaining things, I couldn't keep doing that and it upset me more, ... I would be panicking, not trusting people like that. I ended up in a worse state crying and stuff, because they made me change, and I just ended up refusing to go anywhere.[4]"

Without consistent mental health care, youth may choose other ways to cope, such as distracting themselves and suppressing, ignoring, or refusing to acknowledge negative feelings (Burgund & Zegarac, 2016; Dansey et al., 2018; Downie et al., 2009; Rostill-Brookes et al., 2011). This is evident in comments youth made in some of our studies. For instance, in Australia, some of the youth in kinship care did not seek help but instead withdrew from others in attempts to manage sadness (Burgund & Zegarac, 2016).

Youth also discussed many positive ways they coped and regulated their emotions. Youth in Australia, Sweden, the Netherlands, Serbia, and the United States said they coped in productive ways by talking to friends and teachers, expressing their emotions honestly and directly, forming routines, engaging in extracurricular activities, thinking positively about the future, being active in school, practicing religion, playing or listening to music, playing video games, watching movies, journaling, being outdoors, or creating art (Burgund &

Zegarac, 2016; Downie et al., 2009; Hedin et al., 2011a; Hedin et al., 2012; Kalverboer et al., 2017; Kelly et al., 2019; Mitchell et al., 2010). One youth talked about how he used to worry about being open with his feelings in prior placements, but once he felt safe with his foster carers, he began to open up and feel comfortable talking about his emotions–even when he felt angry (Hedin et al., 2012). Some youth used techniques to improve their well-being by avoiding circumstances that could lead to trouble (e.g., fighting with peers, refraining from gossip; Hedin et al., 2011a; Kelly et al., 2019). For example, one youth described how they work to make better choices and walk away from fights. They said that this is how they *know* they are doing well (Kelly et al., 2019).

Many youth described well-being in terms of their ability to cope with adversity (i.e., resiliency).

"I'm actually happy that I was actually left on the bus, coz now, being left so many places on my own, I am not scared of anything now ... every accident that has happened has made me immune to being scared of anything now.[5]"

Some discussed the importance of being able to relax, be happy, and laugh during difficult times and make healthy decisions while in foster care (Kelly et al., 2019). Youth in Portugal who scored high on a standardized measure of resilience (i.e., perseverance, serenity, self-confidence, meaning of life, and self-sufficiency) reported better well-being (Mota & Matos, 2015). Others felt like their experiences in foster care helped them emotionally cope with life in general (Jansen & Haavind, 2011). One youth described how living through difficult life experiences made her feel stronger rather than weaker. She stated how experiencing so much already in her young life–including traversing over fields containing landmines when she fled her native country with her mother and brother–made her feel more like an adult and better equipped to cope with new life challenges.

Social Support

Other youth coped with the support from their peers and adults around them. In a study of support for LGBTQ foster youth in the United States, most youth had several encouraging peers and adults in their lives and at least one lifelong connection within their social networks (Lorthridge et al., 2018). In another study, Wissö et al. (2019) asked foster youth to name members of their close support networks. All of the children included their foster parents in their lists. Children across studies also included peers (e.g., foster siblings), friends, teachers, coaches, other relatives, and people at their churches as those who gave them social support (Burgess et al., 2010; Downie et al., 2009; Hedin et al., 2011b; Kalverboer et al., 2017; Sands et al., 2009; Wissö et al., 2019). Other than the standard adults that one might expect to be part of social networks, youth in some studies found support from other sources, such as school staff, caseworkers, institution staff, and even pets (Burgess et al., 2010; Holland, 2010; Mota & Matos, 2015; Sands et al., 2009). Of note, youth reported that when they *did* feel well it was primarily when they were with other people (Hedin, 2014).

Youth were asked about their thoughts on mentorship (e.g., Diehl et al., 2011; Hedin et al., 2014). Sometimes children were positive about having mentors and people who would listen to them, take them on outings, and check on them. However, some youth had less positive views of mentoring or felt like they did not need support. In the study by Hedin et al. (2014), boys tended to feel like they didn't need support from a social worker or therapist, whereas girls seemed to appreciate having such support. Of note, most of the youth in this study who did not have consistent support from a social worker or therapist were boys. In a quantitative study by Diehl et al. (2011), White youth had significantly more positive views on mentoring than Black youth. The authors suggested that Black youth may have had more negative attitudes about mentoring than White youth, in part, because the mentors available to them were predominately White. Black youth may have been more open to the idea of mentoring if they had options for mentors that they perceived to be more similar to themselves. Moreover, researchers asked youth how much control they felt over their own lives. Youth who perceived that they had more control over their own lives tended to have more negative attitudes about mentoring, which may be because these youth felt more self-reliant and not in need of mentorship (Diehl et al., 2011).

Youth Recommendations

Youth provided recommendations for fellow foster care peers, adults, and how to improve the foster care system in general. One child interviewed in the Mateos et al. (2012) study suggested that Child Protective Services should help their parents, but did not explain further how. Another child stated that more financial support should be provided to families with foster care youth. They also expressed how reducing the number of placement transitions could improve children's lives. One youth suggested that she would not have all the problems she was currently dealing with had she not been moved around frequently (Jansen & Haavind, 2011).

"If you hadn't moved me around to all these places that were damaging to me, I would not have all the problems I have.[6]*"*

Although children may not always provide a concrete recommendation for improvement, these findings show that they do think about how institutional components of the foster care system can affect their individual care.

Mitchell et al. (2010) interviewed several children who had advice for other children going into care. These children offered advice about what to bring to new homes, how to find social support and comfort, and how to self-advocate. They suggested bringing something comforting, such as a stuffed animal or something sentimental. They also emphasized the importance of maintaining and strengthening current and new social relationships and encouraged those going into care to reach out to their friends and biological family to talk, text, and hang out. They said that youth would get to meet new friends and do things they probably would not have done with their birth parents. Additionally, children discussed how being active could help well-being. For instance, they said it can be beneficial to keep busy, watch movies, play video games, or listen to music, or avoid downtime.

The interviewed youth also discussed advocating for mental health services and developing relationships with foster parents. They strongly encouraged children going into care to ask for a counselor so they can have a professional to talk with who can help them cope. They also emphasized the importance of talking to new foster parents about likes, dislikes, and what would make foster care feel more like home. Children recommended that youth remain calm, do not lash out at foster parents, and feel their feelings. They said that new foster youth need to understand that although things start out hard, they eventually get easier over time (Mitchell et al., 2010).

Youth had recommendations for adults as well. Generally youth encouraged practitioners, carers, social workers, and other professionals to *listen* to foster youth, offer many suggestions, be more proactive, engage in more conversations, offer in-home services or drop in options, and find a way to limit therapist turnover since youth get weary of repeating the same information to different therapists (Fargas-Malet & McSherry, 2018; Jansen & Haavind, 2011; Kalverboer et al., 2017). One youth urged adults to ask children if they want to talk about (or not talk about) why they are in foster care. That is, adults should only talk to children about why they are in foster care if children *want* to talk about it (Mitchell et al., 2010).

Developing a Sense of Belonging

Developing a strong sense of belonging in their foster families seemed to positively affect youth's well-being. Many of the studies we reviewed discussed ways in which foster youth can develop this sense. To facilitate belonging, foster families first need to help youth feel welcome, accepted, and secure in their homes.

When youth feel connected and emotionally safe, they feel like they can stay and won't be forced to move to different homes (see e.g., Hedin et al., 2011b; Mitchel et al., 2010). Foster parents can help youth feel emotionally safe by talking to them about what to expect in the future (Mitchell et al., 2010). In the Hedin et al. (2011b) study, many youth described what helped them feel safe and secure in their foster homes. For example, one foster youth in kinship care already knew other children in the home, which helped him ease into the transition and feel at home more quickly. Other youth described how the foster family's rules helped them feel more secure in their placements because they didn't have to worry about what to expect in the household. Another youth explained that while she didn't feel like she belonged to any family (foster or birth), she did feel safe and secure at her new foster home, which was most important for her (Hedin et al., 2011b).

Across studies, foster youth named things that helped relationship building. Many of these involved being treated as a real part of the family. For example, relationships developed when families did everyday things together, ate dinner as a family, engaged with peers and the community, had conversations about the foster parents' own childhoods, joked and laughed, went on family outings, played games, spent time with siblings, were treated as permanent members of their family, and were included in family decisions (Bamba & Haight, 2009; Biehal, 2014; Clarkson et al., 2017; Downie et al., 2009; Hedin et al., 2011b; Hedin et al., 2012; Mitchell et al., 2010; Rees et al., 2012; Schofield et al., 2012; Schwartz, 2010; Selwyn et al., 2010; Skoog et al., 2015).

Two of the studies we reviewed gave specific examples of how children developed belonging. Bamba and Haight (2009) interviewed 11 foster children who lived in residential care in Japan. They asked children where they felt a sense of "Ibasho," which was defined as a place where one feels a sense of well-being, comfort, and belonging. Children experienced Ibasho in places they could call their own. These included bedrooms they had decorated where they could spend time by themselves or with friends doing things they enjoyed. Children also felt Ibasho in the community or the residential home when they played, teased, and talked with other children and when they engaged in activities that interested them, such as sports, reading, and music. Meaningful relationships with adults in the residential home and the community were important to children's sense of belonging. For instance, children felt like they belonged when adults listened to them, when they felt understood, and felt cared for. In an orphanage in Cambodia, Emond (2010) asked children about their experiences caring for themselves and each other. One main theme that came up was doing chores together. Children valued teaching each other how to do chores, and they valued learning to do things themselves. Children felt that working together helped them gain community, independence, and feel more like an integral part of the orphanage (Emond, 2010).

When foster youth felt like they belonged, often their naming conventions for their foster families changed (Burgess et al., 2010; Gayapersad et al., 2019). For example, rather than using the term foster parents, they called their caregivers mum/mom, dad, grandparent, aunt, or uncle (Biehal, 2014; Burgess et al., 2010; Gayapersad et al., 2019). Some children called their foster siblings brothers and sisters (Aldgate, 2009; Biehal, 2014; Clarkson et al., 2017; Emond, 2010). However, in one study terms for foster families were often related to type of placement and amount of contact with biological relatives. That is, when defining "family," youth in residential and kinship care considered blood relatives to be family, whereas foster youth who had no contact with biological relatives considered their foster families to be family (Burgund & Zegarac, 2016).

For some youth, belonging didn't feel possible. For instance, after being in the same placement for seven years, one youth still described his foster sisters as "foster mum's daughters" and said they didn't like him (Biehal, 2014, p. 964). In another study, youth had difficulty accepting love, warmth, and positive affirmations from their foster parents because they internalized negative things their birth parents had said to them (Madigan et al., 2013). A few children perceived their placements as conditional. In the study by Burgess et al. (2010), youth said that when they argued with foster parents or siblings, caregivers threatened to put them back into the system. In Kenya, some foster youth lived in residential care facilities funded by international donors (e.g., Christian missionaries; Gayapersad et al., 2019). In these facilities, placement was truly conditional. Youth were expected to strictly adhere to Christian beliefs. They were required to attend family Bible studies, were not allowed to socialize outside the placement facility, and did not have access to their cultural traditions and languages. Moreover, children's heads were shaved and boys were circumcised as part of a coming of age ritual. Children who did not conform to Christian values (e.g., got pregnant, didn't do well in school) were kicked out (See Chapter 10 for more on cultural responsiveness).

However, some youth felt like they were excluded from the family and like they didn't belong, even when the foster carers expressed otherwise (Biehal, 2014). One foster carer stated that the child felt completely part of their family, whereas the child described feeling unloved and disconnected from them. Another child mentioned that during large family gatherings, he felt more aware of being a foster youth and not a biological family member. In another study, one youth described feeling less a part of the family as she got older. When the family went on vacation, they took all the foster siblings, but did not extend an invitation to her (Holland, 2010). Other youth didn't fit in due to feeling a lack of community, feeling out of place, being treated differently than the rest of the family, or being jealous of other children (Kelly et al., 2019; Madigan et al., 2013; Rees et al., 2012; see Chapter 10 for more on foster youth being treated differently than other children).

Not having a sense of belonging meant that youth were more likely to worry about their futures. In their study of foster youth satisfaction with residential care, Southwell and Fraser (2010) found that while most of the youth felt safe in their current care, several expressed worry over future potential moves. Skoog et al. (2015) described one youth who always expected to be given away to someone else, another who expected to be told to leave, and yet another who put up emotional walls against their foster family and stayed in other rooms to avoid becoming attached. Some youth interviewed by Mitchell & Kuczynski (2010) said they didn't know anyone; felt disconnected from their birth families, foster families, and/or friends; and like they did not belong anywhere.

Conversely, when youth felt secure and like they belonged, they were less likely to worry about their futures. For example, when the youth had strong bonds to their foster families, they were confident that their foster carers would keep them and they felt more secure in their placements (Ellingsen et al., 2011).

"He belongs here. And that's that" (Foster parent).[7]

Moreover, youth who felt like they belonged, expected to be with their foster families long-term (Farmer et al., 2013; Gayapersad et al., 2019; Hunt et al., 2010; Skoog et al., 2015). Many children intended to maintain connections once leaving foster care (Biehal, 2014; Christiansen et al., 2013;

Gayapersad et al., 2019; Selwyn et al., 2010). As an example, one youth in Kenya stated that their caregivers would be considered grandparents to their future children. A thirteen year old from England imagined remaining in contact with and living in close proximity to both her biological mother and her foster parent when she was an adult (Biehal, 2014). Some children envisioned staying with foster parents long into adulthood. For example, one said that he could not have found a better home and that the family said he could stay until he was 40 (Christiansen et al., 2013). Other youth expressed that they loved their placements so much that they wanted to stay with their foster families until they were 50 (Biehal, 2014) or 100 years old (Selwyn et al., 2010).

Youth Recommendations

Mitchell et al. (2010) collected a series of recommendations by 20 youth in Canada who described how foster families can help them feel more accepted in their new homes. One explained that everyone would probably be nervous when first meeting. They suggested youth and families would feel more comfortable if they engaged in conversations to get to know each other. Especially important to several youth was discussing their favorite colors, activities, places, or foods. Children also said that going on outings together, or doing other types of bonding activities were ways that would help them feel accepted when first arriving at their new homes. Being in the new home also meant not knowing about the household structure. Children recommended the foster parents tell them where things are in the house and if there are any limitations or special rules to follow. They should also make sure that the foster youth have clothes, shoes, preferred foods, bedding, and that foster parents should "share [their] stuff" (Mitchell et al., 2010, p. 181).

> *"Make sure the child is fed, has clothes, a hat, pants, and a room.*[8]*"*

Children expressed how important it is for foster parents to give them choices and include them in decision-making processes in their new home (for more on including youth in the decision-making process, see Chapter 3). One youth suggested that foster parents let children paint their rooms. All of these are great examples of what youth say they need to feel like they belong in their new homes.

Summary

When youth first enter foster care, they may not immediately feel emotionally secure and accepted into their families. Children enter foster care primarily because their biological families cannot care for them properly. Although foster care can provide a safer environment for youth to grow up in, being removed from their home and being placed into foster care can still negatively affect youth well-being. Over time, youth feel more secure when they develop positive relationships with their foster families and others in their lives (see Chapter 6 for more on relationships with foster families; see Chapter 4 for more on relationships with social workers and the impact turnover can have on youth's well-being). In the studies we reviewed, youth who had more social connections reported better well-being compared to youth who lacked these connections. Social support helped youth feel secure and accepted, and like they belonged in their foster families. When youth felt like they belonged, they felt good about their placements, were less fearful about being forced to move or experiencing other significant changes, generally felt cared for, and wanted to maintain long-term contact with their foster families (Bamba & Haight, 2009; Ellingsen et al., 2011; Hedin, 2014; Wissö et al., 2019).

Notes

1 Age 16–17; Kalverboer, 2017, p. 892.
2 Age not given, range 13–18; Buys et al., 2011, p. 1129.
3 This study defines "inner circles" as the "the people who were *most* important to" the youth interviewed (Farmer et al., 2013, p. 29). This means that youth with small inner circles had fewer people who were most important to them.
4 Age not given, range 12+; Fargas-Malet & McSherry, 2018, p. 589.
5 Age 10; Dansey et al., 2018, p. 360.
6 Age 16; Jansen & Haavind, 2011, p. 82.
7 Christiansen, 2013, p. 733.
8 Age 8–9; Mitchell et al., 2010, p. 181.

References

Aldgate, J. (2009). Living in kinship care: A child-centered view. *Adoption & Fostering, 33*(3), 51–63. 10.1177/030857590903300306

Bamba, S., & Haight, W. (2009). Maltreated children's emerging well-being in Japanese state care. *Children and Youth Services Review, 31*(7), 797–806. 10.1016/j.childyouth.2009.02.006

Biehal, N. (2014). A sense of belonging: Meanings of family and home in long-term foster care. *The British Journal of Social Work, 44*(4), 955. 10.1093/bjsw/bcs177

Bulat, L. R. (2010). A longitudinal study of depressiveness in children in public care. *International Journal of Social Welfare*, *19*(4), 412–423. 10.1111/j.1468-2397. 2009.00698.x

Burgess, C., Rossvoll, F., Wallace, B., & Daniel, B. (2010). 'It's just like another home, just another family, so it's nae different' Children's voices in kinship care: A research study about the experience of children in kinship care in Scotland. *Child & Family Social Work*, *15*(3), 297–306. 10.1111/j.1365-2206.2009.00671.x

Burgund, A., & Zegarac, N. (2016). Perspectives of youth in care in Serbia. *Child & Adolescent Social Work Journal*, *33*(2), 151–161. 10.1007/s10560-015-0413-5

Buys, N., Tilbury, C., Creed, P., & Crawford, M. (2011). Working with youth in-care: Implications for vocational rehabilitation practice. *Disability and Rehabilitation*, *33*(13-14), 1125–1135. 10.3109/09638288.2010.521614

Christiansen, Ø., Havnen, K. J. S., Havik, T., & Anderssen, N. (2013). Cautious belonging: Relationships in long-term foster-care. *The British Journal of Social Work*, *43*(4), 720–738. 10.1093/bjsw/bcr198

Clarkson, H., Dallos, R., Stedmon, J., & Hennessy, C. (2017). Exploring the relationship: Joint narratives of foster carers and young people. *Adoption & Fostering*, *41*(1), 35–51. 10.1177/0308575916681711

Damnjanovic, M., Lakic, A., Stevanovic, D., & Jovanovic, A. (2011). Effects of mental health on quality of life in children and adolescents living in residential and foster care: A cross-sectional study. *Epidemiology and Psychiatric Sciences*, *20*(3), 257–262. 10.1017/s2045796011000291

Dansey, D., John, M., & Shbero, D. (2018). How children in foster care engage with loyalty conflict: Presenting a model of processes informing loyalty. *Adoption & Fostering*, *42*(4), 354–368. 10.1177/0308575918798767

Diehl, D. C., Howse, R. B., & Trivette, C. M. (2011). Youth in foster care: Developmental assets and attitudes towards adoption and mentoring. *Child & Family Social Work*, *16*(1), 81–92. 10.1111/j.1365-2206.2010.00716.x

Downie, J. M., Hay, D. A., Horner, B. J., Wichmann, H., & Hislop, A. L. (2009). Children living with their grandparents: Resilience and wellbeing. *International Journal of Social Welfare*, *19*(1), 8–22. 10.1111/j.1468-2397.2009.00654.x

Ellingsen, I. T., Shemmings, D., & Størksen, I. (2011). The concept of 'family' among Norwegian adolescents in long-term foster care. *Child and Adolescent Social Work Journal*, *28*(4), 301–318. 10.1007/s10560-011-0234-0

Emond, R. (2010). Caring as a moral, practical and powerful endeavour: Peer care in a Cambodian orphanage. *The British Journal of Social Work*, *40*(1), 63–81. 10. 1093/bjsw/bcn102

Fargas-Malet, M., & McSherry, D. (2018). The mental health and help-seeking behavior of children and young people in care in Northern Ireland: Making services accessible and engaging. *The British Journal of Social Work*, *48*(3), 578–595. 10. 1093/bjsw/bcx062

Farmer, E., Selwyn, J., & Meakings, S. (2013). 'Other children say you're not normal because you don't live with your parents'. Children's views of living with informal kinship carers: Social networks, stigma and attachment to carers. *Child & Family Social Work*, *18*(1), 25–34. 10.1111/cfs.12030

Fawley-King, K., Trask, E. V., Zhang, J., & Aarons, G. A. (2017). The impact of changing neighborhoods, switching schools, and experiencing relationship disruption on children's adjustment to a new placement in foster care. *Child Abuse & Neglect*, *63*, 141–150. 10.1016/j.chiabu.2016.11.016

Gayapersad, A., Ombok, C., Kamanda, A., Tarus, C., Ayuku, D., & Braitstein, P. (2019). The production and reproduction of kinship in charitable children's institutions in Uasin Gishu County, Kenya. *Child & Youth Care Forum, 48,* 797–828. 10.1007/s10566-019-09506-8

Hedin, L. (2014). A sense of belonging in a changeable everyday life - a follow-up study of young people in kinship, network, and traditional foster families. *Child & Family Social Work, 19*(2), 165–173. 10.1111/j.1365-2206.2012.00887.x

Hedin, L., Höjer, I., & Brunnberg, E. (2011a). Why one goes to school: what school means to young people entering foster care. *Child & Family Social Work, 16*(1), 43–51. 10.1111/j.1365-2206.2010.00706.x

Hedin, L., Höjer, I., & Brunnberg, E. (2011b). Settling into a new home as a teenager: About establishing social bonds in different types of foster families in Sweden. *Children and Youth Services Review, 33*(11), 2282–2289. 10.1016/j.childyouth.2011.07.016

Hedin, L., Höjer, I., & Brunnberg, E. (2012). Jokes and routines make everyday life a good life-on 'doing family' for young people in foster care in Sweden. *European Journal of Social Work, 15*(5), 613–628. 10.1080/13691457.2011.579558

Holland, S. (2010). Looked after children and the ethic of care. *The British Journal of Social Work, 40*(6), 1664–1680. 10.1093/bjsw/bcp086

Hunt, J., Waterhouse, S., & Lutman, E. (2010). Parental contact for children placed in kinship care through care proceedings. *Child and Family Law Quarterly, 22*, 71–92. https://ssrn.com/abstract=1939941

Jansen, A., & Haavind, H. (2011). "If only" and "despite all": Narrative configuration among young people living in residential care. *Narrative Inquiry, 21*(1), 68–87. 10.1075/ni.21.1.04jan

Kalverboer, M., Zijlstra, E., van Os, C., Zevulun, D., ten Brummelaar, M., & Beltman, D. (2017). Unaccompanied minors in the Netherlands and the care facility in which they flourish best. *Child & Family Social Work, 22*(2), 587–596. 10.1111/cfs.12272

Kelly, C., Anthony, E. K., & Krysik, J. (2019). "How am I doing?" Narratives of youth living in congregate care on their social-emotional well-being. *Children and Youth Services Review, 103*, 255–263. 10.1016/j.childyouth.2019.06.001

Lorthridge, J., Evans, M., Heaton, L., Stevens, A., & Phillips, L. (2018). Strengthening family connections and support for youth in foster care who identify as LGBTQ: Findings from the PII-RISE evaluation. *Child Welfare, 96*(1), 53–78. https://www.jstor.org/stable/48628035

Lundström, T., & Sallnäs, M. (2012). Sibling contact among Swedish children in foster and residential care-out of home care in a family service system. *Children and Youth Services Review, 34*(2), 396–402. 10.1016/j.childyouth.2011.11.008

Madigan, S., Quayle, E., Cossar, J., & Paton, K. (2013). Feeling the same or feeling different? An analysis of the experiences of young people in foster care. *Adoption & Fostering, 37*(4), 389–403. 10.1177/0308575913508719

Mateos, A., Balsells, M. À., Molina, M. C., & Fuentes-Peláez, N. (2012). The perception adolescents in kinship foster care have of their own needs. *Revista de Cercetare si Interventie Sociala, 38*, 25–41. http://hdl.handle.net/2445/103325

Mitchell, M. B., & Kuczynski, L. (2010). Does anyone know what is going on? Examining children's lived experience of the transition into foster care. *Children and Youth Services Review, 32*(3), 437–444. 10.1016/j.childyouth.2009.10.023

Mitchell, M. B., Kuczynski, L., Tubbs, C. Y., & Ross, C. (2010). We care about care: Advice by children in care for children in care, foster parents and child welfare workers about the transition into foster care. *Child & Family Social Work, 15*(2), 176–185. 10.1111/j.1365-2206.2009.00657.x

Mota, C. P., & Matos, P. M. (2015). Adolescents in institutional care: Significant adults, resilience and well-being. *Child & Youth Care Forum*, *44*(2), 209–224. 10.1007/s10566-014-9278-6

Rees, A., Holland, S., & Pithouse, A. (2012). Food in foster families: Care, communication and conflict. *Children & Society*, *26*(2), 100–111. 10.1111/j.1099-0860.2010.00332.x

Rostill-Brookes, H., Larkin, M., Toms, A., & Churchman, C. (2011). A shared experience of fragmentation: making sense of foster placement breakdown. *Clinical Child Psychology and Psychiatry*, *16*(1), 103–127. 10.1177/1359104509352894

Sands, R. G., Goldberg-Glen, R. S., & Shin, H. (2009). The voices of grandchildren: A strengths-resilience perspective. *Child Welfare League of America*, *88*(2), 25–45. https://www.jstor.org/stable/48623254

Schofield, G., Beek, M., & Ward, E. (2012). Part of the family: Planning for permanence in long-term family foster care. *Children and Youth Services Review*, *34*(1), 244–253. 10.1016/j.childyouth.2011.10.020

Schwartz, A. E. (2010). "Nobody knows me no more": Experiences of loss among African American adolescents in kinship and non-kinship foster care placements. *Race and Social Problems*, *2*(1), 31–49. 10.1007/s12552-010-9025-z

Selwyn, J., Saunders, H., & Farmer, E. (2010). The views of children and young people on being cared for by an independent foster-care provider. *The British Journal of Social Work*, *40*(3), 696–713. 10.1093/bjsw/bcn117

Skoog, V., Khoo, E., & Nygren, L. (2015). Disconnection and dislocation: Relationships and belonging in unstable foster and institutional care. *The British Journal of Social Work*, *45*(6), 1888–1904. 10.1093/bjsw/bcu033

Southwell, J., & Fraser, E. (2010). Young people's satisfaction with residential care: Identifying strengths and weaknesses in service delivery. *Child Welfare*, *89*(2), 209–228. https://pubmed.ncbi.nlm.nih.gov/20857888/

Wissö, T., Johansson, H., & Höjer, I. (2019). What is a family? Constructions of family and parenting after a custody transfer from birth parents to foster parents. *Child & Family Social Work*, *24*(1), 9–16. 10.1111/cfs.12475

Wojciak, A. S. (2017). 'It's complicated.' Exploring the meaning of sibling relationships of youth in foster care. *Child & Family Social Work*, *22*(3), 1283–1291. 10.1111/cfs.12345

Chapter 10

Feeling Different from Others and Sense of Self

"People were laughing at me because I didn't have a mum"[1]

Often foster youth feel like they are very different from other children, and some feel like those differences decrease their self-worth. These feelings can be compounded by the behavior of friends, peers, and adults. For example, adults may expect less of foster youth than they expect of children who are not in foster care. This can affect youth's overall sense of self and how they view their future selves. Some youth are well-versed in how to address the feelings that arise from feeling "othered," whereas others struggle. In this chapter we discuss how foster youth may feel different from their peers (i.e., from being bullied, feeling stigmatized, or living in a different cultural context), develop a sense of self (through self-advocacy and improving self-esteem), and think about their futures.

Feeling Different from Others

Foster youth across studies described the importance of fitting in with other children, and the stigma associated with being in care was a concern for many of the youth. Children felt like others singled them out for being in foster care (Bamba & Haight, 2009; Buys et al., 2011). Others said they were alone or bullied at school (Bamba & Haight, 2009).

Bullying was a theme that emerged across more than 10% of the studies we reviewed. One third of the youth interviewed by Farmer et al. (2013) felt like other children judged and bullied them because they did not live with their biological parents. These youth said that they were singled out for being "unwanted." In another study, a few were bullied and noted that it was mostly because of their foster care status (Hedin et al., 2011). This led most of the youth to keep their foster care status a secret at their new schools. Two other youth in the same study were bullied for not speaking Swedish well enough and felt extra pressure to fit in. Children interviewed by Madigan et al. (2013) in Scotland frequently described feeling alienated from their peers, witnessing or experiencing bullying, and having difficulties making friends. One youth described how other kids made fun of her and how she realized that before she was in care, she was guilty of engaging in that same

DOI: 10.4324/9781003309215-10

bullying behavior herself. Another youth talked about how she cried when children bullied her, and how that led to more bullying. To adapt, she worked hard to avoid crying in front of her peers to avoid more bullying.

Youth's decisions about whether or not to reveal their foster care status varied across studies. In a study of youth in kinship care in Australia, about half the youth were open about being in care (Downie et al., 2009). For example, one youth felt like it was important to talk about it, so when friends would come over for sleepovers they would better understand why her grandmother was stricter than most parents. In a study of youth also in kinship care, in the United Kingdom, most of the youth discussed their living arrangements, but with close friends only (Farmer et al., 2013). However, some of these youth did not tell *anyone* and few were completely open about living with their kinship carers.

> *"People that I've just met have been quite insensitive and ... be like, 'It's a bit weird you don't live with your parents. Do they hate you?[2]'"*

As youth got older, they were more likely to choose to keep their foster youth status a secret (Farmer et al., 2013). In addition to not wanting to discuss being in care, many youth did not want to talk to others about why they were in care (Aldgate, 2009; Burgess et al., 2010). For instance, several youth preferred to lie about their situation rather than give specific details about their biological parents (Aldgate, 2009).

Many youth felt different or like people treated them differently after learning they were in foster care. One youth was bothered by the fact that while she saw her foster care as a positive thing, her peers' perceptions made her care seem like a bad thing (Madigan et al., 2013). Some youth said that they felt alone; like they were the only ones living in foster care; like they were outsiders; or that they could not do the same things as their peers, such as hanging out with friends and having cell phones (Aldgate, 2009; Emond, 2010; Kelly, 2019; Southwell & Fraser, 2010). Conversely, other youth said they did not feel different from their peers because of being in care (Burgess et al., 2010; Southwell & Fraser, 2010). Several youth who discussed their placement with peers experienced negative interactions that they did not appreciate. For example, peers would feel sorry for them, be overly sympathetic, bring up foster care too often in conversations, or be generally insensitive in their reactions (Farmer et al., 2013; Madigan et al., 2013). One youth felt that people walked on eggshells around him and were overly protective, which eventually led to his exclusion from the group (Madigan et al., 2013). Youth said they would rather people accept their foster care status, understand them, and move on.

Many youth in care felt like they could not escape unwanted labels placed on them by their peers (Madigan et al., 2013). Because of concerns about being labeled as a "foster child" or "looked after child," youth sometimes did not talk to their peers about being in care. Talking to others about being in care is a decision that youth think about seriously—and a decision youth should be able to make for themselves (Madigan et al., 2013). Many youth worried that others would reveal it for them (see e.g., Madigan et al., 2013; Mannay et al., 2017; Mateos et al., 2012). One youth preferred not to discuss her status as a foster youth; however, her teacher mentioned it to her peers without her permission (Madigan et al., 2013). Several youth described having to discuss their foster care status or participate in case reviews in public places, such as school. They did not like this because their foster care status was inadvertently revealed to others, and adults often asked questions about their biological parents and home life before care (Mannay et al., 2017; Mateos et al., 2012).

When youth are treated differently from other children, this can make it difficult for them to feel like they fit in. This can be even more problematic when it occurs within the foster home itself. For example, when adults saw youth as different from their peers, it negatively affected their emotional well-being (Buys et al., 2011). In other studies we reviewed, youth said that privileges and chores differed between children in the same home (see e.g., Flores et al., 2018; Gayapersad et al., 2019). Some crossover youth (youth who are part of both the juvenile justice system and the foster care system) felt that the other noncrossover foster children were given access to more privileges, and those out on probation were isolated, treated unfairly, or disrespected. Youth reported that some carers threatened to call parole officers and did not give them the things they needed, such as their clothing allowances. If children transferred from detention centers into foster homes, they felt like their carers treated them differently because of their backgrounds (Flores et al., 2018). During visitations, youth in charitable institutions in Kenya said that they were not given as much time with their caregivers as other children, and they received fewer gifts than the other children in care (Gayapersad et al., 2019). These institutions had distinctive practices compared to those described in other studies, and this may have contributed to children feeling like they were treated differently from their foster siblings.

Cultural Responsiveness

When children are not placed in families with similar cultural backgrounds, this can contribute to their feeling different from other children. These feelings are compounded when foster carers lack cultural understanding. Children in the studies we reviewed described feeling culturally disconnected from their foster families by race, ethnicity, gender, sexuality, language, and religion. In one study, authors specifically stated that most youth were placed with families of similar backgrounds (Kalverboer et al., 2017). However, many of these youth said that they had experienced racism outside of their foster homes. In Schwartz's (2010) study of kinship versus nonkinship care for Black adolescents in the United States, one child mentioned feeling like she stood out in her school and neighborhood because most of the people were White and not her "color" or ethnicity. In another study, one youth wanted to go to a certain school, but their carers advised against it, saying the youth's ethnicity and native language would prevent them from being socially accepted (Schiller & de Wet, 2018).

As described above, cultural responsiveness was noted in some of the studies we reviewed. However, only a small portion of the 83 studies specifically addressed foster youth's cultural needs (see e.g., Ashley & Brown, 2015; Dove & Powers, 2018; Gayapersad et al., 2019; Lorthridge et al., 2018). Two of these studies specifically looked at Black girls' experiences around their hair care needs (Ashley & Brown, 2015; Dove & Powers, 2018). The issue of Black hair care also came up during interviews with crossover youth (Flores, 2018). One study described the needs of LGBTQIA+ youth in the United States and another study was about youth living in charitable institutions in Kenya. We will talk about these four studies in the next paragraphs.

"... they [White foster parents] are so used to what they use ... how they do their hair versus how we do our hair is a totally different concept.[3]*"*

In studies conducted by Ashley and Brown (2015) and Dove and Powers (2018), Black children reported that hair was an important part of their identity. However, foster carers and caseworkers often lacked awareness about the cultural importance of Black hair and how to care for it properly. For example, one young woman said that her foster family did not consider proper hair care to be a basic need. Instead, they only allowed her to get her hair done as a reward. Another said that many of her foster caregivers had been White and did not understand they couldn't care for Black hair the same way they cared for White hair (Dove & Powers, 2018).

This lack of understanding was detrimental to the children's sense of cultural belonging, and some felt uncomfortable discussing their hair care needs with White caseworkers and caregivers. Ashley and Brown (2015) addressed this issue by providing "Attachment tHAIRapy," a combination of hair care and mental health therapy that helped Black youth feel valued and respected. Participants reported improved self-esteem, better relationships, and greater satisfaction with foster care. Recommendations from youth included placing children with caregivers who know how to do hair or feel comfortable asking for help. Youth also recommended that foster parents take initiative to do the research on hair products and ask the youth directly what would be best for them (Dove & Powers, 2018).

Youth who defined themselves outside of the cis/binary gender/sexuality spectrum experienced unique challenges while in care. Lorthridge et al. (2018) evaluated Recognize, Intervene, Support, Empower (RISE), a program that was created by the Los Angeles LGBT Center to address these challenges. The RISE program was offered to foster parents to increase awareness and understanding of LGBTQ+ (which the organization described as Lesbian, Gay, Bisexual, Transgender, Queer and/or Questioning plus)[4] youth needs. The program led to an improvement in youth well-being, feelings of being accepted and understood, and comfort with discussing gender and sexuality. The RISE program helped youth to feel like they really belonged to their community. Three of the foster youth sought out the RISE program to meet other LGBTQ+ peers. Another youth began engaging in LGBTQ+ activities and support organizations after participating in RISE (Lorthridge et al., 2018). The RISE program helped one foster family find and join a support group. This program is an excellent example of how LGBTQIA+ youth can be supported in foster care in finding identity within, and feeling connected to, their community.

Children's sense of belonging and cultural well-being in their communities can be negatively affected moving into foster care. Southwell and Fraser (2010) asked Aboriginal and Torres Strait Islander youth if they were still connected with their cultural communities after entering residential care and one third reported that they were not. Living conditions within foster care can disrupt children's connections from their communities. Gayapersad et al. (2019) conducted a study on youth living in charitable institutions in Kenya and found that some of them were subjected to practices that resulted in a disconnection from their communities and loss of cultural identity. The researchers highlighted examples such as forcing children to shave their heads, circumcising boys, and prohibiting children from practicing their own culture, religion, and language. As a consequence, when these children aged out of institutional care, they faced difficulties integrating back into society due to the suppression of their cultural identity (Gayapersad et al., 2019).

The studies we reviewed included some examples of how foster caregivers and caseworkers engaged in better cultural awareness, and a few examples of where cultural responsiveness was missing entirely. However, attention to youth's cultures was conspicuously missing from many of the studies identified for our systematic literature review. Further research is needed on foster youth's experiences related to their culture along with ways social workers and foster carers can help youth stay connected with their communities.

Sense of Self

Foster youth are expected to exit the foster care system and become contributing members of society. This requires developing important qualities, such as self-advocacy, self-esteem, and confidence, all of which affect youth's future aspirations. These qualities are complexly interconnected and can affect how well youth integrate into society in adulthood. For instance, if youth are not supported in their self-advocacy, they may have lower self-confidence to try again in the future. This in turn can negatively impact their self-esteem. Conversely, having healthy self-esteem and confidence can increase the ability to self-advocate, which can positively affect youth's futures. The youth interviewed across studies described a range of experiences related to their sense of self, which we will outline in the following sections.

Self-Advocacy

In the studies we reviewed, successful (or unsuccessful) development of self-advocacy was something that youth discussed often. In many cases, youth described feeling like they were the only ones who could or would advocate for them (Barnes, 2012; Burgund & Zegarac, 2016; Buys et al., 2011). When youth advocated for themselves, they felt a sense of maturity and self-sufficiency (Emond, 2010; Hedin et al., 2011; Jansen & Haavind, 2011; Pert, 2017). For instance, children in Cambodia took pride in self-improvement, self-care, and looking after their own well-being (Emond, 2010). One youth in Norway described how it was important to take care of herself and advocate for her own success and well-being. Another youth was not removed from home by Child Protective Services, but instead *chose* to move into foster care. Her parents objected, but she felt this was the best thing for her to do (Jansen & Haavind, 2011). Two youth in Sweden were unhappy in their placements and took the initiative to successfully find new foster families (Hedin, 2014). Pert et al. (2017) found that in review meetings, children in England appreciated when their foster carers supported them in speaking up for themselves. Overall, it was important and beneficial for youth to advocate for themselves and to be active participants in decisions made about their own lives (see Chapter 3 for more about youth's involvement in the decision-making process).

There are times in which youth attempt to self-advocate but are blocked in one way or another. In the research we reviewed, there were youth who knew which services they needed, but were denied because of lack of funds (Buys et al., 2011).

> *"I asked them for a private tutor for English, but they reckon it's too much money. That's all they say ... No I can't help you, it's too much money.*[5]*"*

Other youth described having little say over their own personal space (Hedin et al., 2011). In the study by Morrison et al. (2011) in Canada, youth tried to be involved in scheduling visitation with parents, but they were unsure of who to talk to about it and social workers did not provide any guidance. In another study, a youth expressed interest in moving back home with his birth family, but his social worker did not help (Hedin 2014). This led to him to report feeling stressed, depressed, and pessimistic about having a say in his living arrangements. Sometimes youth needed help with specific problems. Southwell and Fraser (2010) found that 26 of the 169 youth (15%) in their study expressed difficulty with health issues and 23% of those youth had not been seen for these issues by the end of their study. Further, youth reported that educational needs were the least likely to be met. Specifically, 30% of the youth currently attending school in the Southwell and Fraser study were unable to get help with school problems, even though they had asked for help. Another study surveyed youth to better understand the level of control they felt in their lives. They found that white male youth felt more in control of their lives, while Black female youth felt the least amount of control (Diehl et al., 2011). A lower sense of perceived control may deter youth from self-advocating.

Self-advocating was especially challenging for children with disabilities or those who had difficulty expressing their needs (Barnes, 2012). For other youth, fear kept them from discussing their concerns about health, safety, or basic human necessities (Flores et al., 2018). For instance, youth described feeling embarrassed, worrying about making their caregivers uncomfortable, or feeling guilty about advocating on their own behalf (Fargas-Malet & McSherry, 2018; Kuyini et al., 2009). In multiple studies (Barnes, 2012; Flores et al., 2018; Kuyini et al., 2009) there were youth who described being afraid of what would happen if they talked about their concerns or asserted their perceived rights. In some cases, these fears were warranted. In two studies (one in the United States and one in Australia) some of the youth interviewed had been beaten for speaking up. In other cases, caregivers threatened to report youth for property damage or physical assault, even when those things didn't happen. While these circumstances were described in only a few of the studies we reviewed, it is important to be aware that there are some places where youth cannot advocate for themselves because of opposition from the adults who are caring for them.

A few youth in one of the studies gave recommendations to other children in care to help them advocate for themselves (Mitchell et al., 2010). They suggested that youth should talk to social workers if things do not go well at the foster home. They also explained that foster parents are probably nervous about care and recommended that children be polite, remain calm when expressing emotions, and ask for what they need. Paying close attention to foster children's recommendations can help us better support the needs of youth in care.

Self-Esteem and Self-Confidence

Benefits of a strong sense of self include increased self-esteem and self-confidence. Burgund and Zegarac (2016) interviewed 16 foster youth in Serbia in an effort to understand how they perceived themselves and their own strengths. Nearly all the youth were initially unwilling to describe their positive characteristics, some being too humble to state their achievements directly. It is possible that youth needed some encouragement to think about their favorable qualities because by the end of the interviews, all youth had shared something good about themselves. They labeled themselves as good with people and their schoolwork, being caring and communicative, and having perseverance. Youth interviewed by Kelly et al. (2019) said that when they learned to be happy despite their difficult circumstances, and received encouragement from adults, they felt better about themselves and their achievements. These youth described feeling pride in doing well in school and looking toward a brighter academic future. In many studies, youth's self-esteem and self-confidence were positively influenced by engaging in more activities, accepting their LGBTQIA+ identity (by others and themselves), scoring high on assets/prosocial behavior measures, having supportive caregivers/birth mothers/

peers, having "good hair," and thinking about the future (Burgess et al., 2010; Diehl et al., 2011; Dove & Powers, 2018; Farineau et al., 2013; Farmer et al., 2013; Fernandez, 2009; Lorthridge et al., 2018).

Several factors influenced self-esteem and confidence in a negative direction. For example, Black girls' self-esteem was negatively affected when they felt like their natural hair wasn't good enough or they did not have time or resources to care for their hair. In some cases, Black girls called their natural hair "ugly" (Dove & Powers, 2018). Other variables that negatively impacted youth's self-esteem and self-confidence included being bullied, unaccepted by others, alienated by peers, and blaming themselves for being in care (Hedin et al., 2011; Madigan et al., 2013; Mateos et al., 2012). In a study of 188 youth in the United States, Farineau et al. (2013) found that negative relationships with foster parents was strongly related to lower self-esteem. Foster caregivers and social workers need to be aware of ways they can support or impede youth mental health and well-being.

Future Aspirations

The future is uncertain for most adolescents in our society, and this is no different for foster youth. Even with this uncertainty, most of the youth in our studies expressed optimism about the future and their expectations for themselves (Traube et al., 2012). Many youth said they knew what they wanted to do and how to achieve it (Burgund & Zegarac, 2016; Mateos et al., 2012). For example, they described wanting to become self-sufficient, go to college, become independent, start careers, and have families (Burgund & Zegarac, 2016; Mateos et al., 2012). Moreover, youth who felt encouraged by caregivers and social workers were more likely to aim high in their career aspirations (Burgess et al., 2010).

Some youth encountered barriers in achieving their goals. Some in the study by Kalverboer et al. (2017) aspired to careers that require advanced degrees, but they were not doing well enough in high school to meet their goals. Other youth in the same study felt like it was useless to try hard at school because they worried that they might have to change schools in the future.

"How can I think about my future if I don't have security?[6]"

Youth interviewed in Australia by Buys et al. (2011) described difficulties other than those related to school. Most felt like they received little assistance or support when it came to work or life skills, and that they did not know how to attain stable economic futures for themselves (see also Kelly et al., 2019). In addition, youth said their foster parents had low expectations for them and were not good models for future employment, which led to feelings of depression and low self-esteem.

Regardless of difficulties associated with school, many youth across studies described how doing well in school is one of the most important ways to achieve future goals (Buys et al., 2011; Hedin et al., 2011; Kalverboer et al., 2017; Kelly et al., 2019; Mannay et al., 2017). For example, one youth said that the only way to break the negative cycle of his biological family's circumstance was to refrain from drugs and go to college after high school (Kelly et al., 2019).

> *"I used to break the rules and run away at my old group home. But now I try and follow the rules and stay out of trouble. I'm doing really good and focusing on my goals. I have to keep doing good because I want to get a scholarship to go to college.*[7]*"*

Another youth said he worked hard in his classes so he would have better opportunities in high school (Hedin et al., 2011). With proper support, self-confidence, and self-advocacy, youth's sense of self can be developed to help them achieve their future aspirations.

Summary

When youth feel a strong sense of self, this can have a positive effect on their confidence, ability to advocate for themselves, and their future aspirations. Adults can hinder or support youth's sense of self. Some ways that adults can help youth develop and cultivate this sense of self is to be respectful of children's cultures, help them stay connected with their communities, treat them like they do children who are not in care, and encourage children to pursue their goals and education.

Notes

1 Age not given, range 8–16; Aldgate, 2009, p. 60.
2 Age 17; Farmer et al., 2013, p. 28.
3 Age not given, range 13–17; Dove & Powers, 2018, p. 373.
4 The current term is LGBTQIA+, which represents "Lesbian, Gay, Bisexual, Transgender, Queer and/or Questioning, Intersex, Asexual, … and the countless affirmative ways in which people choose to self-identify" (Emerson College, n.d.).
5 Age not given, range 13–18; Buys et al., 2011, p. 1131.
6 Age 16–17; Kalverboer et al., 2017, p. 593.
7 Age not given, range 12–17; Kelly et al., 2019, p. 259.

References

Aldgate, J. (2009). Living in kinship care: A child-centered view. *Adoption & Fostering, 33*(3), 51–63. 10.1177/030857590903300306

Ashley, W., & Brown, J. C. (2015). Attachment tHAIRapy: A culturally relevant treatment paradigm for African American foster youth. *Journal of Black Studies, 46*(6), 587–604. 10.1177/0021934715590406

Bamba, S., & Haight, W. (2009). Maltreated children's emerging well-being in Japanese state care. *Children and Youth Services Review, 31*(7), 797–806. 10.1016/j.childyouth.2009.02.006

Barnes, V. (2012). Social work and advocacy with young people: Rights and care in practice. *The British Journal of Social Work, 42*(7), 1275–1292. 10.1093/bjsw/bcr142

Burgess, C., Rossvoll, F., Wallace, B., & Daniel, B. (2010). 'It's just like another home, just another family, so it's nae different' Children's voices in kinship care: A research study about the experience of children in kinship care in Scotland. *Child & Family Social Work, 15*(3), 297–306. 10.1111/j.1365-2206.2009.00671.x

Burgund, A., & Zegarac, N. (2016). Perspectives of youth in care in Serbia. *Child & Adolescent Social Work Journal, 33*(2), 151–161. 10.1007/s10560-015-0413-5

Buys, N., Tilbury, C., Creed, P., & Crawford, M. (2011). Working with youth in-care: Implications for vocational rehabilitation practice. *Disability and Rehabilitation, 33*(13-14), 1125–1135. 10.3109/09638288.2010.521614

Diehl, D. C., Howse, R. B., & Trivette, C. M. (2011). Youth in foster care: Developmental assets and attitudes towards adoption and mentoring. *Child & Family Social Work, 16*(1), 81–92. 10.1111/j.1365-2206.2010.00716.x

Dove, L. M., & Powers, L. E. (2018). Exploring the complexity of hair and identity among African American female adolescents in foster care. *Children and Youth Services Review, 95*, 368–376. 10.1016/j.childyouth.2018.10.043

Downie, J. M., Hay, D. A., Horner, B. J., Wichmann, H., & Hislop, A. L. (2009). Children living with their grandparents: Resilience and wellbeing. *International Journal of Social Welfare, 19*(1), 8–22. 10.1111/j.1468-2397.2009.00654.x

Emerson College. (n.d.). *Glossary of LGBTQIA+ terms.* Intercultural Student Affairs. https://emerson.edu/departments/intercultural-student-affairs/resources/glossary-lgbtqia-terms

Emond, R. (2010). Caring as a moral, practical and powerful endeavour: Peer care in a Cambodian orphanage. *The British Journal of Social Work*, *40*(1), 63–81. 10. 1093/bjsw/bcn102

Fargas-Malet, M., & McSherry, D. (2018). The mental health and help-seeking behavior of children and young people in care in Northern Ireland: Making services accessible and engaging. *The British Journal of Social Work*, *48*(3), 578–595. 10. 1093/bjsw/bcx062

Farineau, H. M., Wojciak, A. S., & McWey, L. M. (2013). You matter to me: Important relationships and self-esteem of adolescents in foster care. *Child & Family Social Work*, *18*(2), 129–138. 10.1111/j.1365-2206.2011.00808.x

Farmer, E., Selwyn, J., & Meakings, S. (2013). 'Other children say you're not normal because you don't live with your parents'. Children's views of living with informal kinship carers: Social networks, stigma and attachment to carers. *Child & Family Social Work*, *18*(1), 25–34. 10.1111/cfs.12030

Fernandez, E. (2009). Children's wellbeing in care: Evidence from a longitudinal study of outcomes. *Children and Youth Services Review*, *31*(10), 1092–1100. 10.1016/ j.childyouth.2009.07.010

Flores, J., Hawes, J., Westbrooks, A., & Henderson, C. (2018). Crossover youth and gender: What are the challenges of girls involved in both the foster care and juvenile justice systems? *Children and Youth Services Review*, *91*, 149–155. 10.1016/ j.childyouth.2018.05.031

Gayapersad, A., Ombok, C., Kamanda, A., Tarus, C., Ayuku, D., & Braitstein, P. (2019). The production and reproduction of kinship in charitable children's institutions in Uasin Gishu County, Kenya. *Child & Youth Care Forum*, *48*, 797–828. 10.1007/s10566-019-09506-8

Hedin, L. (2014). A sense of belonging in a changeable everyday life - a follow-up study of young people in kinship, network, and traditional foster families. *Child & Family Social Work*, *19*(2), 165–173. 10.1111/j.1365-2206.2012.00887.x

Hedin, L., Höjer, I., & Brunnberg, E. (2011). Settling into a new home as a teenager: About establishing social bonds in different types of foster families in Sweden. *Children and Youth Services Review*, *33*(11), 2282–2289. 10.1016/j.childyouth.2011.07.016

Jansen, A., & Haavind, H. (2011). "If only" and "despite all": Narrative configuration among young people living in residential care. *Narrative Inquiry*, *21*(1), 68–87. 10. 1075/ni.21.1.04jan

Kalverboer, M., Zijlstra, E., van Os, C., Zevulun, D., ten Brummelaar, M., & Beltman, D. (2017). Unaccompanied minors in the Netherlands and the care facility in which they flourish best. *Child & Family Social Work*, *22*(2), 587–596. 10.1111/ cfs.12272

Kelly, C., Anthony, E. K., & Krysik, J. (2019). "How am I doing?" Narratives of youth living in congregate care on their social-emotional well-being. *Children and Youth Services Review*, *103*, 255–263. 10.1016/j.childyouth.2019.06.001

Kuyini, A. B., Alhassan, A. R., Tollerud, I., Weld, H., & Haruna, I. (2009). Traditional kinship foster care in northern Ghana: The experiences and views of children, carers and adults in Tamale. *Child & Family Social Work*, *14*(4), 440–449. 10.1111/j.1365-2206.2009.00616.x

Lorthridge, J., Evans, M., Heaton, L., Stevens, A., & Phillips, L. (2018). Strengthening family connections and support for youth in foster care who identify as LGBTQ: Findings from the PII-RISE evaluation. *Child Welfare*, *96*(1), 53–78. https://www. jstor.org/stable/48628035

Madigan, S., Quayle, E., Cossar, J., & Paton, K. (2013). Feeling the same or feeling different? An analysis of the experiences of young people in foster care. *Adoption & Fostering*, *37*(4), 389–403. 10.1177/0308575913508719

Mannay, D., Evans, R., Staples, E., Hallett, S., Roberts, L., Rees, A., & Andrews, D. (2017). The consequences of being labelled 'looked-after': Exploring the educational experiences of looked-after children and young people in Wales. *British Educational Research Journal*, *43*(4), 683–699. 10.1002/berj.3283

Mateos, A., Balsells, M. À., Molina, M. C., & Fuentes-Peláez, N. (2012). The perception adolescents in kinship foster care have of their own needs. *Revista de Cercetare si Interventie Sociala*, *38*, 25–41. http://hdl.handle.net/2445/103325

Mitchell, M. B., Kuczynski, L., Tubbs, C. Y., & Ross, C. (2010). We care about care: Advice by children in care for children in care, foster parents and child welfare workers about the transition into foster care. *Child & Family Social Work*, *15*(2), 176–185. 10.1111/j.1365-2206.2009.00657.x

Morrison, J., Mishna, F., Cook, C., & Aitken, G. (2011). Access visits: Perceptions of child protection workers, foster parents and children who are Crown wards. *Children and Youth Services Review*, *33*(9), 1476–1482. 10.1016/j.childyouth.2011.03.011

Pert, H., Diaz, C., & Thomas, N. (2017). Children's participation in LAC reviews: A study in one English local authority. *Child & Family Social Work*, *22*(S2), 1–10. 10.1111/cfs.12194

Schiller, U., & de Wet, G. (2018). Communication, indigenous culture and participatory decision making amongst foster adolescents. *Qualitative Social Work*, *17*(2), 236–251. 10.1177/1473325016662329

Schwartz, A. E. (2010). "Nobody knows me no more": Experiences of loss among African American adolescents in kinship and non-kinship foster care placements. *Race and Social Problems*, *2*(1), 31–49. 10.1007/s12552-010-9025-z

Southwell, J., & Fraser, E. (2010). Young people's satisfaction with residential care: Identifying strengths and weaknesses in service delivery. *Child Welfare*, *89*(2), 209–228. https://pubmed.ncbi.nlm.nih.gov/20857888/

Traube, D. E., James, S., Zhang, J., & Landsverk, J. (2012). A national study of risk and protective factors for substance use among youth in the child welfare system. *Addictive Behaviors*, *37*(5), 641–650. 10.1016/j.addbeh.2012.01.015

Chapter 11

Summary and Youth Recommendations

"Take the time to listen to what we have to say[1]"

When we pay attention to the perspectives of foster youth, we are better able to meet youth's needs and facilitate healing. To that end, the purpose of this book was to spotlight foster youth's perspectives about their experiences in care. We conducted a systematic review and meta-analysis[2] of research in which current foster youth were asked about their perceptions of and experiences in foster care (see Appendix A). The review encompassed over 80 studies that were conducted around the globe over a period of 10 years. Of interest, foster youth consistently discussed similar issues across all studies. They shared their pain and victories; they described what they appreciated and liked about foster care; and they told researchers what they needed and what they felt could be better.

We have pulled together this research and these perspectives into one place to provide you with a more complete picture of the challenges and realities faced by youth in foster care. Each of our chapters covered a different theme. However, there was some overlap among chapters because these issues affected youth across multiple domains of their lives. For example, transitions into, out of, and between foster care have implications for youth's knowledge of the foster care system (Chapter 2), their desire to have a say in decisions that are made about placement (Chapter 3), the process itself (Chapter 7), mental health and well-being (Chapter 9), etc.

Across studies, youth described how they often did not understand what was happening, were not consulted, and how they wished adults would include them in the decision-making process, or at the very least, explain to them what was going on (Chapter 2). Transitions into, out of, and between foster care can be confusing for youth. Therefore, it is important that adults support youth, prepare them for these transitions through open communication, and be transparent about what to expect in the upcoming transitions (Chapter 7). Overall, youth frequently expressed a desire to be actively listened to and have their voices matter in decisions that affect them (Chapters 3–4).

Youth described several benefits to being in foster care. They said that compared to living with their biological families, many felt happier and safer, were more engaged in school, were allowed to explore new extracurricular

DOI: 10.4324/9781003309215-11

activities, and made new friends (Chapter 6). After transitioning into their new foster homes, foster families were key in helping youth adapt to their new living environments (Chapter 8). However, foster care placement has the potential to negatively affect youth well-being, which can be mitigated through the development of strong social connections (such as with friends and foster families). For instance, strong social connections and support can help youth feel secure, accepted, and valued in their foster families (Chapter 9). Foster families can strengthen youth's sense of connectedness and belonging by being sensitive to their cultures, encouraging future aspirations, treating them like members of the family, and helping them maintain ties with their communities (Chapter 10). Youth can strengthen their own sense of belonging by engaging in school, exploring new extracurricular activities, and building relationships with peers, friends, and foster families (Chapter 8).

Relationships with social workers were also important to youth. Youth sometimes felt that social workers did not have enough time to build relationships with them (due to heavy caseloads or other reasons) or involve them in important decisions (Chapter 4). For example, youth wanted to have more agency and actively participate in conversations regarding contact visits, rather than having adults make decisions on their behalf (Chapters 3–4). For some youth, their experiences of previous trauma leads them to decide that contact visits with biological families are not in their best interest. However, in other cases, youth find contact visits to be positive experiences and want to maintain and nurture relationships with biological families (Chapter 5).

Many chapters in this book include specific recommendations from foster youth for other foster youth, adults, social workers, and/or foster parents. Below are many recommendations youth made throughout the book about easing transitions, self-advocating, maintaining relationships, how to provide support as adults, and well-being.

Easing Transitions

Recommendations for foster youth from other foster youth

- Bring something comforting to your new foster home, such as a stuffed animal or a sentimental item (Mitchell et al., 2010).
- Keep busy, watch movies, play video games, listen to music, or avoid downtime to help positively cope (Mitchell et al., 2010).
- Talk to your new foster parents about your likes, dislikes, and what would make foster care feel more like home (Mitchell et al., 2010).
- Understand that although things start out hard, they eventually get easier over time (Mitchell et al., 2010).

- When you move to a new home, you will get to meet new friends and do things you probably wouldn't have done with your birth parents (Mitchell et al., 2010).

Recommendations for foster parents from foster youth

- Engage in conversations with youth to get to know each other. Discuss their favorite colors, activities, places, or foods. Talk to them about how you felt when you were a child (Mitchell et al., 2010).
- Go on outings together or do other types of bonding activities (Mitchell et al., 2010).

Recommendations for social workers from foster youth

- Be open about yourself. Describe who you are and your role (Mitchell et al., 2010).
- Help make children feel more comfortable during transition into foster care by actively listening to and alleviating their concerns as much as possible, going with them to meet their new foster parents, and telling them what to expect in care (Mitchell et al., 2010).
- Talk to the child about the upcoming move, explain what to expect during the process, describe what the foster family is like, and tell them if there are pets at the new home. If you are able to drive them to the new foster home, discuss these topics along the way (Mitchell et al., 2010).
- Consider if children need to rush to leave their current homes, if the family can spend one last day together, if you can give children time to work through their emotions, pack, or say goodbyes, if they want to know why they are being placed in care, and if there are significant items children need beyond basic necessities (Mitchell et al., 2010).
- When leaving their biological home to meet their new foster family, have a prior foster youth accompany you to help answer any questions that the new foster youth might have (Mitchell et al., 2010).

Self-Advocating

Recommendations for foster youth from other foster youth

- Talk to your social worker if things do not go well at your foster home (Mitchell et al., 2010).
- Foster parents are probably nervous about care so try to be polite, remain calm when expressing emotions, and ask for what you need (Mitchell et al., 2010).

Recommendations for foster parents from foster youth

- Give foster youth choices and include them in decision-making processes in their new homes (Mitchell et al., 2010).
- Let children paint their rooms so they can feel accepted in their new homes (Mitchell et al., 2010).
- Get to know the foster youth. This can lead to understanding each other's likes and dislikes and you may be more likely to provide the things that they prefer (Mitchell et al., 2010).

Recommendations for social workers from foster youth

- Acknowledge foster youth's agency, don't push them into family contact, and let them make choices for themselves (Kiraly & Humphreys, 2013).
- Ask children which schools they preferred to attend, whether or not they wished to visit their families, and if they needed anything from their old homes (Mitchell et al., 2010).

Maintaining Relationships

Recommendations for foster youth from other foster youth

- Maintain and strengthen current and new social relationships by reaching out to your friends and biological family to talk, text, and hang out (Mitchell et al., 2010).
- Stay connected with old friends by texting, make as many new friends as possible, and get out and do stuff with your friends (Mitchell et al., 2010).

Support from Adults

Recommendations for foster parents from foster youth

- Tell them where things are in the house and if there are any limitations or special rules to follow (Mitchell et al., 2010).
- Make sure that they have clothes, shoes, preferred foods, bedding, and you should "share your stuff" (Mitchell et al., 2010, p. 181).
- Ask children if they want to talk about (or not talk about) why they are in foster care (Mitchell et al., 2010).
- Some Black youth found that White foster parents were not culturally sensitive to their hair care needs. They recommended White families educate themselves about Black hair as well as ask and listen to their foster children regarding what they need to care for their hair (Dove & Powers, 2018).

Recommendations for social workers from foster youth

- Engage in open communication, ensure confidentiality, be more organized, and make more frequent contacts (Pölkki et al., 2012; Selwyn et al., 2010; Skoog et al., 2015).
- Talk more about what youth do well and less about what they do wrong or don't do well (Skoog et al., 2015).

Well-Being

Recommendations for all adults from foster youth

- There were several ways that youth desired support for psychological and socioemotional well-being. Generally youth encouraged practitioners, carers, social workers, and other professionals to *listen* to foster youth, include them in the decision-making process, offer many suggestions, be more proactive, engage in more conversations, offer in-home services or drop in options, and find a way to limit therapist turnover since youth get weary of repeating the same information to different therapists (Fargas-Malet & McSherry, 2018; Jansen & Haavind, 2011; Kalverboer et al., 2017).

Notes

1 Age 16; Fylkesnes et al., 2021, p. 1994.
2 Specifically, we conducted a meta-analysis examining the number of foster youth who had contact with their biological mothers compared with their biological fathers.

References

Dove, L. M., & Powers, L. E. (2018). Exploring the complexity of hair and identity among African American female adolescents in foster care. *Children and Youth Services Review*, *95*, 368–376. 10.1016/j.childyouth.2018.10.043

Fargas-Malet, M., & McSherry, D. (2018). The mental health and help-seeking behavior of children and young people in care in Northern Ireland: Making services accessible and engaging. *The British Journal of Social Work*, *48*(3), 578–595. 10. 1093/bjsw/bcx062

Fylkesnes, M., Larsen, M., Havnen, K., Christiansen, Ø., & Lehmann, S. (2021). Listening to advice from young people in foster care—from participation to belonging. *The British Journal of Social Work*, *51*(6), 1983–2000. 10.1093/bjsw/bcab138

Jansen, A., & Haavind, H. (2011). "If only" and "despite all": Narrative configuration among young people living in residential care. *Narrative Inquiry*, *21*(1), 68–87. 10. 1075/ni.21.1.04jan

Kalverboer, M., Zijlstra, E., van Os, C., Zevulun, D., ten Brummelaar, M., & Beltman, D. (2017). Unaccompanied minors in the Netherlands and the care facility in which they flourish best. *Child & Family Social Work*, *22*(2), 587–596. 10.1111/cfs.12272

Kiraly, M., & Humphreys, C. (2013). Perspectives from young people about family contact in kinship care: "Don't push us—listen more". *Australian Social Work*, *66*(3), 314–327. 10.1080/0312407x.2012.715658

Mitchell, M. B., Kuczynski, L., Tubbs, C. Y., & Ross, C. (2010). We care about care: Advice by children in care for children in care, foster parents and child welfare workers about the transition into foster care. *Child & Family Social Work*, *15*(2), 176–185. 10.1111/j.1365-2206.2009.00657.x

Pölkki, P., Vornanen, R., Pursiainen, M., & Riikonen, M. (2012). Children's participation in child-protection processes as experienced by foster children and social workers. *Child Care in Practice*, *18*(2), 107–125. 10.1080/13575279.2011. 646954

Selwyn, J., Saunders, H., & Farmer, E. (2010). The views of children and young people on being cared for by an independent foster-care provider. *The British Journal of Social Work*, *40*(3), 696–713. 10.1093/bjsw/bcn117

Skoog, V., Khoo, E., & Nygren, L. (2015). Disconnection and dislocation: Relationships and belonging in unstable foster and institutional care. *The British Journal of Social Work*, *45*(6), 1888–1904. 10.1093/bjsw/bcu033

Systematic Literature Search Methodology

The systematic literature review and findings described in this book are an extension of a systematic literature search and review that was conducted for the Swedish Board of Health and Welfare in 2014 (Saywitz et al., 2014). The purpose of the current project was to expand the search from 2014 to 2019 and to synthesize the body of research about the needs of foster children currently in care. Due to changes in library databases, the search strategy was somewhat complex. We describe this search below and in Appendix C.

Research Questions

Based on the extant literature, we focused on the following research questions:

1 What are current foster children's perceptions of and experiences with care?
2 What are the needs of foster children, as voiced by the children who are currently in care?

Data Sources and Search Strategy

The original systematic literature review for the Swedish Board of Health and Welfare spanned the years 1990 to 2014. We searched six electronic databases [PsycInfo, PubMed, Sociological Abstracts, Social Services Abstracts, Web of Knowledge (now Web of Science), and Cochrane Central (now Cochrane Library)]. The search yielded 1,346 studies. We identified 35 studies published in the years 1999 to 2013 to include in the original report. For details on the original systematic literature review, search strategy, and study coding, see Saywitz et al. (2014).

The current systematic literature review spanned the years 2009 to 2019 and included the six electronic databases listed above, with the addition of one other electronic database (CINAHL). We conducted our current search in three phases. In the first phase, we identified all papers from the previous systematic literature review that were published from 2009 to 2013. We planned to use the search terms from the original study to search databases from the years 2014 to 2019. Unfortunately, due to changes to some databases, we were unable to use the same search terms and strategies from the 2014 study. We solicited assistance from university librarians who helped create search strings that were comparable to both the original search strings and across all seven databases. In the second phase, because search strings and strategies had changed, we conducted new searches in all seven databases to locate possible additional papers missed in the original systematic literature review for the years 2009 to 2013. In the third phase, we searched for papers published from 2014 to 2019. (see Appendix C for search terms and strategies).

Search Results and Coding

In the original systematic literature search, there were 428 papers published from 2009 to 2013. The second search of publications dating 2009 to 2013 yielded an additional 975 papers. The search of publications dating 2014 to 2019 yielded 1,819 papers. A total of 3,222 papers were reviewed and coded for the current study (428 as part of the original review and 2,794 in our extension of the original work).

Thirty-one journal articles from the original systematic literature review were published from 2009 to 2013. Based on the predetermined exclusionary criteria listed below coders rated the additional studies. Two raters jointly coded 30 papers to establish interrater reliability. They then separately coded 200 papers achieving 94% reliability ($\gamma = .98$). The two raters individually coded the remaining papers (69% by one rater and 31% by the other rater), with discussion between raters, as they deemed necessary. All selected papers were evaluated again by the first and second author. A total of 3,142 papers were excluded, leaving 80 studies. During coding, we identified 3 additional papers to include, bringing our total to 83 (20 quantitative, 57 qualitative, and 6 mixed). Occasionally, to provide additional context to our findings, we referred to research not identified in this systematic search. In all cases, we made note of this to avoid ambiguity and maintain transparency.

Study Selection and Exclusion Criteria

Studies from all phases were coded against the following predetermined exclusionary criteria.

1 Article is not in English.
2 Article is not published in a peer-reviewed journal from 2009 to 2019.

3 Subjects were recruited because of existing medical or psychological diagnosis.[1]
4 Article is not a write up of an empirical research study.
5 Children were not informants.
6 Primary focus is not on eliciting children's perceptions about their experiences in or their satisfaction with foster care through face-to-face interaction.
7 Most participants are not between the ages 4 and 18 and currently in foster care.[2]

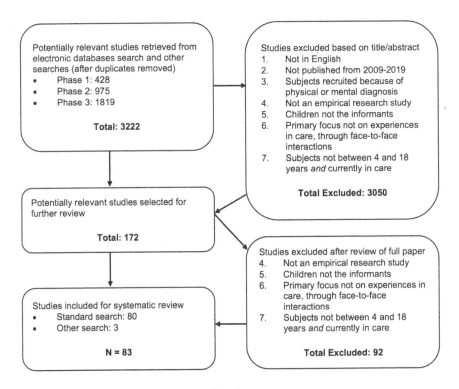

Figure A.1 Systematic literature review flowchart.

Sample Characteristics

The reviewed studies came from several regions across 27 countries (Australia, Austria, Botswana, Bulgaria, Cambodia, Canada, England, Finland, France, Ghana, Greece, Ireland, Israel, Italy, Japan, Kenya, the Netherlands, Norway, Portugal, Romania, Scotland, Serbia, South Africa, Spain, Sweden, the United States, and Wales). Twelve studies were conducted across several countries within the United Kingdom (but did not specify which individual countries were included or exactly where the youth lived). The children ranged in age from 0 to 29, two studies included youth younger than 4, seventeen studies included youth over 18, one study did not describe the specific ages (yet the context indicated that they were young based on being described as "children"), and 61 studies included participants within the age range of 4–18, the focus of the current study. For the studies with youth over 18, the researchers made every effort to include their contributions only if they were still in care (see Jones, 2019 for a review on foster care after age 18 in the United States). Sample sizes for quantitative studies ranged from 22 to 827 youth. Sample sizes for qualitative studies ranged from 2 to 169 youth. Sample sizes for mixed methods studies ranged from 18 to 180 youth. Sample characteristics are shown in Appendix B.

Study Quality Assessments

Sixty-four (57 qualitative and 7 mixed methods) papers were evaluated for study quality using the National Institute for Health and Care Excellence Quality Appraisal Checklist for qualitative studies (NICE, 2018). Two raters jointly coded five papers to achieve interrater reliability then separately coded seven papers (98 items) to test reliability. High reliability was achieved (.90; $\gamma = .97$). The remaining papers were coded individually (32 by one coder and 20 by the other). The NICE consists of 14 items in six categories (theoretical approach, study design, data collection, trustworthiness, analysis, and ethics). Each item is scored on a range of -1 to 1, and possible total scores for journal articles range from -14 to 14. Scores ranged from -3 to 14 ($M = 9.23$, $SD = 4.49$). Forty-four papers scored at the mean or one standard deviation above, eight scored within one standard deviation below the mean, and 12 scored between one and two standard deviations below the mean. Twelve papers earned perfect scores.

Twenty-seven (20 quantitative and 7 mixed methods) papers were evaluated for quality using the Checklist for Measuring Quality (Downs & Black, 1998). All papers were jointly coded by two coders, and disagreements were resolved with discussion. Papers were scored on 27 items in five categories (reporting, external validity, internal validity/bias, internal validity/selection bias, and power). Twenty-six items were scored on a range of 0 to 1, and one item was scored on a range of 0 to 2. For 20 items, papers could earn a score of zero for not meeting the criteria or because coders were unable to determine if the study met the criteria. Possible scores ranged from 0 to 28. Actual scores ranged from 9 to 24 ($M = 17.56$, $SD = 3.97$). See Appendix B for NICE (2018) and D&B, 1998 scores.

Data Extraction and Synthesis

Data extraction was conducted jointly by the first two authors. Journal articles were closely examined for views and concerns expressed by foster youth themselves. Some studies included interviews with additional parties (e.g., foster parents, social workers). However, as the purpose of the current study was to identify and analyze research in which children were interviewed about their experiences in care, data from additional parties were generally not considered[3]. Many of the studies investigated several topics, rather than focusing on a single theme. See Appendix B for a description of interview topics in each study. Many common themes were found across studies. However, data extraction was not limited to common themes, as it is important to consider all concerns voiced by youth in care.

Meta-Analysis

Despite the large number of studies included in the systematic review, they rarely contained information similar enough to be included in a meta-analysis. The only common piece of information contained in enough studies on which to conduct a meta-analysis was the number of foster youth who had seen their biological mothers and biological fathers. This information was sought from all the studies in the systematic review, but this information was found in only 13 of them.

These 13 studies were included in the meta-analysis. The N, mean and standard deviation from contacts with biological mothers and fathers were recorded from each study. The data from mothers (i.e., contact with biological mother or not) were considered the "treatment" group in the meta-analysis, while the data from the fathers (i.e., contact with biological father or not) were considered the "control" group. The decision regarding "treatment" and "control" groups was arbitrary. Stata 17 (StataCorp, 2021a) was used for all analyses.

The effect size Hedges' g was calculated for each study. Hedges' g is very similar to Cohen's d and was used because it corrects for possible bias due to small sample sizes in studies included in the meta-analysis (Borenstein et al., 2009). A random-effects restricted maximum likelihood model was run (Langan, et al., 2019).

The overall Hedges' g was 0.69 with a 95% confidence interval of 0.66 to 0.73. This value is statistically significant with a p-value of 0.00, meaning that 0.69 is different from 0. Substantively, this indicates that there was more contact with biological mothers than with biological fathers.

The output below shows the results of the analysis. The first column gives the author(s) and date of each study included in the meta-analysis. The next three columns provide the number of observations, mean and standard deviation for the data from mothers (i.e., the treatment group), respectively. The next three columns provide the number of observations, mean and standard deviation for the fathers (i.e., the control group), respectively. Next, the plot of the value of Hedges' g with the corresponding 95% confidence interval is given; the same information is given in the next column in text form. Finally, the weight (as a percent) is given in the final column. The weight indicates how much influence each study has in the calculation of the overall effect size (0.693).

The overall Hedges' g and its 95% confidence interval is given below the list of studies. Below that, the heterogeneity measures tau-squared, I-squared and H-squared are given, followed by the test of theta.

Study	N	Treatment Mean	SD	N	Control Mean	SD		Hedges's g with 95% CI	Weight (%)
Ahmed, et. al., 2015	11	.5455	.52223	12	.1667	.38925		0.80 [-0.02, 1.62]	0.18
Aldgate, 2009	28	.7857143	.4178554	28	.4285714	.5039526		0.76 [0.23, 1.30]	0.41
Burgund and Zegarac, 2016	16	.3125	.4787136	8	.125	.3535534		0.41 [-0.42, 1.24]	0.17
Dansey, et. al., 2018	15	.9333333	.2581989	15	.4	.3535534		1.68 [0.86, 2.49]	0.18
Dolan, et. al., 2011	5,873	.922016	.2681692	5,873	.6519666	.4763872		0.70 [0.66, 0.74]	85.37
Fernandez, 2009	59	.9152542	.2808936	59	.6101695	.4918981		0.76 [0.39, 1.13]	0.86
Hedin, et. al., 2012	3	.6666667	.5773503	3	1	.0001		-0.65 [-1.99, 0.68]	0.07
Hunt, et. al., 2010	113	.6106195	.4897818	113	.2654867	.443559		0.74 [0.47, 1.00]	1.64
Kiraly and Humphreys, 2013	21	.8095238	.4023739	21	.4285714	.5070926		0.82 [0.20, 1.44]	0.31
Martinez et al., 2016	104	.5288462	.5015845	104	.2403846	.4293864		0.62 [0.34, 0.89]	1.54
McWey and Cui, 2017	423	.7825059	.4130299	346	.4768786	.5001885		0.67 [0.53, 0.82]	5.57
Schofield, et. al., 2012	230	.6913043	.4629628	230	.4	.4909664		0.61 [0.42, 0.80]	3.40
Schwartz, 2010	18	.6666667	.4850713	18	.6176298	.4860019		0.10 [-0.54, 0.74]	0.29
Overall								0.69 [0.66, 0.73]	

Heterogeneity: τ^2 = 0.00, I^2 = 0.00%, H^2 = 1.00

Test of $\theta_i = \theta_j$: Q(12) = 15.00, p = 0.24

Test of θ = 0: z = 39.46, p = 0.00

-2   0   2

Random-effects REML model

Figure A.2 Forest plot of contact with mothers and fathers.

In this analysis, there was minimal heterogeneity (tau-squared = 0.00; I-squared = 0.00), so no tests to explain heterogeneity were considered. Tau-squared is the variance of the true effect sizes. Of course, we cannot know the "true" effect sizes, so this is an estimate based on our sample of studies. It is in the same metric as the effect sizes used in the meta-analysis. I-squared is a kind of signal-to-noise ratio: " … the ratio of the true heterogeneity to total variance across the observed effect estimates. … The I-squared statistic is a descriptive statistic and not an estimate of any underlying quantity." (Borenstein et al., 2009, pp. 117–118).

A Galbraith plot is also presented. It is useful not only for displaying the results of the meta-analysis, but also for visualizing heterogeneity and for detecting potential outliers. In the graph below, two things are obvious.

The first is that the overall effect size is not 0 (because the regression line is not close to the line that indicates 0, or no effect). Also, there seems to be one outlier. A sensitivity test was conducted to assess the impact of this study on the meta-analysis. The results of this sensitivity analysis are presented after the assessment of potential sources of bias in the current meta-analysis.

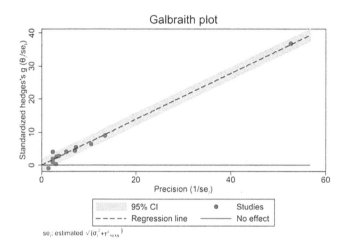

Figure A.3 Galbraith plot of contact with mothers and fathers.

Tests for different types of bias were conducted. Three tests were used to assess the possibility of publication bias. Publication bias is a potential problem for meta-analyses and occurs when smaller studies, often with statistically non-significant results, are not included in the meta-analysis because they were not published in the literature. To assess possible publication bias, both the Egger test and Begg's test were run. The p-value from the Egger test was 0.50, and the p-value from Begg's test was 0.43. The non-parametric "trim-and-fill" method was also used. The observed Hedges' g was 0.69 with a 95% confidence interval of 0.66 to 0.73. The observed plus imputed Hedges' g value was 0.69 with a 95% confidence interval of 0.66 to 0.73.

A funnel plot was also created because it can help assess the possibility of small-study effects, which are often associated with publication bias. A funnel plot is a scatterplot with the effect sizes from each study on the x-axis and some measure of precision on the y-axis. In the graph shown here, the measure of precision is the standard error. The dots on the graph, which represent each study in the meta-analysis, will be approximately symmetrical if there are no small-study effects. Also, the studies with smaller numbers of observations are expected to have more variability and thus be plotted towards the lower part of the funnel plot (StataCorp, 2021b). We see no evidence of small-study effects in the funnel plot associated with our meta-analysis.

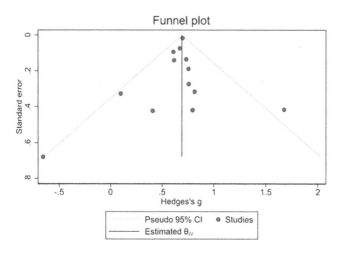

Figure A.4 Funnel plot of contact with mothers and fathers.

While publication bias is one common reason that asymmetry may be seen in a funnel plot, it is not the only reason. Other possible causes of asymmetry include between-study heterogeneity, the type of effect size plotted, a moderator that is correlated with the effect sizes, or chance. One way to try to determine if publication bias is the cause of the observed asymmetry is to make a contoured funnel plot. The contours on the plot correspond to ranges of alpha values: 1–5%, 5–10% and greater than 10%. Publication bias may be present if studies are missing from the statistically non-significant regions of the graph.

The contoured funnel plot was created. There do seem to be some studies missing from the darker (i.e., statistically non-significant) regions of the graph.

In addition to publication bias, meta-analyses may have other types of biases, such as language bias, availability bias and cost bias. Language bias occurs when the search for articles meeting the eligibility requirements of the meta-analysis uses only one or only a few languages. Our search included only articles in English because none of the authors speak any other language. It is unclear how much, if any, bias this causes in our analysis. Availability bias can occur when you do not have access to major databases of articles. This was not an issue for this meta-analysis, because the authors had access to all of the databases accessible through both the University of California and

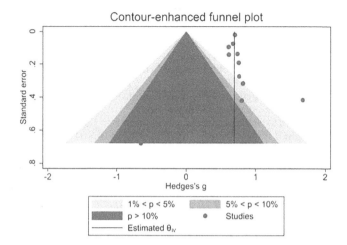

Figure A.5 Contour-enhanced funnel plot of contact with mothers and fathers.

the California State University system. Access to these databases was free for the authors, so cost bias (the bias that may be caused because the authors of meta-analyses cannot afford to access databases) was not an issue.

Looking at the results of the meta-analysis, it is clear that one study, Dolan et al. (2011), had a weight much higher than any other study. This is, of course, because the sample size in this study is much larger than in any other study. As a sensitivity analysis, the meta-analysis was rerun with this study excluded.

The results are essentially the same: the overall Hedges' *g* is 0.66, with a 95% confidence interval of 0.57 to 0.75. The test of this value is statistically significant with a p-value of 0.00. As before, there was minimal heterogeneity (tau-squared = 0.00; I-squared = 0.00). The result of the sensitivity analysis shows that the original analysis was not overly influenced by the Dolan et al. (2011) study.

Notes

1 Research focused only on foster youth with a medical or psychological diagnosis were excluded so the findings would be more generalizable.
2 Because the focus of our study is on valuing the lived experiences of foster youth, we excluded all papers in which researchers only surveyed or interviewed people other than foster youth currently in care (e.g., foster parents, social workers, and former foster youth). Although foster youth alumni have valuable insight, viewpoints can change when looking back on experiences and reporting on them retrospectively.
3 Although, depending on the subject, some other perspectives were included. In these cases, we made it explicitly clear that the additional information was outside of the systematic literature review.

References

Ahmed, K., Windsor, L., & Scott, S. (2015). In their own words: Abused children's perceptions of care provided by their birth parents and foster carers. *Adoption & Fostering, 39*(1), 21–37. 10.1177/0308575914565068

Aldgate, J. (2009). Living in kinship care: A child-centered view. *Adoption & Fostering, 33*(3), 51–63. 10.1177/030857590903300306

Borenstein, M., Hedges, L. V., Higgins, J. P. T., & Rothstein, H. R. (2009). *Introduction to Meta-Analysis* (1st ed.). John Wiley & Sons.

Burgund, A., & Zegarac, N. (2016). Perspectives of youth in care in Serbia. *Child & Adolescent Social Work Journal, 33*(2), 151–161. 10.1007/s10560-015-0413-5

Dansey, D., John, M., & Shbero, D. (2018). How children in foster care engage with loyalty conflict: Presenting a model of processes informing loyalty. *Adoption & Fostering, 42*(4), 354–368. 10.1177/0308575918798767

Dolan, M., Smith, K., Casanueva, C., & Ringeisen, H. (2011). *NSCAW II baseline report: Caseworker characteristics, child welfare services, and experiences of children placed in out-of-home care (Report No. 2011-27e).* National Survey of Child and Adolescent Well-Being. https://www.acf.hhs.gov/sites/default/files/documents/opre/nscaw2_cw.pdf

Downs, S. H., & Black, N. (1998). The feasibility of creating a checklist for the assessment of the methodological quality of both randomised and non-randomised studies of healthcare interventions. *Journal of Epidemiology and Community Health, 52*(6), 377–384.

Fernandez, E. (2009). Children's wellbeing in care: Evidence from a longitudinal study of outcomes. *Children and Youth Services Review, 31*(10), 1092–1100. 10.1016/j.childyouth.2009.07.010

Hedin, L., Höjer, I., & Brunnberg, E. (2012). Jokes and routines make everyday life a good life-on "doing family" for young people in foster care in Sweden. *European Journal of Social Work, 15*(5), 613–628. 10.1080/13691457.2011.579558

Hunt, J., Waterhouse, S., & Lutman, E. (2010). Parental contact for children placed in kinship care through care proceedings. *Child and Family Law Quarterly, 22*, 71–92. https://ssrn.com/abstract=1939941

Jones, L. (2019). Remaining in foster care after age 18 and youth outcomes at the transition to adulthood: A review. *Families in Society: The Journal of Contemporary Social Services, 100*(3), 260–281. 10.1177/104438941984732

Kiraly, M., & Humphreys, C. (2013). Perspectives from young people about family contact in kinship care: "Don't push us—listen more". *Australian Social Work, 66*(3), 314–327. 10.1080/0312407x.2012.715658

Langan, D., Higgins, J. P. T., Jackson, D., Bowden, J., Veroniki, A. A., Kontopantelis, E., Viechtbauer, W., & Simmonds, M. (2019). A comparison of heterogeneity variance estimators in simulated random-effect meta-analyses. *Research Synthesis Methods, 10*(1), 83–98. 10.1002/jrsm.1316

Martínez, M. D. S., Fuentes, M. J., Bernedo, I. M., & García-Martín, M. A. (2016). Contact visits between foster children and their birth family: The views of foster children, foster parents and social workers. *Child & Family Social Work, 21*(4), 473–483. 10.1111/cfs.12163

McWey, L. M., & Cui, M. (2017). Parent–child contact for youth in foster care: Research to inform practice. *Family Relations, 66*(4), 684–695. 10.1111/fare.12276

National Institute for Health and Care Excellence. (2018). *Methods for the development of NICE public health guidance (third edition): Process and Methods.* https://www.nice.org.uk/process/pmg4/

Saywitz, K. J., Larson, R. P., Hobbs, S. D., & Wells, C. (2014). *Listening to children in foster care: Eliciting reliable reports from children: Review of influential factors.* The Swedish National Board of Health and Welfare. http://www.socialstyrelsen.se/publikationer2015/2015-1-17

Schofield, G., Beek, M., & Ward, E. (2012). Part of the family: Planning for permanence in long-term family foster care. *Children and Youth Services Review, 34*(1), 244–253. 10.1016/j.childyouth.2011.10.020

Schwartz, A. E. (2010). "Nobody knows me no more": Experiences of loss among African American adolescents in kinship and non-kinship foster care placements. *Race and Social Problems, 2*(1), 31–49. 10.1007/s12552-010-9025-z

StataCorp. (2021a). *Stata Statistical Software: Release 17.* StataCorp LLC.

StataCorp. (2021b). *Stata 17 Base Reference Manual.* Stata Press.

Descriptive Summary of Included Studies, Including Quality Assessment Scores

Authors (Year)	Country	N	Age Range (years)	Type of Care[A]	NICE Score	D&B Score	Interview Topics
Ahmed et al. (2015)	United Kingdom	12	13–15	Foster	10		Relationships (foster and birth parents); feeling cared for; belonging
Aldgate (2009)	Scotland	30	8–16	Kinship	3		Relationships (birth families, peers, and social workers); feeling cared for; belonging; difficulties in placement; feeling different from other children
Ashley and Brown (2015)	United States	9	11–17	Foster	–2		Hair care for African American girls; cultural responsiveness
Baker et al. (2013)	United States	112	8–20	Foster		16	Psychological maltreatment by caregivers; differences between birth and foster family
Balsells et al. (2017)	Spain	30	6–18+	Foster, Kinship, and Family Reunification	14[B]		Difficulties with placement; self-advocacy
Bamba and Haight (2009)	Japan	9	10–15	Residential	14[B]		Relationships (birth parents and peers); trust; feeling cared for; difficulties with placement; belonging
Barnes (2012)	United Kingdom	20	12–20	Foster and Residential	10		Relationships (social workers); self-advocacy
Biehal (2014)	England	13	9–17	Foster and Kinship	7		Relationships (birth parents); feeling cared for; belonging differences between birth family and foster family; self-advocacy
Block et al. (2010)	United States	85	7–10	Foster, Residential, and Group		18	Self-advocacy; attitudes/knowledge of the dependency court system
Brown et al. (2019)	United Kingdom	13	12–20	Foster, Residential, Independent, and Biological family	13		Relationships (social worker and foster parents); feeling cared for

(Continued)

Authors (Year)	Country	N	Age Range (years)	Type of Care[A]	NICE Score	D&B Score	Interview Topics
Bulat (2010)	Republic of Croatia	139	10–21[C]	Residential and Foster		19	Difficulties in placement; mental health
Burgess et al. (2010)	United Kingdom	12	11–17	Kinship	9		Relationships (birth families, peers, social workers, and other adults); differences between with birth and foster family; feeling cared for; difficulties with care, placement, and school; mental health; self-advocacy; self-confidence; belonging
Burgund and Zegarac (2016)	Serbia	16	13–18	Foster, Kinship, Residential	11		Relationships (birth parents, peers, social workers); difficulties in placement; differences between birth and foster family; belonging; self-confidence; future aspirations
Buys et al. (2011)	Australia	65	13–18	Foster, Kinship, Residential, and Other	13		Relationships (teachers and other adults); future aspirations; self-advocacy; mental health
Christiansen et al. (2013)	Norway	37	13–20	Foster, Kinship, and Other	12		Relationships (birth parents and caregivers); feeling cared for; self-advocacy
Clarkson et al. (2017)	United Kingdom	6	15–18	Foster	12		Relationships (caregivers); belonging
Daly (2009)	Australia	14	8–17	Foster	10		Self-advocacy
Damnjanovic et al. (2011)	Serbia	216	8–18	Foster and Residential		17	Quality of life; comparing types of care; mental health
Dansey et al. (2018)	England	15	7–14	Foster	3		Relationships (birth parents and peers); instability; belonging; mental health; self-confidence; self-advocacy

Study	Country	N	Age	Care type	No.	Themes
Diehl et al. (2011)	United States	54	10–17	Foster	18	Relationships (mentors); self-advocacy; self-confidence
Dolan et al. (2011)	United States	5873	0–17	Reunification, Kinship, Foster, and Residential	10	Relationships (social workers)
Dove and Powers (2018)	United States	11	13–17	Kinship, Foster, and Adoption	14[B]	Hair care for African American girls; difference between birth and foster parents; challenges with care; cultural responsiveness; self-confidence; self-advocacy
Downie et al. (2009)	Australia	20	8–15	Kinship	21	Relationships (birth parents, siblings, peers, teachers, extended family, and caregivers); differences between birth and foster families; feeling cared for; feeling different from other children; belonging
Dunn et al. (2010)	United States	180	9–11	Foster, Kinship, and Residential	20	Comparing types of care; feeling cared for; difficulties in placement
Ellingsen et al. (2011)	Norway	22	13–18	Foster (long-term, specifically)	17	Relationships (birth parents); feeling cared for; belonging
Emond (2010)	Cambodia	19	4–18	Residential	10	Relationships (peers and other children living with them); experiences of living in residential care; belonging; self-advocacy
Euser et al. (2014)	Netherlands	315	12–17	Foster and Residential	24	Placement; relationships (caregivers)
Fargas-Malet and McSherry (2018)	Ireland	25	1–22	Foster, Kinship, Residential, and Biological family	8	Relationships (birth parents and social worker); mental health; self-advocacy

(Continued)

Authors (Year)	Country	N	Age Range (years)	Type of Care[A]	NICE Score	D&B Score	Interview Topics
Farineau et al. (2013)	United States	188	11–16	Foster, Kinship, Residential, and Other		18	Relationships (caregivers); comparing types of care; self-esteem
Farmer et al. (2013)	United Kingdom (4 countries unidentified)	80	8–18	Kinship	8		Relationships (birth parents)
Fawley-King et al. (2017)	United States	152 M = 12		Kinship and Foster		20	Placement; mental health
Fernandez (2009)	Australia	59	7–12+	Foster		14	Relationships (birth families, caregivers, and foster siblings); placement; self-confidence
Flores et al. (2018)	United States	15	14–17	Foster (residing in juvenile detention)	14[B]		Placement; feeling different than other children; self-advocacy
Gayapersad et al. (2019)	Kenya	30	11–23	Residential	14[B]		Placement; feeling different than other children; belonging; cultural responsiveness; self-advocacy
Hedin et al. (2011a)	Sweden	17	13–16[D]	Foster, Kinship, and Network	10		Relationships (birth parents, peers, teachers, caregivers, other children in care); comparing types of care; belonging; self-advocacy
Hedin et al. (2011b)	Sweden	17	13–16[D]	Foster	10		Belonging; difference between living with birth parents and being in care; school performance; mental health; self-confidence; future aspirations; self-advocacy
Hedin et al. (2012)	Sweden	3	13–16[D]	Foster, Kinship, and Network	10		Relationships (birth parents); difficulties in placement; belonging; self-advocacy

Author (year)	Country	N	Age	Placement			Themes
Hedin (2014)	Sweden	15	14–18	Foster, Kinship, and Network	10		Relationships (birth parents, peers, social worker, caregiver); belonging; self-advocacy; mental health
Holland (2010)	United Kingdom	8	10–20	Foster and Kinship	13		Relationships (birth families, social worker, general support network); feeling cared for; belonging; feeling heard
Hunt et al. (2010)	England	14	5–14	Kinship	0		Relationships (birth parents and caregivers); feeling cared for; belonging
Jansen and Haavind (2011)	Norway	12	14–18	Residential	10		Self-advocacy; mental health; attitudes of the system
Kalverboer et al. (2017)	Netherlands	132	16–17	Foster and Residential	13	18	All youth were unaccompanied minors and refugee children; Relationships (general support network, other children in care); feeling cared for; cultural responsiveness; belonging; self-advocacy; future aspirations
Kelly et al. (2019)	United States	20	12–17	Residential	14[B]		Relationships (peers; caregivers; other children in care); feeling cared for; belonging; difficulties in placement; feeling different than other children; self-advocacy; mental health; self-confidence; future aspirations
Kiraly and Humphreys (2013)	Australia	21	10–29	Kinship	14[B]		Relationships (birth parents, birth siblings, extended family); self-advocacy
Kuyini et al. (2009)	Ghana	27	10–19	Foster	2		Relationships (birth parents, other children in care); difficulties in placement; self-advocacy

(Continued)

Authors (Year)	Country	N	Age Range (years)	Type of Care[A]	NICE Score	D&B Score	Interview Topics
Larkins et al. (2015)	England	160	7–22	Foster[E]	10		Relationships (birth parents and social worker); self-advocacy
Leichtentritt (2013)	Israel	12	7–14	Residential	10		Relationships (siblings)
Lindahl and Bruhn (2017)	Sweden	53	11–19	Foster	12		Relationships (social worker)
Lorthridge et al. (2018)	United States	23	13–17	Foster	10	14	All youth were LGBTQ: Relationships (general support network and caregivers); cultural responsiveness; self-confidence
Lundström and Sallnäs (2012)	Sweden	240	13–18	Foster and Residential	24		Relationships (birth families); mental health
Madigan et al. (2013)	Scotland	9	12–16	Foster	12		Relationships (peers and teachers); belonging; feeling different from other children; belonging; mental health; self-confidence
Malinga-Musamba (2015)	Botswana	15	10–17	Kinship	3		Relationships (caregivers); feeling different from other children
Mannay et al. (2017)	Wales	67	6–16[F]	Foster, Kinship, Residential, and "other"	14[B]		Relationships (teachers); feeling different from other children; future aspirations
Martinez et al. (2016)	Spain	104	5–17	Foster		19	Relationships (birth parents); differences between birth and foster family
Mateos et al. (2012)	Spain	57	12–16	Kinship	4		Relationships (birth families and caregivers); feeling cared for; difference between birth parents and caregivers; difficulties in placement and school; feeling different than other children; self-confidence; future aspirations; attitudes and knowledge of the system

Mazzone et al. (2019)	Bulgaria, France, Greece, Italy, and Romania	123	6–22	Residential	9	9	Relationships (peers and caregivers)
McMahon and Curtin (2013)	Ireland	21	13–17	Foster[G]	0	9	Relationships (birth parents, peers, and extended family); difficulties in placements
McWey and Cui (2017)	United States	452	6–17	Foster, Kinship, and Residential		21	Relationships (birth parents)
Mitchell and Kuczynski (2010)	Canada	20	8–15	Foster	14[B]		Relationships (birth parents and caregivers); difficulties with placement; belonging; knowledge of the system; self-advocacy
Mitchell et al. (2010)	Canada	20	8–15	Foster	4		Relationships (peers, social workers, and caregivers); difficulties in placement; belonging; self-advocacy; mental health
Morrison et al. (2011)	Canada	24	8–12	Foster	14[B]		Relationships (birth parents, social workers, other adults, and caregivers); difficulties in placement; self-advocacy; knowledge of the system
Mota and Matos (2015)	Portugal	246	12–18	Residential		18	Relationships (peers and caregivers)
Pears et al. (2012)	United States	75	10–12	Foster and Kinship		21	Relationships (social workers); self-advocacy; self-confidence; attitudes and knowledge of the system
Pert et al. (2017)	England	25	8–17	Foster	7		Relationships (other adults); mental health
Põlkki et al. (2012)	Finland	8	7–17	Foster and Residential	10		Relationships (birth parents, peers, sand social workers); differences between birth and foster families; difficulties with placement; self-advocacy; feeling heard

(Continued)

Authors (Year)	Country	N	Age Range (years)	Type of Care[A]	NICE Score	D&B Score	Interview Topics
Rees et al. (2012)	United Kingdom	16	9–16	Foster	12		Relationships (social workers and caregivers); belonging; differences between birth and foster families
Ridley et al. (2016)	United Kingdom	169	7–23	Foster, Kinship, and Residential	12		Relationships (social workers); feeling cared for; feeling heard; self-advocacy
Rostill-Brookes et al. (2011)	United Kingdom	5	9–15	Foster and Residential	10		Relationships (social workers); difficulties with placement; mental health; feeling heard; self-advocacy
Sala (2009)	Kenya	37	Not provided	Foster	0		Difficulties with placement
Schiller and de Wet (2018)	South Africa	29	12–19	Foster	14[B]		Difficulties with placement; feeling heard; future aspirations; self-advocacy
Schofield et al. (2012)	England	20	9–17	Foster and Kinship	5		Relationships (birth parents); belonging; difficulties with placement; self-advocacy; attitudes and knowledge of the system
Schwartz (2010)	United States	18	11–14	Foster and Kinship	14[B]	17	Relationships (birth families, peers, overall support network, and caregivers); difficulties with placement; cultural responsiveness; belonging
Selwyn et al. (2010)	United Kingdom	160	8–14	Foster	4	14	Relationships (birth parents, peers, and social workers); belonging; differences between birth and foster families; difficulties with placement; mental health; self-advocacy; knowledge of the system

Study	Country	N	Age range	Type of care	Score	Themes
Skoog et al. (2015)	Sweden	12	8–18	Foster, Kinship, Residential, and Institutional	10	Relationships (birth parents, social workers, and caregivers); difficulties with placement; belonging; mental health
Skovdal (2010)	Kenya	69	11–17	Foster and Kinship	13	Relationships (caregivers)
Southwell and Fraser (2010)	Australia	169	6–18	Residential	19	Relationships (birth parents, social workers, caregivers, and other children in care); feeling cared for; difficulties with placement; feeling different from other children; cultural responsiveness; belonging; self-advocacy
Sting (2013)	Austria	9	12–14	Residential	6	Relationships (siblings); difficulties with placement
Traube et al. (2012)	United States	827	11–14	Foster, Kinship, and Residential	23	Feeling cared for; future aspirations
Ward (2009)	United Kingdom	242	11–14	Foster, Kinship, and Residential	−3	Relationships (caregivers and other children in care); difficulties with placement
Weisz et al. (2011)	United States	93	8–18	Not provided[H]	13	Attitudes and knowledge of the system
Wissö et al. (2019)	Sweden	11	14–19	Foster	6	Relationships (birth parents, peers, social workers, and overall support network); belonging
Wojciak (2017)	United States	197	6–18	Foster	6	Relationships (siblings); mental health

[A]Type of care was defined using the descriptions from the original studies.

[B]This was the highest possible score.

[C]Youth were interviewed across two intervals; this number reflects the youngest at time one and the oldest at time two. =

[D]Age was not directly stated but could be assumed based on the context of the article.

[E]Research compared pilot care with independent foster care agencies that involve less bureaucracy against typical foster care offered by local authorities. The paper does not indicate if care was residential, foster care or kinship care.

[F]Youth and adults up to age 27 were included in focus, outside the scope of the study. We focused on the youth who were interviewed.

[G]Type of care was not explicitly labeled but was assumed based on the context of the article.

[H]All youth were in the abuse/neglect court system. Approximately 25% lived with at least one biological parent; the living arrangements for the other 75% were not stated.

References

Ahmed, K., Windsor, L., & Scott, S. (2015). In their own words: Abused children's perceptions of care provided by their birth parents and foster carers. *Adoption & Fostering, 39*(1), 21–37. 10.1177/0308575914565068

Aldgate, J. (2009). Living in kinship care: A child-centered view. *Adoption & Fostering, 33*(3), 51–63. 10.1177/030857590903300306

Ashley, W., & Brown, J. C. (2015). Attachment thAIRapy: A culturally relevant treatment paradigm for African American foster youth. *Journal of Black Studies, 46*(6), 587–604. 10.1177/0021934715590406

Baker, A. J. L., Brassard, M. R., Schneiderman, M. S., & Donnelly, L. J. (2013). Foster children's report of psychological maltreatment experiences. *Journal of Public Child Welfare, 7*(3), 235–252. 10.1080/15548732.2013.779624

Balsells, M. Á., Fuentes-Peláez, N., & Pastor, C. (2017). Listening to the voices of children in decision-making: A challenge for the child protection system in Spain. *Children and Youth Services Review, 79*, 418. 10.1016/j.childyouth.2017.06.055

Bamba, S., & Haight, W. (2009). Maltreated children's emerging well-being in Japanese state care. *Children and Youth Services Review, 31*(7), 797–806. 10.1016/j.childyouth.2009.02.006

Barnes, V. (2012). Social work and advocacy with young people: Rights and care in practice. *The British Journal of Social Work, 42*(7), 1275–1292. 10.1093/bjsw/bcr142

Biehal, N. (2014). A sense of belonging: Meanings of family and home in long-term foster care. *The British Journal of Social Work, 44*(4), 955. 10.1093/bjsw/bcs177

Block, S. D., Oran, H., Oran, D., Baumrind, N., & Goodman, G. S. (2010). Abused and neglected children in court: Knowledge and attitudes. *Child Abuse & Neglect, 34*(9), 659–670. 10.1016/j.chiabu.2010.02.003

Brown, R., Alderson, H., Kaner, E., McGovern, R., & Lingam, R. (2019). "There are carers, and then there are carers who actually care"; Conceptualizations of care among looked after children and care leavers, social workers and carers. *Child Abuse & Neglect, 92*, 219–229. 10.1016/j.chiabu.2019.03.018

Bulat, L. R. (2010). A longitudinal study of depressiveness in children in public care. *International Journal of Social Welfare, 19*(4), 412–423. 10.1111/j.1468-2397.1532009.00698.x

Burgess, C., Rossvoll, F., Wallace, B., & Daniel, B. (2010). "It's just like another home, just another family, so it's nae different" Children's voices in kinship care: A research study about the experience of children in kinship care in Scotland. *Child & Family Social Work, 15*(3), 297–306. 10.1111/j.1365-2206.2009.00671.x

Burgund, A., & Zegarac, N. (2016). Perspectives of youth in care in Serbia. *Child & Adolescent Social Work Journal, 33*(2), 151–161. 10.1007/s10560-015-0413-5

Buys, N., Tilbury, C., Creed, P., & Crawford, M. (2011). Working with youth in-care: Implications for vocational rehabilitation practice. *Disability and Rehabilitation, 33*(13–14), 1125–1135. 10.3109/09638288.2010.521614

Christiansen, Ø., Havnen, K. J. S., Havik, T., & Anderssen, N. (2013). Cautious belonging: Relationships in long-term foster-care. *The British Journal of Social Work, 43*(4), 720–738. 10.1093/bjsw/bcr198

Clarkson, H., Dallos, R., Stedmon, J., & Hennessy, C. (2017). Exploring the relationship: Joint narratives of foster carers and young people. *Adoption & Fostering, 41*(1), 35–51. 10.1177/0308575916681711

Daly, W. (2009). "Adding their flavour to the mix": Involving children and young people in care in research design. *Australian Social Work, 62*(4), 460–475. 10.1080/03124070903265732

Damnjanovic, M., Lakic, A., Stevanovic, D., & Jovanovic, A. (2011). Effects of mental health on quality of life in children and adolescents living in residential and foster care: A cross-sectional study. *Epidemiology and Psychiatric Sciences*, *20*(3), 257–262. 10.1017/s2045796011000291

Dansey, D., John, M., & Shbero, D. (2018). How children in foster care engage with loyalty conflict: Presenting a model of processes informing loyalty. *Adoption & Fostering*, *42*(4), 354–368. 10.1177/0308575918798767

Diehl, D. C., Howse, R. B., & Trivette, C. M. (2011). Youth in foster care: Developmental assets and attitudes towards adoption and mentoring. *Child & Family Social Work*, *16*(1), 81–92. 10.1111/j.1365-2206.2010.00716.x

Dolan, M., Smith, K., Casanueva, C., & Ringeisen, H. (2011). *NSCAW II baseline report: Caseworker characteristics, child welfare services, and experiences of children placed in out-of-home care (Report No. 2011-27e)*. National Survey of Child and Adolescent Well-Being. https://www.acf.hhs.gov/sites/default/files/documents/opre/nscaw2_cw.pdf

Dove, L. M., & Powers, L. E. (2018). Exploring the complexity of hair and identity among African American female adolescents in foster care. *Children and Youth Services Review*, *95*, 368–376. 10.1016/j.childyouth.2018.10.043

Downie, J. M., Hay, D. A., Horner, B. J., Wichmann, H., & Hislop, A. L. (2009). Children living with their grandparents: Resilience and wellbeing. *International Journal of Social Welfare*, *19*(1), 8–22. 10.1111/j.1468-2397.2009.00654.x

Downs, S. H., & Black, N. (1998). The feasibility of creating a checklist for the assessment of the methodological quality both of randomised and non-randomised studies of health care interventions. *Journal of Epidemiology and Community Health*, *52*(6), 377–384. 10.1136/jech.52.6.377

Dunn, D. M., Culhane, S. E., & Taussig, H. N. (2010). Children's appraisals of their experiences in out-of-home care. *Children and Youth Services Review*, *32*(10), 1324–1330. 10.1016/j.childyouth.2010.05.001

Ellingsen, I. T., Shemmings, D., & Størksen, I. (2011). The concept of "family" among Norwegian adolescents in long-term foster care. *Child and Adolescent Social Work Journal*, *28*(4), 301–318. 10.1007/s10560-011-0234-0

Emond, R. (2010). Caring as a moral, practical and powerful endeavour: Peer care in a Cambodian orphanage. *The British Journal of Social Work*, *40*(1), 63–81. 10.1093/bjsw/bcn102

Euser, S., Alink, L. R. A., Tharner, A., van Ijzendoorn, M. H., & Bakermans-Kranenburg, M. J. (2014). Out of home placement to promote safety? The prevalence of physical abuse in residential and foster care. *Children and Youth Services Review*, *37*, 64–70. 10.1016/j.childyouth.2013.12.002

Fargas-Malet, M., & McSherry, D. (2018). The mental health and help-seeking behavior of children and young people in care in Northern Ireland: Making services accessible and engaging. *The British Journal of Social Work*, *48*(3), 578–595. 10.1093/bjsw/bcx062

Farineau, H. M., Wojciak, A. S., & McWey, L. M. (2013). You matter to me: Important relationships and self-esteem of adolescents in foster care. *Child & Family Social Work*, *18*(2), 129–138. 10.1111/j.1365-2206.2011.00808.x

Farmer, E., Selwyn, J., & Meakings, S. (2013). "Other children say you're not normal because you don't live with your parents". Children's views of living with informal kinship carers: Social networks, stigma and attachment to carers. *Child & Family Social Work*, *18*(1), 25–34. 10.1111/cfs.12030

Fawley-King, K., Trask, E. V., Zhang, J., & Aarons, G. A. (2017). The impact of changing neighborhoods, switching schools, and experiencing relationship disruption on children's adjustment to a new placement in foster care. *Child Abuse & Neglect, 63*, 141–150. 10.1016/j.chiabu.2016.11.016

Fernandez, E. (2009). Children's wellbeing in care: Evidence from a longitudinal study of outcomes. *Children and Youth Services Review, 31*(10), 1092–1100. 10.1016/ j.childyouth.2009.07.010

Flores, J., Hawes, J., Westbrooks, A., & Henderson, C. (2018). Crossover youth and gender: What are the challenges of girls involved in both the foster care and juvenile justice systems? *Children and Youth Services Review, 91*, 149–155. 10.1016/j. childyouth.2018.05.031

Fylkesnes, M., Larsen, M., Havnen, K., Christiansen, Ø., & Lehmann, S. (2021). Listening to advice from young people in foster care—from participation to belonging. *The British Journal of Social Work, 51*(6), 1983–2000. 10.1093/bjsw/ bcab138

Gayapersad, A., Ombok, C., Kamanda, A., Tarus, C., Ayuku, D., & Braitstein, P. (2019). The production and reproduction of kinship in charitable children's institutions in Uasin Gishu County, Kenya. *Child & Youth Care Forum, 48*, 797–828. 10.1007/s10566-019-09506-8

Hedin, L. (2014). A sense of belonging in a changeable everyday life—A follow-up study of young people in kinship, network, and traditional foster families. *Child & Family Social Work, 19*(2), 165–173. 10.1111/j.1365-2206.2012.00887.x

Hedin, L., Höjer, I., & Brunnberg, E. (2011a). Why one goes to school: What school means to young people entering foster care. *Child & Family Social Work, 16*(1), 43–51. 10.1111/j.1365-2206.2010.00706.x

Hedin, L., Höjer, I., & Brunnberg, E. (2011b). Settling into a new home as a teenager: About establishing social bonds in different types of foster families in Sweden. *Children and Youth Services Review, 33*(11), 2282–2289. 10.1016/j.childyouth.2011. 07.016

Hedin, L., Höjer, I., & Brunnberg, E. (2012). Jokes and routines make everyday life a good life-on "doing family" for young people in foster care in Sweden. *European Journal of Social Work, 15*(5), 613–628. 10.1080/13691457.2011.579558

Holland, S. (2010). Looked after children and the ethic of care. *The British Journal of Social Work, 40*(6), 1664–1680. 10.1093/bjsw/bcp086

Hunt, J., Waterhouse, S., & Lutman, E. (2010). Parental contact for children placed in kinship care through care proceedings. *Child and Family Law Quarterly, 22*, 71–92. https://ssrn.com/abstract=1939941

Jansen, A., & Haavind, H. (2011). "If only" and "despite all": Narrative configuration among young people living in residential care. *Narrative Inquiry, 21*(1), 68–87. 10.1075/ni.21.1.04jan

Kalverboer, M., Zijlstra, E., van Os, C., Zevulun, D., ten Brummelaar, M., & Beltman, D. (2017). Unaccompanied minors in the Netherlands and the care facility in which they flourish best. *Child & Family Social Work, 22*(2), 587–596. 10.1111/ cfs.12272

Kelly, C., Anthony, E. K., & Krysik, J. (2019). "How am I doing?" Narratives of youth living in congregate care on their social-emotional well-being. *Children and Youth Services Review, 103*, 255–263. 10.1016/j.childyouth.2019.06.001

Kiraly, M., & Humphreys, C. (2013). Perspectives from young people about family contact in kinship care: "Don't push us—listen more". *Australian Social Work, 66*(3), 314–327. 10.1080/0312407x.2012.715658

Kuyini, A. B., Alhassan, A. R., Tollerud, I., Weld, H., & Haruna, I. (2009). Traditional kinship foster care in northern Ghana: The experiences and views of children, carers and adults in Tamale. *Child & Family Social Work, 14*(4), 440–449. 10.1111/j.1365-2206.2009.00616.x

Larkins, C., Ridley, J., Farrelly, N., Austerberry, H., Bilson, A., Hussein, S., Manthorpe, J., & Stanley, N. (2015). Children's, young people's and parents' perspectives on contact: Findings from the evaluation of social work practices. *The British Journal of Social Work, 45*(1), 296–312. 10.1093/bjsw/bct135

Leichtentritt, J. (2013). "It is difficult to be here with my sister but intolerable to be without her": Intact sibling placement in residential care. *Children and Youth Services Review, 35*(5), 762–770. 10.1016/j.childyouth.2013.01.022

Lindahl, R., & Bruhn, A. (2017). Foster children's experiences and expectations concerning the child-welfare officer role--prerequisites and obstacles for close and trustful relationships. *Child & Family Social Work, 22*(4), 1415–1422. 10.1111/cfs.12362

Lorthridge, J., Evans, M., Heaton, L., Stevens, A., & Phillips, L. (2018). Strengthening family connections and support for youth in foster care who identify as LGBTQ: Findings from the PII-RISE evaluation. *Child Welfare, 96*(1), 53–78. https://www.jstor.org/stable/48628035

Lundström, T., & Sallnäs, M. (2012). Sibling contact among Swedish children in foster and residential care-out of home care in a family service system. *Children and Youth Services Review, 34*(2), 396–402. 10.1016/j.childyouth.2011.11.008

Madigan, S., Quayle, E., Cossar, J., & Paton, K. (2013). Feeling the same or feeling different? An analysis of the experiences of young people in foster care. *Adoption & Fostering, 37*(4), 389–403. 10.1177/0308575913508719

Malinga-Musamba, T. (2015). The nature of relationships between orphans and their kinship carers in Botswana. *Child & Family Social Work, 20*(3), 257–266. 10.1111/cfs.12121

Mannay, D., Evans, R., Staples, E., Hallett, S., Roberts, L., Rees, A., & Andrews, D. (2017). The consequences of being labelled "looked-after": Exploring the educational experiences of looked-after children and young people in Wales. *British Educational Research Journal, 43*(4), 683–699. 10.1002/berj.3283

Martínez, M. D. S., Fuentes, M. J., Bernedo, I. M., & García-Martín, M. A. (2016). Contact visits between foster children and their birth family: The views of foster children, foster parents and social workers. *Child & Family Social Work, 21*(4), 473–483. 10.1111/cfs.12163

Mateos, A., Balsells, M. À., Molina, M. C., & Fuentes-Peláez, N. (2012). The perception adolescents in kinship foster care have of their own needs. *Revista de Cercetare si Interventie Sociala, 38*, 25–41. http://hdl.handle.net/2445/103325

Mazzone, A., Nocentini, A., & Menesini, E. (2019). Bullying in residential care for children: Qualitative findings from five European countries. *Children and Youth Services Review, 100*, 451–460. 10.1016/j.childyouth.2019.03.025

McMahon, C., & Curtin, C. (2013). The social networks of young people in Ireland with experience of long-term foster care: Some lessons for policy and practice. *Child & Family Social Work, 18*(3), 329–340. 10.1111/j.1365-2206.2012.00849.x

McWey, L. M., & Cui, M. (2017). Parent–child contact for youth in foster care: Research to inform practice. *Family Relations, 66*(4), 684–695. 10.1111/fare.12276

Mitchell, M. B., & Kuczynski, L. (2010). Does anyone know what is going on? Examining children's lived experience of the transition into foster care. *Children and Youth Services Review, 32*(3), 437–444. 10.1016/j.childyouth.2009.10.023

Mitchell, M. B., Kuczynski, L., Tubbs, C. Y., & Ross, C. (2010). We care about care: Advice by children in care for children in care, foster parents and child welfare workers about the transition into foster care. *Child & Family Social Work, 15*(2), 176–185. 10.1111/j.1365-2206.2009.00657.x

Morrison, J., Mishna, F., Cook, C., & Aitken, G. (2011). Access visits: Perceptions of child protection workers, foster parents and children who are Crown wards.

Children and Youth Services Review, 33(9), 1476–1482. 10.1016/j.childyouth.2011.03.011

Mota, C. P., & Matos, P. M. (2015). Adolescents in institutional care: Significant adults, resilience and well-being. *Child & Youth Care Forum, 44*(2), 209–224. 10.1007/s10566-014-9278-6

National Institute for Health and Care Excellence (2018). *Methods for the Development of NICE Public Health Guidance (third Edition): Process and Methods.* https://www.nice.org.uk/process/pmg4/

Pears, K. C., Kim, H. K., & Leve, L. D. (2012). Girls in foster care: Risk and promotive factors for school adjustment across the transition to middle school. *Children and Youth Services Review, 34*(1), 234–243. 10.1016/j.childyouth.2011.10.005

Pert, H., Diaz, C., & Thomas, N. (2017). Children's participation in LAC reviews: A study in one English local authority. *Child & Family Social Work, 22*(S2), 1–10. 10.1111/cfs.12194

Pölkki, P., Vornanen, R., Pursiainen, M., & Riikonen, M. (2012). Children's participation in child-protection processes as experienced by foster children and social workers. *Child Care in Practice, 18*(2), 107–125. 10.1080/13575279.2011.646954

Rees, A., Holland, S., & Pithouse, A. (2012). Food in foster families: Care, communication and conflict. *Children & Society, 26*(2), 100–111. 10.1111/j.1099-0860.2010.00332.x

Ridley, J., Larkins, C., Farrelly, N., Hussein, S., Austerberry, H., Manthorpe, J., & Stanley, N. (2016). Investing in the relationship: Practitioners' relationships with looked-after children and care leavers in social work practices. *Child & Family Social Work, 21*(1), 55–64. 10.1111/cfs.12109

Rostill-Brookes, H., Larkin, M., Toms, A., & Churchman, C. (2011). A shared experience of fragmentation: Making sense of foster placement breakdown. *Clinical Child Psychology and Psychiatry, 16*(1), 103–127. 10.1177/1359104509352894

Sala, M. A. (2009). The quality of food, clothing and shelter provided to orphaned children under foster care in Kibera slums in Kenya. *East African Journal of Public Health, 6*(3), 312–316. https://pubmed.ncbi.nlm.nih.gov/20803926/

Sands, R. G., Goldberg-Glen, R. S., & Shin, H. (2009). The voices of grandchildren: A strengths-resilience perspective. *Child Welfare League of America, 88*(2), 25–45. https://www.jstor.org/stable/48623254

Schiller, U., & de Wet, G. (2018). Communication, indigenous culture and participatory decision making amongst foster adolescents. *Qualitative Social Work, 17*(2), 236–251. 10.1177/1473325016662329

Schofield, G., Beek, M., & Ward, E. (2012). Part of the family: Planning for permanence in long-term family foster care. *Children and Youth Services Review, 34*(1), 244–253. 10.1016/j.childyouth.2011.10.020

Schwartz, A. E. (2010). "Nobody knows me no more": Experiences of loss among African American adolescents in kinship and non-kinship foster care placements. *Race and Social Problems, 2*(1), 31–49. 10.1007/s12552-010-9025-z

Selwyn, J., Saunders, H., & Farmer, E. (2010). The views of children and young people on being cared for by an independent foster-care provider. *The British Journal of Social Work, 40*(3), 696–713. 10.1093/bjsw/bcn117

Skoog, V., Khoo, E., & Nygren, L. (2015). Disconnection and dislocation: Relationships and belonging in unstable foster and institutional care. *The British Journal of Social Work, 45*(6), 1888–1904. 10.1093/bjsw/bcu033

Skovdal, M. (2010). Children caring for their "caregivers": Exploring the caring arrangements in households affected by AIDS in Western Kenya. *AIDS Care, 22*(1), 96–103. 10.1080/09540120903016537

Southwell, J., & Fraser, E. (2010). Young people's satisfaction with residential care: Identifying strengths and weaknesses in service delivery. *Child Welfare*, *89*(2), 209–228. https://pubmed.ncbi.nlm.nih.gov/20857888/

Sting, S. (2013). Sibling relations in alternative child care results of a study on sibling relations in SOS Children's Villages in Austria. *Kriminologija & Socijalna Integracija*, *21*(1), 119–128. https://www.proquest.com/scholarly-journals/sibling-relations-alternative-child-care-results/docview/1450029344/se-2?accountid=10358

Traube, D. E., James, S., Zhang, J., & Landsverk, J. (2012). A national study of risk and protective factors for substance use among youth in the child welfare system. *Addictive Behaviors*, *37*(5), 641–650. 10.1016/j.addbeh.2012.01.015

Ward, H. (2009). Patterns of instability: Moves within the care system, their reasons, contexts and consequences. *Children and Youth Services Review*, *31*(10), 1113–1118. 10.1016/j.childyouth.2009.07.009

Weisz, V., Wingrove, T., Beal, S. J., & Faith-Slaker, A. (2011). Children's participation in foster care hearings. *Child Abuse & Neglect*, *35*(4), 267–272. 10.1016/j.chiabu.2010.12.007

Wissö, T., Johansson, H., & Höjer, I. (2019). What is a family? Constructions of family and parenting after a custody transfer from birth parents to foster parents. *Child & Family Social Work*, *24*(1), 9–16. 10.1111/cfs.12475

Wojciak, A. S. (2017). "It's complicated." Exploring the meaning of sibling relationships of youth in foster care. *Child & Family Social Work*, *22*(3), 1283–1291. 10.1111/cfs.12345

Search Strategy for Efficacy of Interview Methods with Children in Foster Care

PubMed Strategy for Initial and Follow-up Search

Search string: ("interview, psychological"[Mesh] OR "interviews as topic"[Mesh] OR interview* OR question*) AND ("foster home care"[Mesh] OR "foster child*" OR "foster care" OR "out of home") AND ("child"[Mesh] OR "child, preschool"[Mesh] child* OR youth*)

- Allowed database to search for variations of words
- Limited for:

    - Final Date—(2009–2019)[1]
    - Language—English
    - (No publication type limiters were used in this database)
    - Age—Child (6–12 years), Preschool Child (2–5 years)[2]

Cochrane CENTRAL Initial Search

Search string: ("interview, psychological"[Mesh] OR "interviews as topic"[Mesh] OR interview* OR question*) AND ("foster home care"[Mesh] OR "foster child*" OR "foster care" OR "out of home") AND ("child"[Mesh] OR "child, preschool"[Mesh] child* OR youth*)

- Limited for:

    - Final Date—(2009–2019)
    - (No language limiters were used in this database)
    - (No publication type limiters were used in this database)
    - (No age limiters were used in this database)

Cochrane Library (replaced Cochrane CENTRAL) Follow-up Search

Search string: ("interview, psychological"[Mesh] OR "interviews as topic"[Mesh] OR interview* OR question*) AND ("foster home care"[Mesh] OR "foster child*" OR "foster care" OR "out of home") AND ("child"[Mesh] OR "child, preschool"[Mesh] child* OR youth*)

- Limited for:
  - Final Date—After (2009–2019)
  - (No language limiters were used in this database)
  - (No publication type limiters were used in this database)
  - (No age limiters were used in this database)

PsycInfo Initial Search

Search string: (SU.EXACT("foster care") OR "foster child*" OR "foster care" OR "out of home") AND (SU.EXACT("interviewing") OR SU. EXACT("questioning") OR interview* OR question*) AND (child* OR youth*) AND (stype.exact("scholarly journals") AND su.exact("school age (6–12 yrs)" OR "preschool age (2–5 yrs)") AND la.exact("ENG") AND yr(1990–2019))

- Limited for:
  - Final Date—(2009–2019)
  - Language—English
  - Publication—Scholarly Peer Reviewed
  - Age—School Age (6–12 yrs) and Preschool Age (2–5 yrs)

PsycInfo Follow-up Search

Search String: ((DE "foster care") OR "foster child*" OR "foster care" OR "out of home") AND ((DE "interviewing") OR (DE "questioning") OR interview* OR question*) AND (child* or youth*)

- Limited for:
  - Final Date—(2009–2019)
  - Language—English
  - Publication type—Peer Reviewed Journal
  - Age—School Age (6–12 yrs) and Preschool Age (2–5 yrs)

CINAHL New Search

Search String: ((DE "foster care") OR "foster child*" OR "foster care" OR "out of home") AND ((DE "interviewing") OR (DE "questioning") OR interview* OR question*) AND (child* or youth*)

- Limited for:
  - Final Date—(2009–2019)

- Language—English
- Publication—Peer Reviewed Journal
- Age—School Age (6–12 yrs) and Preschool Age (2–5 yrs)

Social Services Abstracts Initial Search

Search String: (SU.EXACT("foster care") OR "foster child*" OR "foster care" OR "out of home") AND (SU.EXACT("interviewing") OR SU.EXACT("questioning") OR interview* OR question*) AND (child* OR youth*) AND (stype.exact("scholarly journals") AND la.exact("ENG") AND yr(1990–2019)

- Limited for:

  - Final Date—(2009–2019)
  - Language—English
  - Publication—Scholarly Peer Reviewed
  - (No age limiters were used in this database)

Social Services Abstracts Follow-up Search

Search string: ((SU.EXACT("foster care")) OR "foster child" OR "foster children" OR "foster care" OR "out of home") AND ((SU.EXACT("interviewing")) OR SU.EXACT("questioning") OR interview* OR question*) AND (child* OR youth*) AND stype.exact("scholarly journals") AND la.exact("ENG") AND yr(2014–2019)

- Limited for:

  - Final Date—(2009–2019)
  - Language—English
  - Publication—Scholarly Peer Reviewed
  - (No age limiters were used in this database)

Sociological Abstracts Initial and Follow-up Search

Search string: (SU.EXACT("foster care") OR "foster child*" OR "foster care" OR "out of home") AND (SU.EXACT("interviewing") OR SU.EXACT("questioning") OR interview* OR question*) AND (child* OR youth* OR adolescent*) AND (stype.exact("scholarly journals") AND la.exact("ENG") AND yr(1990–2019))

- Limited for:

  - Final Date—(2009–2019)
  - Language—English

- Peer Reviewed
- (No age limiters were used in this database)

Web of Knowledge Initial and Follow-up Search

Search string: TOPIC: (("foster child*" OR "foster care" OR "out of home")) AND TOPIC: ((interview* OR question*)) AND TOPIC: ((child* OR youth*))

- Keyword only search—Subject headings were not used due to the database's search restrictions.
- Limited for:
  - Final Date—(2009–2019)
  - Language—English
  - Publication—Journal Article
    - In the follow-up search, there was no filter for "publication type."
  - (No age limiters were used in this database)

Notes

1 The original search spanned 1990–2009. The final date range for included articles was 2009–2019.
2 The original search was focused on young children. However, all searches returned articles including foster youth of all ages.

Author Index

Subject Index